Seventh Workshop on the Use of Computational Methods in the Study of Endangered Languages (ComputEL 2024)

St. Julian's, Malta
21-22 March 2024

ISBN: 978-1-7138-9452-0

Printed from e-media with permission by:

Curran Associates, Inc.
57 Morehouse Lane
Red Hook, NY 12571

Some format issues inherent in the e-media version may also appear in this print version.

Association for Computational Linguistics
209 N. Eighth Street
Stroudsburg, Pennsylvania 18360

Phone: 1-570-476-8006
Fax: 1-570-476-0860

acl@aclweb.org

Additional copies of this publication are available from:

Curran Associates, Inc.
57 Morehouse Lane
Red Hook, NY 12571 USA
Phone: 845-758-0400
Fax: 845-758-2633
Email: curran@proceedings.com
Web: www.proceedings.com

ComputEL 2024

The Seventh Workshop on the Use of Computational Methods in the Study of Endangered Languages

Proceedings of the Workshop

March 21-22, 2024

Association for Computational Linguistics (ACL)
209 N. Eighth Street
Stroudsburg, PA 18360
USA
Tel: +1-570-476-8006
Fax: +1-570-476-0860
acl@aclweb.org

Introduction

These proceedings contain the papers presented at the 7th Workshop on the Use of Computational Methods in the Study of Endangered Languages, held as a hybrid event March 21-22, 2024 in St. Julians, Malta, and co-located with the 18th Conference of the European Chapter of the Association for Computational Linguistics. As the name implies, this is the seventh workshop held on the topic—the first meeting was co-located with the ACL main conference in Baltimore, Maryland in 2014 and the second, third, fourth and sixth ones in 2017, 2019, 2021 and 2023 were co-located with the 5th, 6th, 7th, and 8th editions of the International Conference on Language Documentation and Conservation (ICLDC) at the University of Hawai'i at Mānoa. The fifth iteration of the workshop was held in 2022 alongside the 60th Association of Computational Linguistics (ACL) conference in Dublin, Ireland. This is the third time this workshop has been co-located with the ACL main conference.

The primary aim of the workshop is to continue narrowing the gap between computational linguists interested in methods for endangered languages, field linguists documenting these languages, and the language communities who are striving to maintain their languages. The intention of the workshop is not merely to allow for the presentation of research, but also to build a network of computational linguists, documentary linguists, and community language activists who are able to effectively join together and serve their common interests. The organizers are pleased with the range of papers, many of which highlight the importance of interdisciplinary work and interaction between the various communities that the workshop is aimed towards.

In addition to the regular program, we hosted a special theme session discussion at the workshop. The theme for this Special Session is "Partnerships in Practice". The goal of this Special Session is to increase our shared understanding of how best to work together across disciplinary and cultural boundaries to support community goals for language revitalization.

We received 34 submissions as papers or extended abstracts or submissions to the Special Session. After a thorough review process, 19 submissions were accepted of which 13 were selected to be published in the ACL Anthology excluding the extended abstracts.

The Organizing Committee would like to thank the Program Committee for their thoughtful review of the submissions. We would moreover want to acknowledge the support of the organizers of EACL 2024.

Program Committee

Chairs

Sarah Moeller, University of Florida
Godfred Agyapong, University of Florida
Christopher Cox, Carleton University
Aditi Chaudhary, Google Research
Shruti Rijhwani, Google DeepMind
Ryan Henke, University of Wisconsin–Madison
Alexis Palmer, University of Colorado Boulder
Daisy Rosenblum, University of British Columbia, Canada
Lane Schwartz, University of Alaska-Fairbanks, USA
Antti Arppe, University of Alberta

Program Committee

Steven Abney, Univ of Michigan
Antonios Anastasopoulos, George Mason University
Alexandre Arkhipov, Universität Hamburg
Tara Azin, Carleton University
Dorothee Beermann, Norwegian University of Science and Technology
Martin Benjamin, Kamusi Project International
Claire Bowern, Yale University
Rolando Coto-Solano, Dartmouth College
Vera Ferreira, CIDLeS - Interdisciplinary Centre for Social and Language Documentation
Luke Gessler, University of Colorado, Boulder
Michael Ginn, University of Colorado
Jeff Good, University at Buffalo
Michael Goodman, LivePerson, Inc.
Atticus Harrigan, University of Alberta
Gary Holton, University of Hawaii
Raphael Iyamu, University of Florida
Marie-Odile Junker, Carleton University
Anna Kazantseva, National Research Council Canada
Frantisek Kratochvil, Palacky University Olomouc
Roland Kuhn, National Research Council of Canada
Ritesh Kumar, Dept. of Linguistics, Dr. Bhimrao Ambedkar University, Agra
Ngoc Tan Le, Universite du Quebec a Montreal
Éric Le Ferrand, Boston College
Gina-Anne Levow, University of Washington
Zoey Liu, Department of Linguistics, University of Florida
Olga Lovick, University of Saskatchewan
Jean Maillard, Meta AI
Ali Marashian, University of Colorado at Boulder
Bradley McDonnell, University of Hawai'i at Mānoa
Alexis Michaud, CNRS - LACITO
Steven Moran, Université de Neuchâtel
Saliha Muradoglu, The Australian National University
Claire Post, University of Colorado Boulder

Emily Prud'hommeaux, Boston College
Karthick Narayanan Ramakrishnan, Krea University
Enora Rice, University of Colorado Boulder
Daisy Rosenblum, UBC
Elizabeth Salesky, Johns Hopkins University
Olivia Sammons, First Nations University of Canada
Nay San, Stanford University
Emmanuel Schang, Université d'Orléans
Yves Scherrer, University of Oslo
Miikka Silfverberg, University of British Columbia
Gary Simons, SIL International
Sonal Sinha, K.M.Institute of Hindi and Linguistics, Dr. B. R Ambedkar University
Nick Thieberger, University of Melbourne
Paul Trilsbeek, Max Planck Institute for Psycholinguistics
Francis Tyers, Indiana University
Daan Van Esch, Google Research
Borui Zhang, University of Florida

Table of Contents

Program

Thursday, March 21, 2024

09:30 - 10:00	*Day-1 Welcome + Opening Remarks*
10:00 - 10:30	*Day-1 Session A*
	A Finite State Model for the Morphological Analysis of Eyak Olivia Waring and Gary Holton
	Akha, Dara-ang, Karen, Khamu, Mlabri and Urak Lawoi' language minorities' subjective perception of their languages and the outlook for development of digital tools Joanna Dolinska, Shekhar Nayak and Sumittra Suraratdecha
10:30 - 11:00	*Day-1 Break*
11:00 - 12:30	*Day-1 Session B*
	T is for Treu, but how do you pronounce that? Using C-LARA to create phonetic texts for Kanak languages Pauline Welby, Fabrice Wacalie, Manny Rayner and Chatgpt-4 C-Lara-Instance
	End-to-End Speech Recognition for Endangered Languages of Nepal Marieke Meelen, Alexander O'neill and Rolando Coto-Solano
	MunTTS: A Text-to-Speech System for Mundari Varun Gumma, Rishav Hada, Aditya Yadavalli, Pamir Gogoi, Ishani Mondal, Vivek Seshadri and Kalika Bali
12:30 - 14:00	*Day-1 Lunch*
14:00 - 15:30	*Day-1 Session C*
	Fitting a Square Peg into a Round Hole: Creating a UniMorph dataset of Kanien'kéha Verbs Anna Kazantseva, Akwiratékha Martin, Karin Michelson and Jean-Pierre Koenig
	Machine-in-the-Loop with Documentary and Descriptive Linguists Sarah Moeller and Antti Arppe

Language Root Empowering Indigenous Communities through a Community-Centric Approach to Language Revitalization via an Innovative Mobile Application
Stephanie Witkowski

15:30 - 16:00 *Day-1 Break*

16:00 - 17:30 *Day-1 Special Session I Partnerships in North America*

Data-mining and Extraction: the gold rush of AI on Indigenous Languages
Marie-Odile Junker

Creating Digital Learning and Reference Resources for Southern Michif
Heather Souter, Olivia Sammons and David Huggins Daines

Cloud-based Platform for Indigenous Language Sound Education
Min Chen, Chris Lee, Naatosi Fish, Mizuki Miyashita and James Randall

Friday, March 22, 2024

09:00 - 10:30	*Day-2 Special Session II Partnerships in Europe and Australia*
	Computel partnerships in practice Flammie Pirinen and Tromsø Troms og Finnmark
	How collaboration between Celtic language communities has improved Leena Farhat and Preben Vangberg
	Designing Indigenous PhD Projects Steven Bird
10:30 - 11:00	*Day-2 Break*
11:00 - 12:30	*Day-2 Session D*
	Automatic Transcription of Grammaticality Judgements for Language Documentation Éric Le Ferrand and Emily Prud'hommeaux
	Creating a Multimedia Online Dictionary for an Endangered Language Yarjis Xueqing Zhong
	Investigating the productivity of Passamaquoddy medials: A computational approach James Roberts
	DEVELOPING A NEPALBHĀSĀ E-CORPUS & CHALLENGES IN ENCODING ADJUSTMENT Shahani Shrestha and Prajwal Shrestha
12:30 - 14:00	*Day-2 Lunch*
14:00 - 15:30	*Day-2 Session E*
	The platform Open Text Collections as a provider of interoperable high-quality curated interlinear glossed text Sebastian Nordhoff, Christian Döhler and Mandana Seyfeddinipur

Technology and Language Revitalization: A Roadmap for the Mvskoke Language
Julia Mainzinger

Looking within the self: Investigating the Impact of Data Augmentation with Self-training on Automatic Speech Recognition for Hupa
Nitin Venkateswaran and Zoey Liu

Phonetic Granularity Effects on Forced Alignment Across Panãra and English
Emily Ahn, Eleanor Chodroff, Myriam Lapierre and Gina-Anne Levow

15:30 - 15:45 *Day-2 Closing Remarks*

Cloud-based Platform for Indigenous Language Sound Education

Min Chen
University of Washington-Bothell
minchen2@uw.edu

Chris Lee
University of Washington-Bothell
leec351@uw.edu

Naatosi Fish
Blackfeet Community College/Blackfeet Nation
naatosifish@gmail.com

Mizuki Miyashita
University of Montana
mizuki.miyashita@umontana.edu

James Randall
University of Montana
james.randall@umontana.edu

Abstract

Blackfoot is challenging for English speaking instructors and learners to acquire because it exhibits unique pitch patterns. This study presents MeTILDA (Melodic Transcription in Language Documentation and Application) as a solution to teaching pitch patterns distinct from English. Specifically, we explore ways to improve data visualization through a visualized pronunciation teaching guide called Pitch Art. The working materials can be downloaded or stored in the cloud for further use and collaboration. These features are aimed to facilitate teachers in developing curriculum for learning pronunciation, and provide students with an interactive and integrative learning environment to better understand Blackfoot language and pronunciation.

1 Introduction

Blackfoot is referred to as a pitch accent language where some words can differ in meaning based only on changes in pitch (Frantz, 2017). Consider the example below where the pronunciation of the Blackfoot word apssiw has two distinct meanings based only on where the high pitch – marked with an acute symbol – is placed.

ápssiw	H*L	'it is an arrow'
apssíw	LH*	'it is a fig; snowberry'

In our previous work, a cloud-based system called MeTILDA (Melodic Transcription in Language Documentation and Application) was developed to assist in analyzing the pitch movement of individual Blackfoot words (Lee at el, 2021), and to create a visual aid called Pitch Art for learning pitch (Fish and Miyashita 2017). We are expanding on this work to support language education by improving MeTILDA's data processing, sharing, and visualization capabilities.

- Data processing: We explore working with the relative pitch differences between syllables to enhance users' understanding of pronunciation.
- Data Sharing: We are committed to community-based-research (Czaykowska-Higgins, 2009) and are extending the data storage services so users can collaboratively utilize the data-reuse capabilities of a cloud-based system when working with Pitch Art.

Proceedings of the The Seventh Workshop on the Use of Computational Methods in the Study of Endangered Languages, pages 1–6
March 21-22, 2024

- Data visualization: We explore ways to filter results and improve data visualization to help users identify pitch patterns in the data.

2 Related Work

2.1 Existing Linguistics Tools

Currently, existing software systems fail to address the urgent need of Indigenous language education. Language learning tools such as Babbel (n.d.) and Rosetta Stone (n.d.) are advertised as effective for language education, but they largely focus on commonly spoken languages and only have limited support for typologically distinct Indigenous languages. It is even rarer to find support for languages described by their pitch counters. Studies show that pronunciation learning technique is significantly understudied in Indigenous languages (McIvor, 2015). Pitch movements are often not explicitly represented in instructions and remain unclear to learners. On the other hand, existing linguistics tools such as Praat (Boersma and Weenink, 2013) provide essential support for linguistic research on pitch in languages. Praat is a standalone tool for acoustic analysis, providing tools to analyze sound waves and sound based spectrogram. It includes visualized pitch contours, and a feature to annotate speech sounds. However, Praat was not designed for language education because it lacks learnability and pedagogical components, and its PC-based setup does not support a collaborative learning environment that enhances education. In our previous study (Lee et al., 2021), an initial effort was done to migrate several Praat functions that are commonly used for studying pitch, such as speech synthesis, audio features extractions and a spectrum analysis. While Praat can be helpful in building collaborative linguistics training sessions for linguists and teachers, it is not intuitive for students who do not have linguistics background.

2.2 Blackfoot, Pitch Art, and MeTILDA

Previous studies on Blackfoot have identified pitch movement patterns using recordings of Blackfoot native speakers (Fish and Miyashita, 2017; Miyashita and Weber, 2020). One of these studies, conducted by a team consists of a community linguist who is also a language instructor and a formally trained linguist, became the basis for Pitch Art (Fish and Miyashita, 2017), a visual representation of pitch movement throughout a word serving as a visual aid for teachers and learners of Blackfoot (Bird and Miyashita 2018). Originally, the creation of Pitch Art involved manual processes using multiple tools such as Praat, excel, and drawing software. To lessen the burden of time-consuming procedure, MeTILDA was developed to automate the Pitch Art creation in one application (Lee et al., 2021). It also provides initial visualization to analyze and compare the speech of native speakers and that of language learners, which serves as a foundation to extend this study to assist in analyzing and teaching the Blackfoot language. The current version focuses more on teacher support, and the implementation of the system for further analysis and documentation will be conducted in the future.

3 Methods

As illustrated in Figure 1 (below), MeTILDA follows a multi-tier architecture pattern to support language education and research. It provides four major components as web services, namely Creation, Learning, and User and Content Management. All web services are deployed to the Heroku cloud platform and are made publicly available for other developers to adopt and extend the functionality in their own applications.

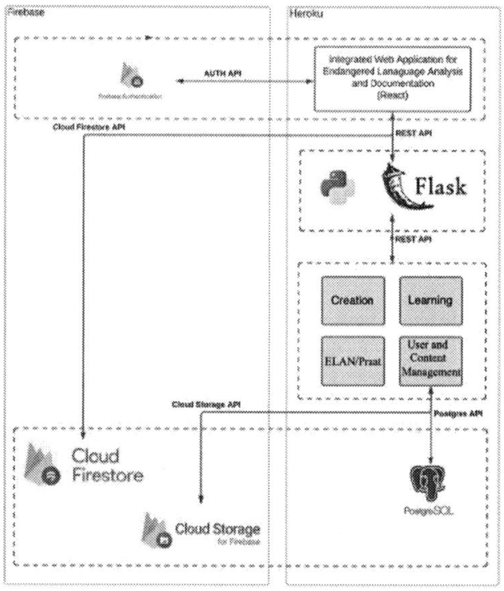

Figure 1: High-level system architecture

In addition, creating this platform as opposed to using an existing market software was drawn from the language specific community-based-research practice, which is explained in the next section where describes its Creation feature.

3.1 Creation

Previous research on Blackfoot has shown Blackfoot prosody in terms of unique patterns in pitch movement. (Fish and Miyashita, 2017; Miyashita and Weber, 2020). The shape of the pitch movement is predictable once the accent location, which interacts with pitch declination, is determined as shown in Figure 2. The declination starts from a mid-point in a speaker's pitch range; pitch is raised at the accented syllable which are the first syllable in (a), second syllable in (b), and the third syllable in (c) and gradually drops toward the target boundary low tone (Miyashita and Weber, 2020).

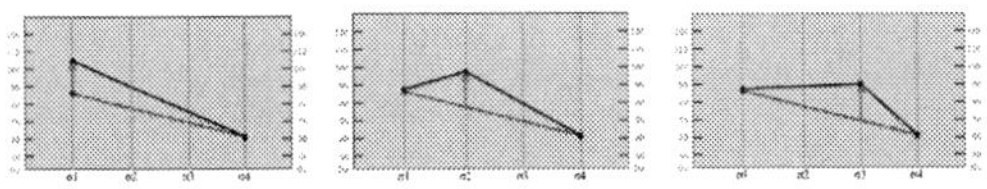

Figure 2: The pitch accent is on the (a) first, (b) second, and (c) third syllable.

Therefore, being able to transcribe pitch patterns becomes an important part of study in language teaching and learning techniques. Currently, Pitch Art used in some language classes (Fish and Miyashita, 2017; Bird and Miyashita, 2018). As mentioned previously, the creation of Pitch Art prior to the development of MeTILDA involved several steps and multiple tools, represented in Figure 3: (a) measuring the fundamental frequency (F0) of each vowel in Praat, (b) inputting values in an Excel spreadsheet to create a graph, (c) modifying the graph according to a perceptual scale, and (d) applying a design to the graph lines to make them more aesthetically pleasing.

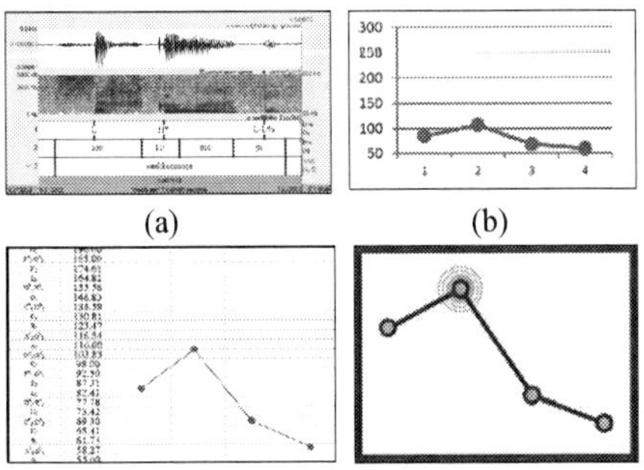

Figure 3: (a) frequency measures in Praat; (b) graph based on frequency; (c) graph on perceptual scale; (d) Pitch Art

The incorporation of a perceptual scale was determined in order to normalize the speaker-specific pitch ranges. In addition, it is challenging to identify a perceptual scale to properly reflect how pitches are auditorily perceived by human. In our previous study (Miyashita et al., 2021), we developed a MeT perceptual scale by adopting and extending the equal temperament scale in western music. The MeT scale enables the visualization of pitch data by aligning pitch data (in Hz) to a repeating series of 12 notes that form an octave. This allows users to focus on the melody or contour of the word, while disregarding the speakers' actual pitch ranges, which can vary due to age, gender, or other physical factors. We developed a feature in MeTILDA (Creation) for users to upload and process speech recordings, and to automate the creation of Pitch Art. Since the selection of parts that pitch are extracted requires knowledge in acoustic phonetics, users of the Create feature are researchers and teachers who has linguistics backgrounds. Note that the current version focuses of relative pitch movement, and it does not necessarily correspond the timing of syllable intervals.

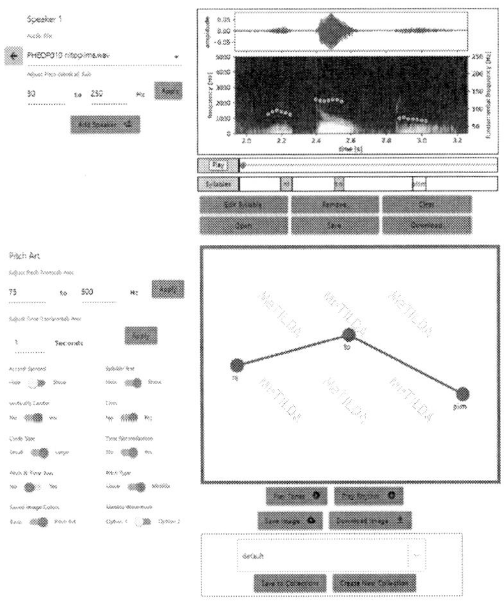

Figure 4: Creation: Audio Analysis (top) and Pitch Art (bottom)

As shown in Figure 4, the Create feature contains two main sub-components: Audio Analysis and Pitch Art. In the Audio Analysis sub-component, users can view an audio waveform and a spectrogram of speech recordings uploaded to the cloud database. Users can either upload their own recordings or access the already-existing databases. Tools are provided for users to identify vowels and enter their orthographic symbols. We have also implemented the MeT perceptual scale in MeTILDA so pitch can be calculated and represented in both a frequency scale and a perceptual scale (Miyashita et al., 2021). Once users analyze pitch, the program automatically creates Pitch Art which then can be downloaded. Additionally, users can save Pitch Art images, measurement data, listen to the tones of the word melody, and toggle a variety of appearance options (e.g., displaying orthography, showing pitch in an F0 contour or by average, showing pitch in Hz or as transcribed to a psychoacoustic scale). The Creation component can directly contribute to the training of community linguists in acoustic phonetics and to the production of teaching materials including pronunciation guides.

3.2 Learning

The Learning component provides tools for users to learn pitch patterns, practice word pronunciations, and visualize the similarity/difference between learners' and native speakers' pronunciations as shown in Figure 5.

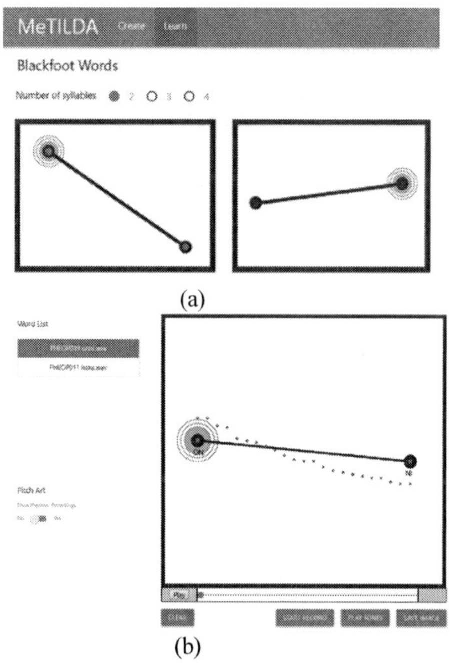

Figure 5: The Learning component

To use the Learning feature shown in Figure 5 (a), users choose a syllable pattern which is determined based on the number of syllables and the location of a pitch accent in a word (Miyashita and Weber, 2020), and listen to a native speaker's utterance. Then a Pitch Art of a sample word created based on the recording of a native speaker is shown on the screen. Then looking at the Pitch Art, users pronounce the word and record themselves, and immediately pitch tracking of the users' utterances is printed as a dotted line over the sample Pitch Art as shown in Figure 4 (b). Thus, users can compare their own pitch performance with the sample. All the recorded sounds can be saved for future access. This saving feature enables an implementation for a language course supplement, such that a teacher can students' performances.

3.3 User and Content Management

The User and the Content Management component provides the functionality to administer the MeTILDA system create or remove users, upload, move, delete files, and other administrative tasks. This component can be used to facilitate curriculum development and administer class setup/process.

Data Type	Use Case	Storage Service
Audio File (wav)	Users upload wav files for analysis.	Firebase Cloud Storage
JSON File (json)	Users save the Pitch Art data as a .json file from the Create Page.	
Image File (png)	Users save an image of the Pitch Art as .png file from the Create Page.	
Metadata about users, including user roles, and audio, image and JSON file information	Transparent to the user, this data is used by the application.	PostgreSQL
Audio Analysis Data: Words and Letter properties.	Implementation exists in the services tier to save word and letter data (e.g. time and frequency) to tables however it is not included in the front end.	
Audio Analysis Data: Words and Letter properties.	Users save the Pitch Art data as a json document from the Create Page. Introduced for the Collections feature.	Firebase Firestore

Table 1. MeTILDA Data Objects

The MeTILDA data tier makes use of multiple services in a hybrid SQL-NoSQL architecture, taking advantage of the benefits of each service for the specific data types used within the system. Table 1 describes each data type, explains its use in the system and how it maps to a service in the data storage tier. Google's Firebase Cloud Storage (Firebase, n.d.) is optimal for BLOB (binary large object) storage and is used to persist audio (wav), analysis (json), and image (png) files while Heroku

PostgreSQL (Heroku, n.d.) stores the metadata necessary for the operation of the system such as users, user roles, and metadata related to audio, analysis, and image files. In this project we introduce the use of Google Firebase Firestore, a document database optimized for real time access, to store the AudioAnalysis objects that are created as part of the Pitch Art process. To improve data re-use and the collaborative capabilities of MeTILDA, we also introduced "Collections." From the Collections page, users can create, view, rename, or delete a collection group as shown at the top of Figure 6. Once a collection group is created, users can save Pitch Art to that collection through Create component. On the Collection page, each word is displayed as a card to accommodate a thumbnail image and initial information about the PitchArt including the user supplied word, word translation, speaker name, the number of syllables in the word, and the date of creation. Clicking on the card redirects to the Learning component for review and practice.

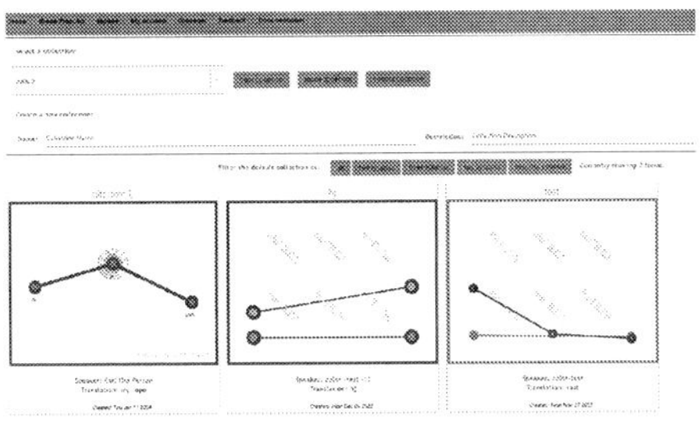

Figure 6: The Collection component

	Researcher	Teacher	Learner
Prosodic Analysis	✓	(✓)	
Upload Audio	✓	(✓)	
Create Pitch Art	✓	(✓)	
View data	✓	✓	✓
Edit Collection	✓	✓	
Play Audio	✓	✓	✓
Record Speech	✓	✓	✓
Submit Work	✓	✓	✓

Table 2. Access to Features by User Category

Users can obtain access to MeTILDA by logging in based on their user category: researcher, teacher, student, or other. These user categories were selected based on the ultimate goal for the tool to contribute to both prosody research and language teaching/learning. Different users have varied access permissions to data in the system. For example, as shown in Table 2, researchers and teachers can access all features: measurement tools, Pitch Art creation, saving, and stored data. Students do not need to create Pitch Art and have access only to play, record, and submit in the Learning component. While teachers can access all, they can optout access to the top three components that require linguistic background, and they can collaborate with researchers or other teachers who have access to all. Teachers can view their students' saved work, while students cannot see each other's submissions.

3.4 Limitations

MeTILDA is hosted on Heroku, a cloud application platform. In general, while cloud service providers implement strict security standards and industry certifications, storing sensitive and/or confidential data on external service providers requires additional measures to ensure security and privacy. Currently, MeTILDA limits the types of raw data to be processed for research activities. For example, only sound files that have acquired authorization for such use can be uploaded to MeTILDA for processing.

4 Usability Studies

While the tool is in-progress, usability surveys of MeTILDA were conducted in a linguistics class with a special topic at the University of Montana (12 students) in Fall 2022. Additionally, several language researchers via the linguist co-author's network participated in the survey. Tested components focused on those who would create Pitch Art and use edit collection features. 11 questions were chosen based on the survey research done in Lund (2001) and focused on user experience, including usefulness, ease of use, ease of learning, and satisfaction. Among them, 10 questions use the Likert format with ratings from 1 to 5 (1 being "Strongly disagree" and 5 "Strongly agree") and 1 open ended question allowing the participants to provide general feedback. A total of 25 users participated of which three were linguists, 21 were students, and 1 was a teacher. By average, the rating for each question is above 4.0 out of 5 and over half of the questions received more than 4.5 ratings, which indicates the overall effectiveness of MeTILDA in supporting the Blackfoot language education. Usability of the Learn feature has not yet been tested. More sample words for this feature need to be added before the component can be tested. However, the students in the class were shown how it works, and they informally expressed that the component is helpful for realizing their own pitch performances.

5 Conclusions

In this paper, we presented MeTILDA, an integrated system for Indigenous language education. It supports speech data processing, analysis, visualization, and sharing via three main components: Creation, Learning, and User and Content Management. The Creation component is especially helpful for the training of community linguists in acoustic phonetics and the production of teaching materials including pronunciation guides. The Learning component helps users to learn pitch patterns, practice word pronunciations, and visualize the similarity/difference between learners' and native speakers' pronunciations using Pitch Art. User and Content Management can be used to facilitate curriculum development and administer class setup/ process. In our future work, we plan to enhance pronunciation education with other Indigenous languages.

Acknowledgments

This work is supported by National Science Foundation (NSF BCS-2109654 & NSF BCS-2109437). We appreciate the late Mr. Earl Old Person and Mr. Rod Scout for their audio recording as native speakers. We also thank students in the linguistics program at the University of Montana for participating in the survey.

References

Arnold M. Lund. 2001. Measuring usability with the USE questionnaire12. *Usability interface*, 8(2):3-6.

Babbel. n.d. Available: https://www.babbel.com/ (Accessed October 14, 2023).

Donald. Frantz. 2017. *Blackfoot Grammar*. Toronto: University of Toronto Press.

E. Czaykowska-Higgins. 2009. Research models, community engagement, and linguistic fieldwork: Reflections on working within Canadian Indigenous communities. *Language Documentation and Conservation*, 3(1):15-50.

Firebase. Available: https://firebase.google.com/ (Accessed October 14, 2023).

Florian R. Hanke. 2017. *Computer supported collaborative language documentation*. PhD. Dissertation, The University of Melbourne.

Heroku. Available: https://devcenter.heroku.com/categories/reference (Accessed October 14, 2023).

Mitchell Lee, Praveena Avula, and Min Chen. 2021. MeTILDA: platform for melodic transcription in language documentation and application. In *Proceedings of the 2021 International Conference on Multimedia Retrieval*. Taipei Taiwan, pp. 607–610.

Mizuki Miyashita, Min Chen, James Randall, and Naatosi Fish. 2021. *Introducing the melodic transcription (MeT) scale for language documentation and application. University of Arizona Research Data Repository.* https://doi.org/10.25422/azu.data.14481825.v1.

Mizuki Miyashita and Ntalie Weber. 2020. Blackfoot Pitch Contour: An Instrumental Investigation. *Papers of the Forty-Ninth Algonquian Conference*. Eds. by Monica Macaulay and Margaret Noodin. 149-166.

Naatosi Fish and Mizuki Miyashita. 2017. *Guiding pronunciation of Blackfoot melody*. In *Honoring Our Teachers*. Eds. by J. Reyhner, J. Martin, L. Lockard & W. Sakiestewa Gilbert. Flagstaff, AZ: NAU, pp. 203-210.

Onowa McIvor. 2015. Adult Indigenous language learning in western Canada: what is holding us back? In *Living Our Languages: Papers from the 19th Stabilizing Indigenous Languages Symposium*. Eds. by Michel, K., Walton, P., Bourassa, E., Miller, J. (Eds.) pp. 37-49.

Paul Boersma and David Weenink. 2013. *Praat: doing phonetics by computer* [Computer program]" Version 5.3.51, http://www.praat.org.

Rosetta Stone. n.d. Available: https://www.rosettastone.com. (Accessed October 14, 2023).

Sonya Bird and Mizuki Miyashita. 2018. Teaching phonetics in the context of Indigenous language revitalization. In *Proceedings of ISAPh 2018 International Symposium on Applied Phonetics*. pp. 39-44.

Technology and Language Revitalization: A Roadmap for the Mvskoke Language

Julia Mainzinger
University of Washington
jmainz@uw.edu

Abstract

Speaking a language is inherent to maintaining cultural identity and pride for many indigenous peoples of the Americas. For the Mvskoke people, a history of removal from tribal lands and colonialism has accelerated language loss. In recent years, there has been a resurgence of tribal members interested in reclaiming their language. This paper is a discussion of how natural language processing (NLP) can come alongside community efforts to aid in revitalizing the Mvskoke language. Presented here is an overview of available resources in Mvskoke, an exploration of relevant NLP tasks and related work in endangered language contexts, and applications to language revitalization.

1 Introduction

As NLP research matures and computational linguistic technologies enter the commercial realm, low-resource and endangered languages are seeing a greater gap between what is possible for high-resource languages, and what is available for endangered language communities. Work is needed to reverse this trend and include diverse languages in the forefront of language technology.

The technology cannot be an end in itself - rather the goal of developing NLP tools should be to support the ongoing work of the endangered language community. The Mvskoke[1] have several ongoing language revitalization efforts. This paper explores some of the techniques that have been employed in other low-data situations and how they might be helpful for the Mvskoke language.

1.1 Mvskoke Language Reclamation

The Mvskoke tribe has been invested in language reclamation efforts for decades. The Muscogee (Creek) Nation established the Mvskoke Language Program more than 25 years ago to collect and create language documentation and educational resources. The tribal college, the College of the Muscogee Nation (CMN), established in 2004, has a Mvskoke Language Studies certificate program, and more recently is offering a Mvskoke Language Teaching certificate.

Though these efforts have been ongoing, the COVID-19 pandemic was a pivotal time for increasing awareness among the broader Mvskoke community. Home isolation drove people to seek online interaction. Mvskoke speakers formed online groups and began holding Mvskoke-only chats. The CMN moved its classes online, allowing students from diverse locations beyond their service area to attend. These online activities provided better access for displaced tribal members and fostered connection within the tribe. Many people began learning their heritage language for the first time.

Since 2020, new initiatives are inviting long-term involvement from community members. In 2022, the inaugural Mvskoke Language Symposium was held. In fall 2023, the CMN established its master-apprentice program, in which eight committed students are studying the language full-time under three master-level first language teachers for a full academic year.

Some of these efforts could benefit from improved computational infrastructure and Mvskoke language NLP tools. Similar surveys of have been done for the Cherokee (Zhang et al., 2022) and Bodwéwadmimwen (Potawatomi) (Lewis, 2023). The hope is that this paper might increase visibility for the needs of the Mvskoke language revitalization community.

Finally, while this author is a citizen of the Muscogee Nation and has spent time in personal conversation and working groups within the tribe over the last several years, my views are by no means representative of the entire tribe. However,

[1]Following the trend of Mvskoke-led scholarship, I will use the spelling "Mvskoke" from the traditional orthography in all cases except when referring to certain legal entities such as the tribal government and tribal college.

Proceedings of the The Seventh Workshop on the Use of Computational Methods in the Study of Endangered Languages, pages 7–12
March 21-22, 2024

I have received feedback from tribal members and leadership on this paper, and I attempt here to summarize some trends within the community.

2 The Mvskoke Language

2.1 Background

The Mvskoke language (also spelled Muscogee or Muskogee) is a member of the Muskogean family, a group of several languages indigenous to the southeastern United States (Martin and Mauldin, 2000). The language is now spoken by residents of the Muscogee (Creek) Nation and Seminole Nation in Oklahoma, and members of the Seminole tribe of Florida. It is estimated that less than 300 first-language speakers remain, and nearly all are over the age of 60[2]. The loss of language was expedited by removal from tribal lands, residential schools, and U.S. federal policies. My grandparents, who spoke Mvskoke as their first language, were encouraged to raise their children exclusively in English in order to encourage assimilation into the "white" American world. Thus my mother, like most in her generation, grew up without speaking the language. Reversing this trend of language loss will require concerted effort in multiple disciplines.

2.2 Linguistic Description

The Mvskoke language has two writing systems. The traditional spelling is a Latin-based orthography of 20 letters, which was developed in the 1800s. A phonemic system was developed by the linguist Mary R. Haas in the 1930s and is used primarily by linguists (Martin and Mauldin, 2000). Most Mvskoke speakers are familiar with the traditional spelling.

Mvskoke is a subject–object–verb (SOV) language that is agglutinating and synthetic (Martin, 2011; Frye, 2020). Subjects and objects are marked by an affix. Verbs have many prefixes, suffixes, and internal grade changes that indicate person, tense, number, and duration, among other things. For example, the verb *liketv* "to sit" could appear in many forms including:

liketv	to sit
likis	"I have sat down"
likes	"S/he sat down"
kakes	"(Of two) They sit down"
vpokes	"(Of three or more) They sit down"
likepvs	"Have a seat!"
likvranis	"I will sit"
ohliketska	"Are you sitting (up there)?"

3 Mvskoke Language Resources

Mvskoke is a smaller language group than Cherokee, which has a growing NLP community, but has more speakers than Seneca, which is seeing great strides in both NLP research and language revitalization (Liu et al., 2021). We can take cues from other indigenous language communities in developing NLP tools for Mvskoke based on the size and type of resources available. This section contains an overview of available resources.

3.1 Text

Mvskoke has a rich history of language documentation, dating back to the 1730s (Frye, 2020). A few of the more recent documentation efforts are highlighted here. A series of 29 traditional stories was written in 1915 by Earnest Gouge. In the 1930s, Mary R. Haas conducted extensive fieldwork documentation, along with James Hill, who wrote down stories, songs, sermons, letters, and descriptions of Mvskoke cultural practices. Beginning in 1992, Dr. Jack Martin and Margaret Mauldin began preserving much of this linguistic work, and published the Earnest Gouge collection in 2004 and the Haas/Hill collection in 2014 (Gouge et al., 2004; Haas et al., 2015). The majority of these texts contain orthographic transcriptions, phonemic transcriptions, morpheme-by-morpheme glosses, and free translation into English. In 2000, Dr. Martin published a dictionary in print, and the FLEx data was published online in 2023[3] (Martin and Mauldin, 2000). The New Testament was translated in the early 1900s and republished in 2011 (Randall and Randall).

3.2 Audio Recordings

The Gouge stories, a portion of the Haas/Hill texts, as well as other stories and letters have been recorded by dictation, and the entire New Testament has been recorded, totalling about 50 hours of read speech. From 2015-2017, the Seminole Nation's Pumvhakv School conducted video interviews of fluent Seminole and Mvskoke speakers. This has led to a collection of nearly 14 hours of transcribed spontaneous speech in ELAN. Other untranscribed audio data includes a series of radio

[2]This estimate is from personal communication with a member of Ekvn-Yefolecv, a community of Mvskoke people.

[3]https://www.webonary.org/muscogee/

recordings from the 1990s as well as audio lessons and story tellings recorded by the Mvskoke Language Program. In the future, the CMN hopes to build a recording studio to conduct interviews and produce other Mvskoke-language media. These resources can be accessed on the Muskogee (Seminole/Creek) Documentation Project website [4].

3.3 Corpus Development and Archiving

The available resources have not yet been centralized into a corpus ready for NLP. Most of the resources exist in various file formats (Word, PDF, mp3, wav, etc) on hard drives, cloud folders, and websites. As part of my speech experiments, I am developing a labeled speech corpus; more information about the data preparation is in Section 4.2. A structured, searchable corpus would be useful for educators, as mentioned in Section 4.4.

Archival versions of many of the audio recordings are housed at the Sam Noble Museum at the University of Oklahoma. The Mvskoke National Library and Archives houses physical documents and cultural objects, as well as a growing digital collection, with moderated access for community members. In similar fashion, an NLP corpus would need to have appropriate viewing access in accordance with the wishes of the families represented.

3.4 Language Learning Technology

A Muscogee language learning app was published several years ago with some limited vocabulary lists, songs, and quiz games. Since 2020, there has been a marked increase in the effort to make learning materials available online. The Muscogee Nation has been releasing video recordings of online and community classes, and a Mvskoke language learning podcast has been proposed. The dictionary website and mobile app are in the final stages of publishing. In order to facilitate communicating in the language over text, I have built a Mvskoke keyboard with limited predictive text based on a simple unigram language model that is currently undergoing community evaluation[5]. NLP tools can support the growing work of Mvskoke language education and revitalization.

4 NLP Roadmap

The goal of any NLP tool development should contribute to the language community's goals. For the Mvskoke people, this includes empowering language educators, producing new language speakers, leading beginning speakers to fluency, and removing obstacles to sharing knowledge within the language community.

4.1 Morphological Analysis

Morphological analysis, the task of splitting words into morphemes, is helpful to many NLP systems. As an agglutinative and synthetic language in which verbs can have hundreds of forms and words can grow quite long, Mvskoke technology could be improved by morphological parsing. For example, a morphological parser could improve dictionary search by being able to split long queries into morphemes. Generative morphology can be implemented in language learning software, as in the case of Kanyen'kʹeha (Mohawk) (Lessard et al., 2018). Furthermore, a morphological parser could be built into the mobile keyboard with predictive text, helping Mvskoke speakers use the language in their daily life.

Current machine learning approaches rely on corpora on the order of millions or more tokens. The amount of text data available for Mvskoke is relatively small in comparison. However, since Mvskoke has a wonderful dictionary and grammar, a rule-base approach may be advantageous over a data-driven approach. Finite-state transducer approaches have seen success in other morphologically complex languages, such as Yup'ik (Strunk and Bender, 2020) and Inuktitut (Farley, 2009). Deep learning techniques are also possible, as seen in the case of Innu-aimun (Le et al., 2022). If deep learning techniques were attempted for Mvskoke, training could be supervised by the interlinear glossed text (IGT) collected in the language documentation, but experimentation is needed to determine if the amount of data is sufficient.

4.2 Speech Recognition

Automatic Speech Recognition (ASR) is the process of using machine learning to produce written text from audio recordings. An ASR model could be used in applications such as speech-to-text input and language learning software. Classically, work in language documentation has viewed ASR as a way to overcome the "transcription bottleneck." Two community members specifically requested assistance with the burden of transcription. However, there are applications for ASR that can go beyond transcription, though transcriptions are im-

[4] https://muskogee.pages.wm.edu

[5] https://github.com/muscogee-language-foundation/muscogee-keyboard

	dev	test
WER	0.27	0.35
CER	0.09	0.06

Table 1: Results of ASR model fine-tuned on 1.12 hours of data of a single speaker.

portant for providing more training data and valuable language documentation. This author agrees with (Bird, 2020) that the goal of speech technology need not be full transcriptions but rather that the diversity of computational methods can facilitate a number of tasks that offer more participatory opportunities for speakers of the language.

One such example application is corpus search, which could allow users to find examples from recordings using an audio query. In low data settings, the high error rates of traditional ASR may render transcriptions unusable. Instead, spoken term detection is an area of research that could be used in place of traditional ASR, to detect isolated terms in a speech collection (Le Ferrand, 2023). Spoken term detection can be accomplished via either ASR with phone recognition, or dynamic time warping (DTW).

I have begun aligning recordings with transcripts at the word and phrase level using the Montreal Forced Aligner (McAuliffe et al., 2017). Only a small portion of the many hours of transcribed audio data is prepared in phrase-transcription pairs. Mvskoke can be easily mapped with a near 1-to-1 grapheme-to-phoneme conversion. Therefore, I am able to map Mvskoke to an English phone set and adapt an English acoustic model to Mvskoke with 2 hours of audio data. Resulting alignments on new transcripts require only minimal correction.

Initial ASR experiments are conducted by finetuning the Massively Multilingual Speech (MMS-1B-l1107) model, a pretrained wav2vec 2.0 model (Pratap et al., 2023; Baevski et al., 2020). The model is trained with 1.12 hours of low-noise data from one speaker. Preliminary results show promise, especially considering the lack of a language model. Forced alignment will allow for improvement by providing more data for supervision, and a language model can improve word accuracy. Results are shown in Table 1 and details of experimentation are in Appendix A.

4.3 Text to Speech

Two instructors at the College of the Muscogee Nation expressed interest in training a text-to-speech synthesis (TTS) model to support language learning software. In their view, engaging with the language outside the classroom would help keep students at the college motivated during school breaks. As Mvskoke language learners are usually surrounded by English on a day-to-day basis, time needs to be set aside for listening to the language. Existing recordings can serve as one resource, but being able to generate new examples can provide a more interactive experience. With so few speakers remaining, TTS can relieve some of the burden of recording elders for language learning applications, especially as recordings for posterity generally take priority.

In a low data situations, TTS traditionally requires careful rule-based construction (Koffi and Petzold, 2022; Chasaide et al., 2015). However, a TTS model for Ojibwe has been trained using a neural approach from scratch with about 12 hours of speech, and is deployed into a web-based language learning platorm (Hammerly et al., 2023), paving the way for other indigenous languages to follow suit in using TTS for language revitalization.

4.4 Corpus Search

Because there is no longer intergenerational language transmission for Mvskoke, we are dependent on teachers to continue passing on the language. Therefore NLP technology for Mvskoke needs to be built with language education in mind. There has been an increase in fluent speakers being willing to teach over the last few years, but pedagogy needs to improve in order to move beginning speakers to fluency (Frye, 2020). One way to support teachers is by providing access to a digital corpus. Currently, some resources are available for access through documentation and archival websites, or can be purchased in print form. But for teachers preparing lessons, an organized and searchable corpus would be hugely beneficial.

Teacher in the Loop was proposed in (Neubig et al., 2020) as an interface for educators to have access to textual language documentation resources. In this type of program, a teacher could not only search the corpus, but could also provide feedback during search to improve the system. Yup'ik developers have built a great example of a dictionary website with in-context examples that are linked to interviews and texts.[6]. Building a searchable corpus with these features would require at least

[6]https://www.yugtun.com/

a morphological analyzer, word embeddings, an indexed digital corpus, a search engine, and a user interface, and is therefore a significant undertaking. In the case of Mvskoke, the main obstacles are lack of funding and human resources.

My current experiments with ASR could aid corpus search in that audio results can be returned by matching text queries to automatically transcribed text. Even if word accuracy is low, spoken term detection techniques could be utilized to match queries to most likely examples as mentioned in section 4.2.

5 Ethical Considerations

Due to the painful history of colonization and even recent data misuse, indigenous people are wary of allowing sensitive documents and recordings to be viewed by those outside the tribe. Therefore, there is an active push for tribes to collect and maintain their own language data. Te Hiku Media, an organization active in Māori language revitalization, has written on concerns about the use of indigenous language data in training AI, and has created guidelines for communities to write their own data licenses (Mahelona et al., 2023; Media, 2022). A digital corpus of Mvskoke language materials would need to be treated with care and dignity, and any use of the data to train NLP systems should benefit the tribal community.

6 Conclusion

This survey presents the current state of resource availability and development of NLP tools for the Muscogee language. Also examined are challenges and steps towards the future development of NLP tools and how they can be applied to the goals of language revitalization in the Muscogee community.

Acknowledgements

I am thankful to faculty at the College of the Muscogee Nation, employees of the Muscogee (Creek) Nation, and Mvskoke friends and community members for their helpful comments. Thank you to my advisor, Gina-Anne Levow for her encouragement and guidance. Thank you to Jack Martin for providing resources and support. And I am especially indebted to our tribal elders who have passed on our language and culture through much adversity. *Mvto*.

References

Alexei Baevski, Henry Zhou, Abdelrahman Mohamed, and Michael Auli. 2020. wav2vec 2.0: A framework for self-supervised learning of speech representations.

Steven Bird. 2020. Sparse transcription. *Computational Linguistics*, 46(4):713–744.

Ailbhe Ní Chasaide, Neasa Ní Chiaráin, Harald Berthelsen, Christoph Wendler, and Andrew Murphy. 2015. Speech technology as documentation for endangered language preservation: The case of irish. In *ICPhS*, volume 2015, page 18th.

B. Farley. 2009. The uqailaut project.

Melanie Frye. 2020. Improving mvskoke (creek) language learning outcomes: A frequency-base approach. *Thesis, University of Oklahoma*.

Earnest Gouge, Edited, Translated by Jack B. Martin, and Juanita McGirt. 2004. *Totkv Mocvse / New Fire: Creek Folktales*. Norman: University of Oklahoma Press.

Mary R. Haas, James H. Hill, Jack B. Martin, Margaret McKane Mauldin, and Juanita McGirt. 2015. *Creek (Muskogee) Texts*. University of California Publications.

Christopher Hammerly, Sonja Fougère, Giancarlo Sierra, Scott Parkhill, Harrison Porteous, and Chad Quinn. 2023. A text-to-speech synthesis system for border lakes Ojibwe. In *Proceedings of the Sixth Workshop on the Use of Computational Methods in the Study of Endangered Languages*, pages 60–65, Remote. Association for Computational Linguistics.

Ettien Koffi and Mark Petzold. 2022. A tutorial on formant-based speech synthesis for the documentation of critically endangered languages. *Linguistic Portfolios*, 11(3).

Ngoc Tan Le, Antoine Cadotte, Mathieu Boivin, Fatiha Sadat, and Jimena Terraza. 2022. Deep learning-based morphological segmentation for indigenous languages: A study case on innu-aimun. In *Proceedings of the Third Workshop on Deep Learning for Low-Resource Natural Language Processing*, pages 146–151.

Eric Le Ferrand. 2023. *Leveraging Speech Recognition for Interactive Transcription in Australian Aboriginal Communities*. Theses, Charles Darwin University.

Greg Lessard, Nathan Brinklow, and Michael Levison. 2018. Natural language generation for polysynthetic languages: Language teaching and learning software for Kanyen'kéha (Mohawk). In *Proceedings of the Workshop on Computational Modeling of Polysynthetic Languages*, pages 41–52, Santa Fe, New Mexico, USA. Association for Computational Linguistics.

Robert Lewis. 2023. A survey of computational infrastructure to help preserve and revitalize bodwéwadmimwen. In *Proceedings of the Sixth Workshop on the Use of Computational Methods in the Study of Endangered Languages*, pages 44–50, Remote. Association for Computational Linguistics.

Zoey Liu, Robert Jimerson, and Emily Prud'hommeaux. 2021. Morphological segmentation for Seneca. In *Proceedings of the First Workshop on Natural Language Processing for Indigenous Languages of the Americas*, pages 90–101, Online. Association for Computational Linguistics.

Keoni Mahelona, Gianna Leoni, Suzanne Duncan, and Miles Thompson. 2023. OpenAI's whisper is another case study in colonisation.

Jack B. Martin. 2011. *A Grammar of Creek (Muskogee)*. University of Nebraska Press.

Jack B. Martin and Margaret McKane Mauldin. 2000. *A Dictionary of Creek/Muskogee*. University of Nebraska Press.

Michael McAuliffe, Michaela Socolof, Sarah Mihuc, Michael Wagner, and Morgan Sonderegger. 2017. Montreal Forced Aligner: Trainable Text-Speech Alignment Using Kaldi. In *Proc. Interspeech 2017*, pages 498–502.

Te Hiku Media. 2022. Data sovereignty and the kaitiakitanga license.

Graham Neubig, Shruti Rijhwani, Alexis Palmer, Jordan MacKenzie, Hilaria Cruz, Xinjian Li, Matthew Lee, Aditi Chaudhary, Luke Gessler, Steven Abney, Shirley Anugrah Hayati, Antonios Anastasopoulos, Olga Zamaraeva, Emily Prud'hommeaux, Jennette Child, Sara Child, Rebecca Knowles, Sarah Moeller, Jeffrey Micher, Yiyuan Li, Sydney Zink, Mengzhou Xia, Roshan S Sharma, and Patrick Littell. 2020. A summary of the first workshop on language technology for language documentation and revitalization.

Vineel Pratap, Andros Tjandra, Bowen Shi, Paden Tomasello, Arun Babu, Sayani Kundu, Ali Elkahky, Zhaoheng Ni, Apoorv Vyas, Maryam Fazel-Zarandi, Alexei Baevski, Yossi Adi, Xiaohui Zhang, Wei-Ning Hsu, Alexis Conneau, and Michael Auli. 2023. Scaling speech technology to 1,000+ languages.

Steve Randall and Monte Randall, editors. *Nak-cokv Mucvsat (The Bible)*. Wiyo Publishing Company.

Lonny Alaskuk Strunk and Emily M. Bender. 2020. A finite-state morphological analyzer for central alaskan yup'ik.

Thomas Wolf, Lysandre Debut, Victor Sanh, Julien Chaumond, Clement Delangue, Anthony Moi, Pierric Cistac, Tim Rault, Rémi Louf, Morgan Funtowicz, and Jamie Brew. 2019. Huggingface's transformers: State-of-the-art natural language processing. *CoRR*, abs/1910.03771.

Shiyue Zhang, Ben Frey, and Mohit Bansal. 2022. How can NLP help revitalize endangered languages? a case study and roadmap for the Cherokee language. In *Proceedings of the 60th Annual Meeting of the Association for Computational Linguistics (Volume 1: Long Papers)*, pages 1529–1541, Dublin, Ireland. Association for Computational Linguistics.

A Appendix. ASR Experimentation

Speech data for training and evaluation consists of low-noise recordings of read speech from one female speaker. Other data is significantly more noisy and therefore omitted for this initial experiment. The clarity of recordings likely lowers the error rate.

The data is separated into training and test sets, and the development set is automatically split at 10% of the training set during the preprocessing step. The training set consists of 1,703 utterances, and the test set consists of 141 utterances, with the lengths shown in the table below (h=hour, m=minute, s=second).

	train+dev	test
Total Length	1.12h	10.2m
Average Length	2.3s	4.4s

Implementation follows the steps detailed by Patrick von Platen to fine-tune the MMS adapter using Huggingface Transformers[7] (Wolf et al., 2019). I fine-tune MMS-1B-l1107 (Pratap et al., 2023), a wav2vec model (Baevski et al., 2020). The following parameters are used during training:

Learning rate: 1e-3
Training epochs: 4
Train batch size: 2
Eval batch size: 8
Gradient accumulation steps: 4

Example output:

Predict:	vtok**k**ehatt**e** vtokfenētk**e** vtoy**ē**hattē
Reference:	vtokyehattē vtokfenētkē vtoyehattē

Mvskoke has geminate consonants, in which clusters of like consonants are slightly longer than single consonants. The model correctly identifies the "tt" geminate but mis-identifies a nongeminate consonant "k". The model also has trouble distinguishing a long "ē" from a short "e", which can be difficult even for speakers.

[7] https://huggingface.co/blog/mms_adapters

Investigating the productivity of Passamaquoddy medials: A computational approach

James Cooper Roberts
Massachusetts Institute of Technology
77 Massachusetts Ave
Cambridge, MA 02139
jcrobert@mit.edu

Abstract

Medials are a class of morphemes in the language Passamaquoddy that are involved in the construction of verbs. Members of this class have an unknown level of productivity. In this work, I investigate the matter by generating a comprehensive list of possible verb and compare it against a text corpus. Given the amount of time and energy traditional fieldwork/lexical decision tasks require, this methodology is adavntageous, particularly for Algonquianists working on similar topics. I ultimately find that 679 of approximately 15 million possible verbs are attested in said corpus. The distribution of medial type frequencies would suggest that a handful of medials are productive (under some metrics for productivity) while many medials are not. It is my hope that this data will inform future fieldwork research on the topic.

1 Introduction

This work is part of a larger research effort on a certain set of morphemes in the endangered language Passamaquoddy (Algonquian, ISO: pqm). In this language, three distinct classes of morphemes are involved in the construction of verb stems. In the literature, these classes are referred to as *inital*, *medial*, and *final* (Bloomfield, 1946; Goddard, 1990).

(1)	$\emptyset$–[$_{stem}$	ut-	ek-	som	] -on
3- [	from	sheet	cut	] -N
. [	**initial**	**medial**	**final**	] .

's/he cuts a slice from it'

[1]The focus of the current study lies with the second of these. Medials in Passamaquoddy and the Algonquian languages in general are linguistically interesting for a number of reasons; some recent works have investigated the (morpho)syntax and semantics of this morphological class (Brittain, 2003; Quinn, 2009; Branigan et al., 2005; Biedny et al., 2021; Whitney et al., 2022; Slavin, 2012), but several questions remain. Crucially, there is the issue of *productivity*—i.e., does the grammar of Passamaquoddy allow speakers to create new verbs with these medials? Claims of productive verb stem construction are sprinkled throughout the literature on Algonquian; Bakker (1997), for example, claims that it is possible "make new [verb stem] combinations [with initials/medials/finals] productively" in Cree. However, he also reports that Cree speakers are unable to "ascribe meanings" to them, which casts some doubt on his initial claim. In more recent work, Mazzoli (2023) argues that some finals can combine with a root in predictable ways (and are therefore productive), while other finals can not.

As far as I am aware, though, there has been no systematic work investigating medial productivity. The answer to this question are consequential not only to our understanding of Passamaquoddy, but also to those interested in the language's revitalization. If verb stem construction is a regular process, second language instructors should impart this knowledge to learners. However, going about a survey on the matter is not a trivial effort, considering that the current estimate on the number of medials in Passamaquoddy is 97. Evaluating productivity with a lexical decision task would require a linguist to run through thousands of possible verbs with a native speaker, which can be time-consuming for both the researcher and the consultant. In any effort to document a language of Passamaquoddy's vitality, time is of the essence. Can this research be streamlined?

In this project, I automate this effort by first generating a list of all possible medial-containing verb stems. I then determine which of them are attested by comparing said list against a text corpus. In 2, I

[1]In this article, Passamaquoddy words are orthographically represented with the Newell-Hale Alphabet. This writing system is largely phonemic, save for some characters. For more details on the orthography and the language's phonology, I direct the reader to Grishin (2023) for an overview.

Proceedings of the The Seventh Workshop on the Use of Computational Methods in the Study of Endangered Languages, pages 13–20
March 21-22, 2024 ©2024 Association for Computational Linguistics

situate this work by providing some details on the Passamquoddy language and its speakers. In 3, I elaborate on the morphophonology of verb stems. This is followed by 4, where I discuss the procedure employed in generating the possible verb stems and running them against the dictionary. I provide a statistical analysis for the data in 5, and conclude with a discussion of my findings and plans for future work in 6.

2 Language background

Passamaquoddy is a member of the Northeastern branch of Eastern Algonquian subfamily, which makes it a close relative of Mi'kmaq, Penobscot, and Abenaki (Oxford). There are two mutually-intelligible dialects of this language, namely Passamaquoddy and Maliseet (an exonym for Wolastoqey, alternatively spelled *Malecite*). The former of these is spoken in Eastern Maine, USA, while the latter is spoken in New Brunswick, Canada (Grishin, 2023). Given their similarities, the language is also referred to as *Passamaquoddy-Maliseet* or *Passamaquoddy-Wolastoqey*. While there are some differences between the two, none of them are consequential to this work as far as I am aware. For the sake of brevity, I refer to the language as simply Passamaquoddy in this article.

Like other Algonquian languages, Passamaquoddy is polysynthetic, which is reflected especially clearly in the domain of verbs. Interestingly, verbs do a large portion of the semantic legwork in the language; based on some preliminary investigations, there are no adjectives proper, no singular "group nouns" (e.g., *team, family*) (Peter Grishin, p.c.), and no non-verb measure functions (e.g., *height, weight, cost*). In Passamaquoddy, equivalent expressions are handled by verbs, which are subject to the tripartite structure introduced in 1. Other features include complex agreement patterns, proximate/obviative marking for third person noun phrases, animate/inanimate distinctions for nouns, and free word order (Grishin, 2023).

Recent estimates claim that there are approximately 500 native speakers of the language (Lewis and Fennig, 2016), the majority of which are over the age of sixty (Crockett-Current, 2020). The risk of language dormancy has spurred the creation of language courses at universities (Crockett-Current, 2020) and grade schools. Detailed knowledge of Passamaquoddy grammar is crucial for such programs, and could aid in non-native speakers achieving native-like fluency in the language.[2]

3 More on verb stems

In this section, I present some facts about Passamaquoddy verb stems and medials that are relevant to this research and/or may be of interest to the reader. Most of the following is based off of LeSourd (1988), Bloomfield (1946) and Goddard (1990).

To begin, some verbs do not include medials, such as that in (2). In Passamaquoddy, a well-formed verb stem consists of at minimum a final. Ergo, some verbs do not include an initial or medial. Note that the existence of a verb stem with a medial does not necessarily entail the existence of a similar verb stem without a medial. For example, (3) is an attested word in the dictionary (see 4), but a corresponding medial-less form *aluwahke* is unattested.

(2)
pehki-	kon
clean	be$_{II}$
initial	final

'it is clean'

(3)
aluw-	al-	ke
aluw	al	ahke
initial	medial	final

's/he goes around causing trouble'

Furthermore, many medials appear noun-like in their translations into other languages, such as *atpe* 'head' in (4). However, the syntax and morphology of Passamaquoddy do not treat these morphemes as though they were nouns.[3] As a result, predicates that may require a transitive verb with an object in other languages can be expressed with a single intransitive verb in Passamaquoddy.[4]

[2]A reviewer wonders whether this specific work presented in this article was requested by the Passamaquoddy and Maliseet communities. There is a desire to produce more speakers of the language, and many members of the community are involved in the aforementioned pedagogical efforts. While this research into medial productivity is beneficial to language pedagogy for the reasons mentioned in 1, this work was not directly requested.

[3]It is worth mentioning that medials often bear no obvious resemblance to their respective noun. For example, the medial translated as 'head' is *atpe*, but the independent noun for head is *woniyakon*.

[4]The argument structure of a verb (specifically, the transitivity of the verb and the animacy of one of its arguments) is determined by the final. The subscripts on the finals in (2), (4), and (5) stand for *inanimate intransitive*, *animate intransitive*, and *transitive inanimate*, respectively.

(4) mask- -atpe -mahsu
smelly head smell_{AI}
initial medial final
's/he has a smelly head/hair'

Medials can not be consistently interpreted as the theme of their respective verb. In (5) for example, *ocok* has an arguably instrumental interpretation.

(5) kopp- ocok- ahm
close mushy by.tool_{TI}
's/he seals it with a sticky substance'

There are a number of (semi-regular) phonological alternations that occur within verb stems. In the remainder of this section, I will briefly summarize these alternations; specifically, I present those that have an overt effect on a verb stem's orthographic representation, as these are most relevant to the current study.

If the synthesis of a word stem creates a consonant cluster at a morpheme boundary, an epenthetic [i] is inserted between the two consonants.

(6) kin naqot
initial final
kininaqot 'it looks big'

Some vowels (*o* in particular) will drop at morpheme boundaries in certain environments. If *o* would otherwise be the first segment of the verb stem, it is dropped. It will also drop to resolve vowel hiatus (7) or to bring two identical sonorants together (8). It is also lost before obstruents (9).

(7) mace olan
initial final
macelan 'it starts raining'

(8) otol olan
initial final
tollan 'it is raining'

(9) kin okil
initial final
kinkil 's/he is big'

[i] and [a] will occasionally drop if they are preceded by a consonant and followed by an hC cluster.

(10) con ahte
initial final
conte 'it is stoped in place'

If an hC cluster ends up before a consonant, [h] is dropped.

(11) ehq ihtahal
initial final
eqtahal 's/he stops sitting'

If a [t] is preceded by an [i] at a morpheme boundary, it undergoes palatilization. This includes the aforementioned epenthetic [i]. Some morphemes such as *essi* and *eyi* "lexically" palatilize a preceding [t] despite not starting with [i].

(12) wikuwat eyi
initial final
wikuwaceyu 'it is fun'

An underlying /i/ is realized as [u] when it is word final.

(13) ahq al omi
initial medial final
ahqalomu 's/he is shy'

In the case of vowel hiatus, a glide (or sometimes [h]) is inserted. The complete list of alternations is presented in Table 1.

		first vowel			
		a	e	i	u
second vowel	a	aya	iya	iya	uwa
	e	aye	iye	iye	uwe
	i	ayi	ihi		uwi
	o	a	e	i	u
	u	ayu	iyu		uwu

Table 1: Vowel hiatus repairs

4 Procedure

Using a Python script, I begin by generating a comprehensive list of medial-bearing possible verb stems. This is produced by exhaustively combining every initial, medial, and final from a machine-readable list.[5] For each verb stem, the phonological rules sketched in 3 are applied. These are modeled computationally using base Python functions (if/elif/else, find-replace functions, truncation, etc.). The phonological alternations are broken into two separate series, which I have dubbed *pre-compounding phonology* and *post-compounding phonology*. As the nomenclature implies, pre-compounding rules act on individual morphemes prior to synthesis into a verb stem, while post-compounding rules apply after. The former houses

[5]See 6.

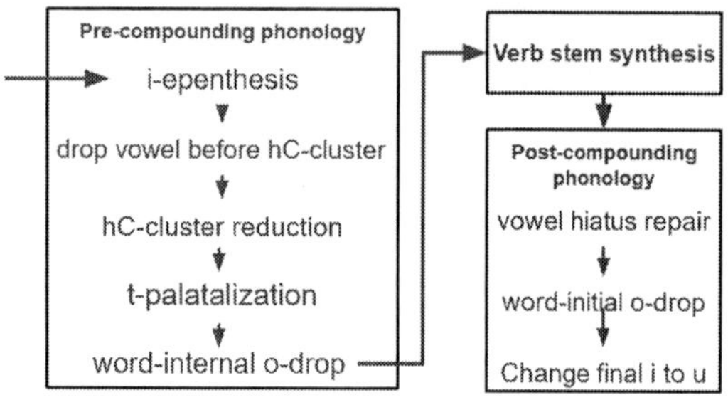

Figure 1: Diagram of simulated phonology rules applied to verb stem.

phonological rules that apply at morpheme boundaries, while the latter is for alternations that apply to the entire verb stem or at the word boundary.

A sketch of the rules and their application order is provided in Figure 1. The ordering is not trivial as some rules appear to feed others (e.g., i-epenthesis and t-palatilization).

This process yields 14,949,058 possible verb stems (502 initials * 97 medials * 307 finals). This list is then compared against a list of verbs from the Passamaquoddy-Maliseet Language Portal (pmp), an online dictionary and language resource. Over a hundred hours of transcribed conversation between native speakers are also available on the language portal. According to the website, at least 85 speakers are represented in the corpus. The transcriptions are particular helpful for finding token frequencies, which is relevant to the quantitative analysis of productivity presented in 5.

It should be noted here that the list of verbs from the dictionary contains only 14,941 elements, so just a fraction of the possible verb stems in the generated list can be attested. This asymmetry in sizes may be jarring, but this analysis will nevertheless provide some insight into the behavior of Passamaquoddy medials.

5 Data & analysis

Of the $\approx$15 million possible verb stems generated, exactly 697 of them had exact matches in the dictionary. 84 of the 97 medials have attested forms, with Figure 2 (see A) showing a Zipf-like distribution in frequency. The highest frequency of any medial was 77 (*atok*), while the lowest was 1 (*akomite*, *altoqe*, many others). A similar graph with additional information on mean token frequency is provided in Figure 3.

With this data, there are a number of ways to calculate the productivity of each medial. One established method in the morphological productivity literature is Baayen's criterion (Baayen and Lieber, 1991). This method defines the productiveness of a morphological process by the function $\frac{n_1}{N}$, where N is the total number of words formed by said process and n_1 is the number of hapax legomena (words that only occur once in a corpus) derived by that process. The greater the number of hapax legomena in a set of derived words, the more productive a process is said to be. Unfortunately, none of the verbs in the corpus used in this study are hapax legomena, so this is not an acceptable option.[6]

Another way of quantifying productivity is Yang's Sufficiency Principle (Yang, 2018), which states that a process is productive if it meets the following criterion:

(14) $(N - M) \leq \theta_N$ where $\theta_N = \frac{N}{lnN}$

...where N is the number of items to which the process can possibly apply, and M is the number of items known to undergo that process. This method seems particularly well-suited to this research, as it does not presuppose knowledge on the number of exceptions to a process. For any given medial, M is the number of attested verbs that contain said medial. It seems reasonable to conclude that every possible pairing of initial and final is the set to which a medial can apply, so N = 154,114 ($n_{initial}$ * n_{final}) and $\theta_N \approx$ 12,901.5. These calculations predict that none of the medials are productive, but they would predict this even if every verb in the corpus were an attested form with a single shared medial (15).

(15) (154,114 - 15,000) $\not\leq$ 12,901.5

One final method I consider in this work compares type frequency (number of forms derived by a process) with the mean token frequency of words formed by that process. Under this method, a construction is said to be more productive when the type frequency is high and the mean token frequency is low (Baayen, 1991). In figure 3, we see evidence for the productivity of some medials under this view. Specifically, *atok*, *amk*, *ek*, *ak*, *apsk*, and *alok* are plausibly so. For medials of lower type frequencies, though, there is no evidence to indicate that they are productive.

[6]The only hapax legomena in the corpus is *u*, an interjection analogous to English *oh*.

6 Concluding discussion

Considering several different techniques for operationalizing productivity, I find evidence to support the productivity of a small handful of medials. At the very least, figure 3 is a helpful indicator of which morphemes are more productive than others. Yang's Sufficiency Principle has a much less charitable view of the data, but this is arguably a case of the method not fitting the data we have. The amount of things a single medial can combine with is massive, and it alone trumps the size of the dictionary many times over.

It is curious why so few of the possible verb stems had attested forms in the dictionary. Of course, there are many things outside of *initial* + *medial* + *final* in the Passamaquoddy verbal lexicon. As previously stated, some verbs lack a medial and even an initial. So, it makes sense that some verbs in the dictionary do not have a companion in the comprehensive verb stem list. More puzzling are the missing medials from the attested forms list. I mention in 5 that only 84 medials are represented in the 697 attested forms; this indicates to me that there may have been an error in generating the possible verb stems. I am uncertain whether this was due to an unforeseen consequence of my own code or the result of a phonology rule I neglected to add, but it warrants further investigation.

Regardless, the results of this study provide a number of interesting avenues for future research. For the seemingly-productive medials, one question is their semantic import. Are their semantics consistent across every verb stem? Do they consistently have instrumental/theme/classificatory interpretations, or are the meanings of their respective verb stems more opaque or idiomatic? Conversely, for medials with less attested forms, are their semantics consistent? Returning to the question of productivity, I plan to continue investigating this matter through lexical decision tasks with native speakers. It would make sense to start with medials that already have a large number of attested cases, then moving on to medials with fewer.

In this work, I present a simple yet (as far as I am aware) novel approach to investigating morphological productivity in an endangered polysynthetic language. While the findings of this study are interesting, Passamaquoddy is only a small part of the full story concerning Algonquian verbal morphology; I am hopeful that the methodology I introduce here will be employed by others working on Algonquian languages with similar questions.

In conclusion, this work proposes a computational approach to to investigating the productivity of medials in Passamaquoddy. For languages with low vitality, such methods are especially valuable for research and revitalization efforts. While only a small number of generated verbs were actually attested in the dictionary, there is evidence for some medials being productive. Regardless, this work provides a foundation for future fieldwork and more "traditional" linguistic inquiry.

Acknowledgments

This work is indebted to Peter Grishin, Jonathan Rawski, Norvin Richards, and three anonymous reviewers. I thank them for their helpful insight and feedback. The lists of initials, medials, and finals used in this project was compiled by Norvin Richards. The PM Portal entry frequency data was compiled by Yadav Gowda. Errors are my own.

7 Data availability statement

For access to the data and code used in this study, please contact me at `jcrobert@mit.edu`.

References

Passamaquoddy-maliseet language portal; language keepers and passamaquoddy-maliseet dictionary project. http://www.pmportal.org.

Harald Baayen. 1991. Quantitative aspects of morphological productivity. In *Yearbook of morphology 1991*, pages 109–149. Springer.

Harald Baayen and Rochelle Lieber. 1991. Productivity and english derivation: A corpus-based study.

Peter Bakker. 1997. *A language of our own: The genesis of Michif, the mixed Cree-French language of the Canadian Métis*, volume 10. Oxford University Press.

Jerome Biedny, Matthew Burner, Andrea Cudworth, and Monica Macaulay. 2021. Classifier medials across algonquian: A first look. *International Journal of American Linguistics*, 87(1):1–47.

Leonard Bloomfield. 1946. Algonquian. In *Linguistic structures of Native America*, pages 85–129. Vinking Fund.

Phil Branigan, Julie Brittain, and Carrie Dyck. 2005. Balancing syntax and prosody in the algonquian verb complex. *Algonquian Papers-Archive*, 36.

Julie Brittain. 2003. A distributed morphology account of the syntax of the algonquian verb. In *Proceedings of the 2003 annual conference of the Canadian Linguistic Association*, pages 25–39.

Sophia Crockett-Current. 2020. Pursuing passamaquoddy-maliseet language revitalization through song.

Ives Goddard. 1990. Primary and secondary stem derivation in algonquian. *International Journal of American Linguistics*, 56(4):449–483.

Peter Grishin. 2023. Lessons from cp in passamaquoddy and beyond. *Dissertation, MIT.* `https://ling.auf.net/lingbuzz/007567`.

Philip S LeSourd. 1988. Accent and syllable structure in passamaquoddy. phd diss.

Simons Gary F. Lewis, M. Paul and Charles D. Fennig. 2016. *Ethnologue: Languages of the World*. SIL International.

Maria Mazzoli. 2023. Productivity, polysynthesis, and the algonquian verb.

Will Oxford. Algonquian language maps. `http://home.cc.umanitoba.ca/~oxfordwr/algling/maps.html#cite`. Accessed: 2024-01-28.

Conor McDonough Quinn. 2009. Medials in the northeast. *Unpublished ms.< http://www. conormquinn. com/MedialsInTheNortheast-AC40writeup. pdf.*

Tanya Slavin. 2012. *The syntax and semantics of stem composition in Ojicree*. University of Toronto (Canada).

Anna Whitney, Garrett Johnson, and Cherry Meyer. 2022. A survey of "classificatory medials" in ojibwe: Classifiers versus incorporation.

Charles Yang. 2018. A formalist perspective on language acquisition. *Linguistic Approaches to Bilingualism*, 8(6):665–706.

A Appendix: Figures

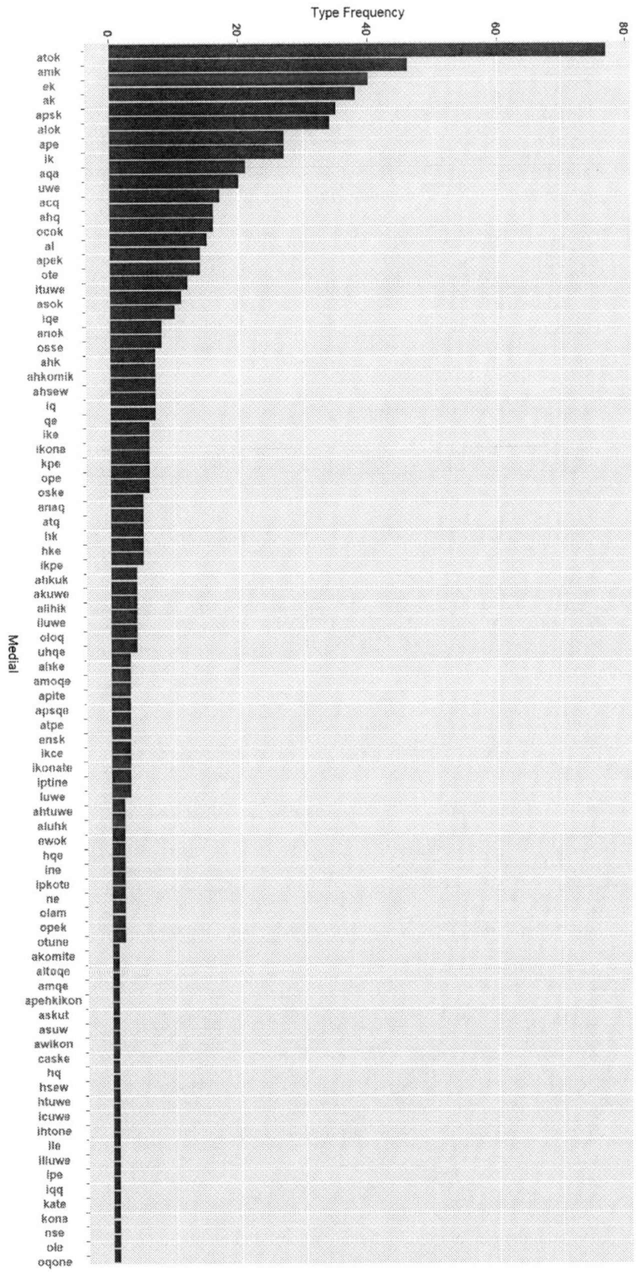

Figure 2: Frequency of medials for attested forms.

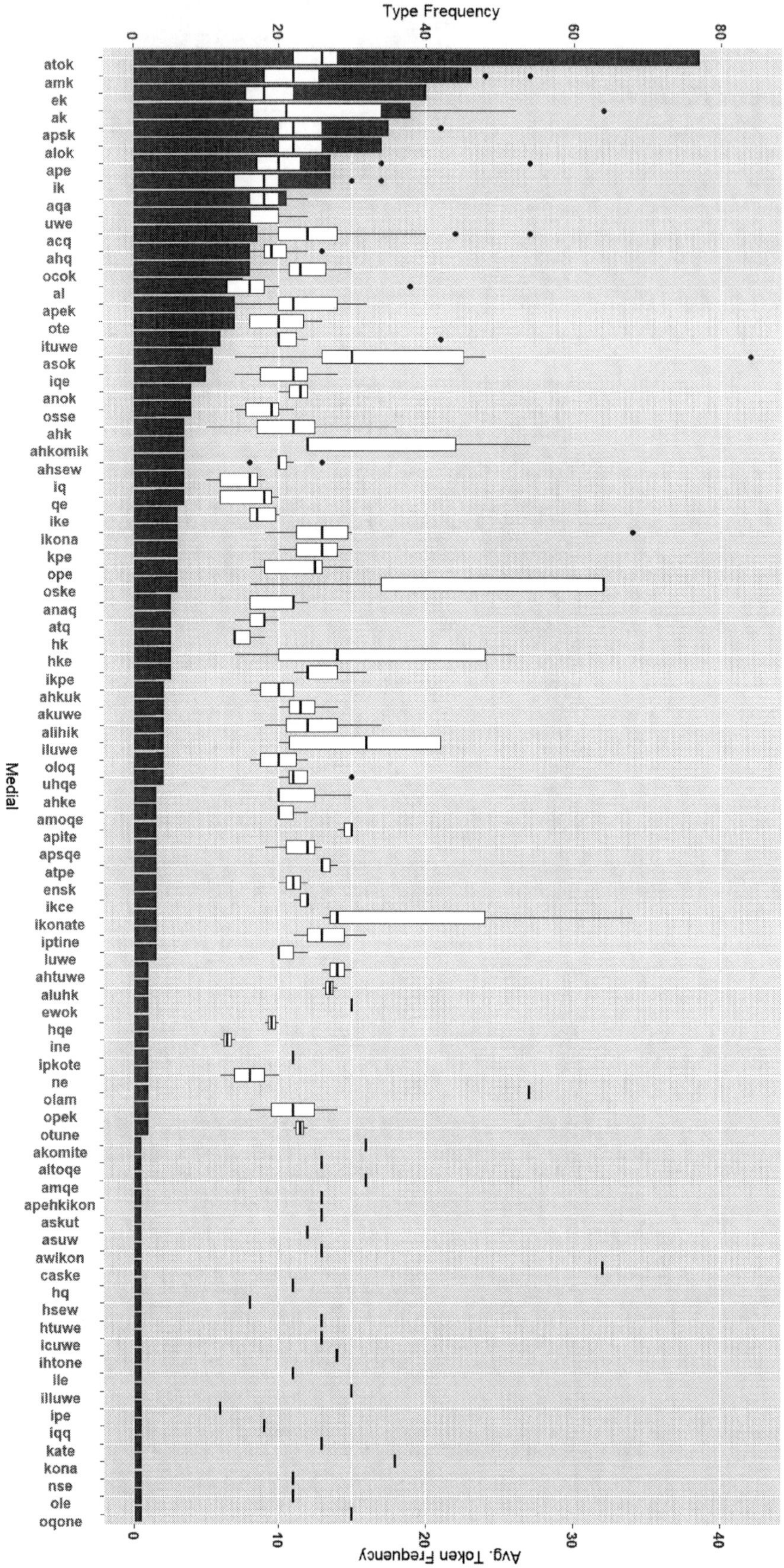

Figure 3: Frequency of medials and average frequency of tokens for attested forms. Columns are associated with the left y-axis, while boxplots are associated with the right.

T is for *Treu*, but how do you pronounce that? Using C-LARA to create phonetic texts for Kanak languages*

Pauline Welby
Aix Marseille Université, CNRS
Laboratoire Parole et Langage
and
Université de la Nouvelle Calédonie
pauline.welby@cnrs.fr

Fabrice Wacalie
Université de la Nouvelle Calédonie
fabrice.wacalie@unc.nc

Manny Rayner
University of South Australia
manny.rayner@unisa.edu.au

ChatGPT-4 C-LARA-Instance
University of South Australia
chatgptclarainstance@proton.me

Abstract

In Drehu, a language of the indigenous Kanak people of New Caledonia, the word *treu* 'moon' is pronounced [tʃe.u]; but, even if they hear the word, the spelling pulls French speakers to a spurious pronunciation [tʁø]. We implement a strategy to mitigate the influence of such orthographic conflicts, while retaining the benefits of written input on vocabulary learning. We present text in "phonetized" form, where words are broken down into components associated with mnemonically presented phonetic values, adapting features from the "Comment ça se prononce ?" multilingual phonetizer. We present an exploratory project where we used the ChatGPT-based Learning And Reading Assistant (C-LARA) to implement a version of the phonetizer strategy, outlining how the AI-engineered codebase and help from the AI made it easy to add the necessary extensions. We describe two proof-of-concept texts for learners produced using the platform, a Drehu alphabet book and a Drehu version of "The (North) Wind and the Sun"; both texts include native-speaker recorded audio, pronunciation re-spellings based on French orthography, and AI-generated illustrations.

1 Introduction

1.1 A challenge: Reading a word and hearing it is often not enough

. In Drehu, a language of the indigenous Kanak people of New Caledonia in the South Pacific, the word *treu* means 'moon', as we can learn in a classic, illustrated children's book (Atti et al., 1995). Books like these can be very useful to the beginning learner; seeing the spelling is a powerful aid for learning words and their meanings (Bürki et al., 2019; Pattamadilok et al., 2022; Welby et al., 2022). "[W]hen faced with speech, which is inherently [] highly variable and fleeting, the orthographic form offers L2 speaker-listeners something stable to 'grab onto"' (Welby et al., 2022).

But how do you pronounce *treu*? Teachers designing classroom activities or heritage learners trying to reclaim their language need to know. Of course, it helps to hear words spoken out loud. Multimodal texts are common in mainstream platforms like LingQ[1]: words are annotated with audio files that can be played by clicking or hovering. Sound has been integrated into online dictionaries and other resources for dozens of endangered or underresourced languages (e.g. A Speaking Atlas of Indigenous Languages of France and its Overseas (Boula de Mareüil et al., 2019), the Swarthmore Talking Dictionaries Project[2], the online dictionary of the Académie Tahitienne[3] and the 50 Words Project for the Indigenous languages of Australia[4], allowing users to read a printed word or phrase and hear its pronunciation. Having these two forms of the word may be sufficient, depending on the goals of a given project and on the user's language and literacy background.

For language learners, however, seeing (reading) the written form of a word and hearing it spoken will often not be enough. This is likely to be the case, for example, for French

* Authors in anti-alphabetical order.

[1] https://www.lingq.com/
[2] https://talkingdictionaries.swarthmore.edu/
[3] https://www.farevanaa.pf/dictionnaire.php/
[4] https://50words.online/languages/

Proceedings of the The Seventh Workshop on the Use of Computational Methods in the Study of Endangered Languages, pages 21–26
March 21-22, 2024 ©2024 Association for Computational Linguistics

speakers who wish to learn Drehu (or any other Kanak language) as an L2 or heritage language. This is because when there is a conflict between what we hear and what we read, the written input often wins out. *Treu* is pronounced [tʃe.u] (*chay-OO*), but knowledge of the letter-to-sound correspondences of French, the main language of schooling and of literacy-based activities in New Caledonia, will pull many Caledonians toward a spurious, French-like pronunciation, a single syllable with T' and 'R' sounds and rhyming with *feu* [fø] 'fire'. We routinely encounter this phenomenon in our experience teaching Kanak languages and linguistics (FW) and living in New Caledonia (FW and PW). The influence of the spelling system of the institutional or literacy-dominant language extends beyond the Caledonian context. Similarly, for the Australian Aboriginal language Barngarla, Bédi et al. (2022) report : "the voiced retroflex plosive [ɖ] ... is written 'rd' as for example in Barngarla *yarda*, 'country'. It is however all too easy for the anglophone reader to interpret this as representing a lengthened preceding vowel followed by [d] as for example in ...'card' or 'herd' ". It has also been shown experimentally that L1 French orthographic conventions pull L2 English speakers to spurious French-link vowel pronunciations (Bürki et al., 2019; Welby et al., 2022).

1.2 The Caledonian context and the Kanak languages and beyond

. Issues of this kind are ubiquitous for people engaging with the Kanak languages. Like other Melanesian islands and countries, New Caledonia is characterized by its linguistic diversity, with just under 30 Kanak languages, most of which are endangered or vulnerable. Many have writing systems, developed first by 19th century missionaries working with native speakers, and revised or expanded by linguists. Twelve have suggested standard orthographies, published or under development as part of the Académie des Langues Kanak's "Propositions d'écriture" series. For some languages there is a long and continuing (e.g. in social media) tradition of writing using French orthographic conventions. All Kanak languages are under-resourced, lacking not only digital resources, but also in pedagogical and reading materials, and many have no such resources at all.

As noted by Welby et al. (2023): "[e]ach of the Kanak languages has its own phonology as well as its own orthographic system.... Learning the grapheme-phoneme correspondences (GPCs) of a second language (L2) is not always straightforward... There is also likely to be interference from the GPCs of the L1 or those of the language in which one typically reads and writes." To give just one example in a handful of languages, the grapheme <j> corresponds to /ð/ in Drehu *jol* 'difficult', /dz/ in Nengone *jo* 'to suffer', /ʒ/ in French *joli* 'pretty', and /dʒ/ in English *Joe*.

The motivation for our project and its challenges extend beyond the Caledonian context. As Welby et al. (2023) note, they will resonate with "other communities where several languages are present to one degree or another (e.g. countries with migrant communities) or in which the L1 (or the literacy dominant language) and the L2 (or L2s) have very different orthographies, for example, English and Irish".

1.3 A proposed solution: including phonetic texts

In this paper, we propose a solution to mitigate the influence of cross-language orthographic conflicts on pronunciation, while retaining the clear benefits of written input on vocabulary learning. We build on theoretical and applied results from two thus far independent projects. The first of these projects, LARA (Learning and Reading Assistant; Akhlaghi et al. 2019, 2020), now reimplemented as C-LARA (ChatGPT-based LARA; Bédi et al. 2023b,a, 2024; `https://www.c-lara.org/`), is a collaborative open source project to develop tools converting plain texts into interactive multimedia language learning resources. The second, "Comment ça se prononce ?" ('How is that pronounced?') is a project to build a multilingual phonetizer bridging between spelling and pronunciation in the many languages of New Caledonia (Welby et al. 2023). Here we implement the Caledonian phonetizer strategy inside the C-LARA platform.

When we began the joint project, we were particularly curious to explore two themes. The first was to use the idea of "pronunciation respellings" based on the orthography of the common language. For example, in the Caledonian context where French fills this role, we present the word *treu* as [tché-ou]. Learners reading e-books report appreciating having phonetic text alongside regular written text (Bédi et al., 2023a), and our experience suggests that for many learners, pronunciation respellings are more user-friendly and thus more usable than phonetic transcription (Welby et al., 2023).

The second theme was to discover what assistance we could obtain in the context of Kanak languages from the newly reimplemented ChatGPT-based version of LARA, "C-LARA". Interestingly, we found that the AI was able to make a very useful contribution, but not in the way one might have anticipated. On the negative side, the late 2023 version appears to have essentially no knowledge of Kanak languages, and is thus unable to do any language-specific work. The AI was however able to make a large contribution in its software engineer role. Its image-generation skills also turned out to be surprisingly helpful in creating high-quality picture book texts.

The rest of the paper is structured as follows. In Section 2, we briefly outline the C-LARA architecture and describe how we were able to use it to repackage the LARA "phonetizer" functionality to make it practically useful, and in particular address the requirements by the Kanak languages. Section 3 describes initial proof-of-concept examples, a "phonetized" alphabet book for Drehu with AI-generated illustrations and a Drehu version of "The Wind and the Sun". The final section summarises and suggests further directions.

2 Adding phonetic text capabilities to C-LARA

We begin this section with a few words about the C-LARA platform, then describe how we added the phonetic text capabilities. C-LARA is an international open source project initiated in March 2023 and currently involving partners in eight countries. As previously indicated, the goal was to perform a complete reimplementation of the earlier LARA project, keeping the same basic functionality of providing a flexible online tool for creating multimodal texts, but adding ChatGPT-4 as the central component. ChatGPT-4 is used in two separate and complementary ways. In the form of GPT-4, it appears as a software *component*, giving the user the option of letting it perform the central language processing operations for languages it understands sufficiently well; it also appears as a software *engineer*, working together with human collaborators to build the platform itself. As described in the initial C-LARA report (Bédi et al., 2023a), the software engineering aspect has proven very successful, with ChatGPT not only writing about 90% of the code, but greatly improving it compared to the earlier LARA codebase. In this paper, where we are interested in small languages that GPT-4 knows little about, the AI cannot play a meaningful role as a language processor. It was however able to contribute effectively as a software engineer, both by having created a well-designed architecture that was easy to extend, and by assisting in the extension process. We start by outlining the structure.

C-LARA is a web app implemented in Python/Django.[5] The code is divided into two layers: a Python core processing layer, which implements all the language processing functions, and a Django web layer which sits on top of it. Nearly all the design decisions in the web layer come from ChatGPT-4, which has created an app with a simple, entirely mainstream structure; this has made it easy for the AI to write most of the web-level code.[6] The AI has also been responsible for the greater part of the design decisions in the core layer. This consists of a set of modules, nearly all of which are of one the four generic types: internalisation (conversion of text into a class-based Python representation); repositories (storing linguistic data into database records accessed through Python classes); rendering (converting inter nal representations into multimedia text); and language processing (usually, invoking the AI to perform operations like segmentation, glossing, lemma tagging etc).

We now move to describing the phonetic text functionality. An initial exploration of the idea of creating phonetic texts was carried out during the earlier LARA project (Bédi et al., 2022). The basic idea was to support a second annotation mode, where instead of

[5] `https://www.djangoproject.com/`

[6] The project codebase is available at `https://github.com/mannyrayner/C-LARA`

dividing pages into segments and words, they are instead divided into words and grapheme-groups; grapheme-groups are annotated with associated phonetic information. Two methods were developed for dividing words into meaningful annotated grapheme-groups. For languages with consistent grapheme-phoneme correspondences (e.g. Arabic, Hebrew, most Australian Indigenous languages), a conversion table and a greedy parsing algorithm gave good results. For languages with complex and/or inconsistent correspondences, a more sophisticated example-based method was implemented where words were aligned against entries taken from a phonetic lexicon.

The method gave good results for English and French (Akhlaghi et al., 2022). Unfortunately, the LARA phonetic text functionality was never integrated into the LARA web platform and could only be accessed through the command-line version of the tool; also, the language-specific resources (grapheme-phoneme conversion tables, links to phonetic lexica, etc) were hard-coded. Although these issues were from a theoretical point of view trivial, in practice they meant that the functionality was hardly used.

With the better-engineered C-LARA codebase and the AI's assistance, we found it was straightforward to solve the problems involved in repackaging the phonetic text functionality to make it easily available in the new context. We carried over the core processing modules (in particular, the dynamic programming grapheme-phoneme alignment code) from the LARA codebase, defined suitable repository modules to store the necessary information, connected them to new views in the Django layer, and generalised the rendering templates so that they worked for phonetic texts as well. Nearly all of this routine work could be carried out by the AI. From the user's point of view, the functionality exposed is the following:

1. A screen on which a language expert can define the relevant phonetic resources for a language. These can be of two types: a grapheme-group-to-phoneme-group correspondence table for languages with consistent GPCs, and a phonetic lexicon, uploaded in file form, which associates words with phonetic entries.

2. A screen on which the user can invoke phonetic processing, if phonetic resources are defined for the language in question, to convert plain text into phonetically decomposed text.

3. A screen on which the user can upload audio files corresponding to the phoneme-groups occurring in a phonetic text. These are stored in a shared language-specific repository, so it is only necessary to upload new files. For languages supported by ipa-reader[7], the files are by default produced automatically and downloaded from the site.

4. A screen on which the user can invoke a rendering process to convert phonetically decomposed text and associated audio into multimedia text.

5. The final result is a flexible multimedia document which can be viewed either as normal or as phonetic text (Fig. 1) and can be posted in the C-LARA social network, where users can rate it and leave comments. It is also possible to link together multiple C-LARA documents in the same language to form a "reading history", a virtual document representing the concatenation of the component documents and including a common concordance.

All of this is described in full detail in the second C-LARA Progress Report (Bédi et al., 2024), which in particular describes more precisely the AI's role in developing the various functionalities.

In the next section, we describe how we have started using these new functionalities for the Kanak language Drehu.

3 Two proof-of-concept examples

As an initial step, we have developed two C-LARA texts for Drehu, the language of the island of Lifou. Drehu, pronounced /dʒehu/ or *jay-hoo*, is the Kanak language with the largest community of speakers (approx. 16,000). It is taught as a subject in some schools and at university, and has a proposed written standard.

[7] `http://ipa-reader.xyz/`

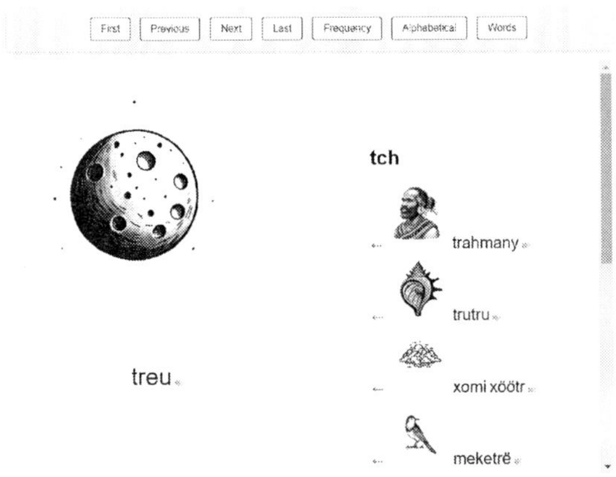

Figure 1: Top of a page from the initial Drehu alphabet book. The user has clicked on the 'tr' in *treu* ("moon"), playing audio and bringing up a concordance for the /tch/ phoneme that shows contexts where it occurs. The text has been arranged so that the associated images are part of these contexts.

The first text is a Drehu alphabet book based on the entries from an introductory booklet produced by the Académie des Langues Kanak (2023). It has almost exactly the same Drehu words and French glosses as this original resource, with 80 entries in total. The C-LARA version of the alphabet book contains one entry per page. Each page can be viewed either in "Words" mode, where words are treated as indivisible entities and hovering over a word shows a French gloss, or in "Sounds" (phonetic text) mode, where words are divided into graphemes. Clicking on the icon next to the word plays the entire word recorded by the Drehu native speaker author. Hovering over a grapheme shows the associated phoneme; clicking on it plays the audio for the associate phoneme and shows a "phonetic concordance" of words which contain the phoneme, each one displayed together with its associated image (see Fig. 1).

We used ChatGPT-4's integrated DALL-E-3 functionality to produce the images. This allowed us to test the abilities of the AI to produce images culturally appropriate to the Melanesian context. Our impression is that it has succeeded well; initial comments from the Drehu community are very positive.

The second text is a C-LARA edition of "Leu me Jö", the Drehu version of Aesop's fable "The (North) Wind and the Sun", a standard text used in studies of many languages including Kanak languages (Boula de Mareüil et al., 2019). The C-LARA functionalities add value as a teaching and learning resource.

Both texts are openly available on the C-LARA site.[8]

4 Further directions

We have three immediate goals. First, we are gathering feedback from users and community members on the proof-of-concept resources, with respect to the accuracy and the usefulness of the phonetic texts, the appropriateness of the AI-generated images, and the usability of the interface. This input will help shape subsequent work. Second, we plan to carry over several features from the "Comment ça se prononce ?" phonetiser project to the C-LARA context. These include: 1. offering two options for phonetic transcriptions: International Phonetic Alphabet (IPA) and French-based orthographic respellings (illustrated in Figure 1), enhanced with pronunciation tips, such as images or video clips of mouth shapes or tongue movement, and 2. rendering text in an interlinear form which alternates lines of plain and phonetic text. Third, we will explore the ways in which community members might participate in creating C-LARA resources, such as glossing and lemma tagging.

As in the phonetizer project, we adopt an incremental approach, developing proof-of-concept resources for one language, here Drehu, which we can then show to members of other communities. We have begun discussions with the Paicî community.

Finally, the work presented here could also serve as a first step towards giving new life to a legacy alphabet book for five Kanak languages, Drehu, Fwaî, Numèè, Paicî, and Yuanga (Atti et al., 1995). If the authors and their communities so desire, a new C-LARA, multimedia edition of the book could retain the rich, evocative illustrations of the original, while linking the written words to their pronunciations. This important cultural document would then be accessible to new generations.

[8] https://c-lara.unisa.edu.au/accounts/rendered_texts/17/phonetic/page_1.html; https://c-lara.unisa.edu.au/accounts/rendered_texts/10/phonetic/page_1.html

References

Académie des Langues Kanak. 2023. *Abécédaire illustré en drehu.* Académie des Langues Kanak, Noumea, New Caledonia.

Elham Akhlaghi, Branislav Bédi, Fatih Bektaş, Harald Berthelsen, Matthias Butterweck, Cathy Chua, Catia Cucchiarini, Gülşen Eryiğit, Johanna Gerlach, Hanieh Habibi, Neasa Ní Chiaráin, Manny Rayner, Steinþór Steingrímsson, and Helmer Strik. 2020. Constructing multimodal language learner texts using LARA: Experiences with nine languages. In *Proceedings of The 12th Language Resources and Evaluation Conference*, pages 323–331.

Elham Akhlaghi, Branislav Bédi, Matthias Butterweck, Cathy Chua, Johanna Gerlach, Hanieh Habibi, Junta Ikeda, Manny Rayner, Sabina Sestigiani, and Ghil'ad Zuckermann. 2019. Overview of LARA: A learning and reading assistant. In *Proc. SLaTE 2019: 8th ISCA Workshop on Speech and Language Technology in Education*, pages 99–103.

Elham Akhlaghi et al. 2022. Reading assistance through LARA, the Learning And Reading Assistant. In *Proceedings of the 2nd Workshop on Tools and Resources to Empower People with REAding DIfficulties (READI) within the 13th Language Resources and Evaluation Conference*, pages 1–8.

Solange Atti, Chantal Bouanou, Helene Diahioue, Jean-Pierre Diahioue, Michele Grynagier, Pierre Hnacipan, Yvette Lepigeon, Paulette Prevaut, and Marcko Waheo (illustrator). 1995. *Et toi, comment-dis tu?* Centre Territorial de Recherche et de Documentation Pedagogique, Noumea, New Caledonia.

Philippe Boula de Mareüil, Frédéric Vernier, Gilles Adda, Albert Rilliard, and [J]acques Vernaudon. 2019. A speaking atlas of indigenous languages of france and its overseas. In *Proceedings of the Language Technologies for All (LT4All), Paris. France*, pages 155—-159.

Audrey Bürki, Pauline Welby, Mélanie Clément, and Elsa Spinelli. 2019. Orthography and second language word learning: Moving beyond “friend or foe?”. *The Journal of the Acoustical Society of America*, 145(4):EL265–EL271.

Branislav Bédi, Hakeem Beedar, Belinda Chiera, Nedelina Ivanova, Christèle Maizonniaux, Neasa Ní Chiaráin, Manny Rayner, John Sloan, and Ghil'ad Zuckermann. 2022. Using LARA to create image-based and phonetically annotated multimodal texts for endangered languages. In *Proceedings of the Workshop on Computational Methods for Endangered Languages.*

Branislav Bédi, ChatGPT-4, Belinda Chiera, Cathy Chua, Catia Cucchiarini, Christèle Maizonniaux, Claudia Mărginean, Neasa Ní Chiaráin, Chadi Raheb, Manny Rayner, Annika Simonsen, Manolache Lucreţia Viorica, Pauline Welby, Zhengkang Xiang, and Rina Zviel-Girshin. 2024. ChatGPT-Based Learning And Reading Assistant: Second report. Technical report. ResearchGate preprint.

Branislav Bédi, ChatGPT-4, Belinda Chiera, Cathy Chua, Catia Cucchiarini, Neasa Ní Chiaráin, Manny Rayner, Annika Simonsen, and Rina Zviel-Girshin. 2023a. ChatGPT-Based Learning And Reading Assistant: Initial report. Technical report. ResearchGate preprint.

Branislav Bédi, ChatGPT-4, Belinda Chiera, Cathy Chua, Neasa Ní Chiaráin, Manny Rayner, Annika Simonsen, and Rina Zviel-Girshin. 2023b. ChatGPT + LARA = C-LARA. Presented at SLaTE 2023.

Chotiga Pattamadilok, Pauline Welby, and Michael D Tyler. 2022. The contribution of visual articulatory gestures and orthography to speech processing: Evidence from novel word learning. *Journal of Experimental Psychology: Learning, Memory, and Cognition*, 48(10):1542.

Pauline Welby, Brigitte Bigi, Antoine Corral, Fabrice Wacalie, and Guillaume Wattelez. 2023. A visit to the Cliffs of Jokin: A role for phonetizers in second language pronunciation and word learning, with an example from the languages of New Caledonia. In *Proc. 2nd Annual Meeting of the ELRA/ISCA SIG on Under-resourced Languages (SIGUL 2023)*, pages 19–23.

Pauline Welby, Elsa Spinelli, and Audrey Bürki. 2022. Spelling provides a precise (but sometimes misplaced) phonological target. orthography and acoustic variability in second language word learning. *Journal of Phonetics*, 94:101172.

Machine-in-the-Loop with Documentary and Descriptive Linguists

Sarah Moeller
University of Florida
smoeller@ufl.edu

Antti Arppe
University of Alberta
arppe@ualberta.ca

Abstract

This paper describes a curriculum for teaching linguists how to apply machine-in-the-loop (MitL) approach to documentary and descriptive tasks. It also shares observations about the learning participants, who are primarily non-computational linguists, and how they interact with the MitL approach. We found that they prefer cleaning over increasing the training data and then proceed to reanalyze their analytical decisions, before finally undertaking small actions that emphasize analytical strategies. Overall, participants display an understanding of the curriculum which covers fundamental concepts of machine learning and statistical modeling.

1 Introduction

This paper outlines the curriculum for "Machine-in-the-Loop for Language Documentation" workshops and shares from the experience we gained while teaching the material in different settings.[1] The workshop material gives instruction in foundational machine learning concepts, natural language processing (NLP) techniques, and statistical modeling. The full version of the material is designed to create an opportunity where documentary and descriptive linguists learn the concepts and apply NLP models to assist them in their documentary and descriptive tasks.

In hopes of increasing the effectiveness of instructors who teach NLP to linguists or who wish to improve inter-disciplinary collaboration and communication, this paper describes patterns that we observed while teaching this material in different settings. We aim the discussion towards instructors who come from a computational angle and will be teaching participants whose degrees or training is primarily in linguistics or related social sciences (We use the term "linguist" as a shorthand for any of these learners.) After teaching the material in whole or part, we noticed similar patterns of interaction with the NLP models emerged. These patterns make sense in light of typical linguistic training that promotes analytical skills and in-depth investigation of language data.

2 Motivation and Background

Unfortunately, current documentary and descriptive methods cannot scale up to match the pace of the language endangerment or provide automated methods to assist documentation (Seifart et al., 2018) because annotating large corpora of potential training data is still done mostly by hand (Duong, 2017; Palmer et al., 2010). This situation can be addressed by providing non-computational linguists with a basic understanding of statistical NLP so they are better equipped to integrate machine learning assistance into their work.

The potential for NLP to increase and improve documentary tasks has been clearly demonstrated (Felt, 2012; Moeller, 2021; Palmer, 2009; Xia et al., 2016). However, NLP research with under-documented languages often does not consider realistic factors sufficiently. For example, research tends to take a linear approach, where initial annotation of training data is the only input from human experts that the NLP system receives. In contrast, the workshop promotes human-in-the-loop approaches in realistic settings. The goal of human-in-the-loop techniques is to make optimal use and also reduce expensive human annotation while improving model performance (Bridgwater, 2016). We use the term "machine-in-the-loop (MitL)" to emphasize our conviction that technology's role is to assist humans (Zhang et al., 2022), not *vice versa*.

Although Lin et al. (2016) indicate that "reactive" learning that uses simple uncertainty sampling for denoising a corpus is not ideal, the workshop code implements this basic method, we choose this simple method because, unfortunately,

[1] https://github.com/sarahrmoeller/AI_Workshop

Proceedings of the The Seventh Workshop on the Use of Computational Methods in the Study of Endangered Languages, pages 27–32

a short pedagogical event is not ideal for active learning experimentation or complex strategies. It may be worth noting that Lin et al. assume that the examples sampled by the algorithm as most "uncertain" are the only examples that will be relabeled, whereas we allow the linguists to choose what examples they will work with. Humans can analyze why a data point might have been selected as most uncertain by the algorithm and whether they agree that relabeling it for the next training cycle is likely to be impactful. Also, humans can generalize from the algorithm's simple calculations and then find and re-label multiple examples that they feel are similar in nature. These abilities may counteract some of the noted drawbacks of simple uncertainty sampling.

3 Overview of Curriculum and Workshops

The goal of the curriculum is to help linguists better understand concepts that will, hopefully, make them comfortable integrating NLP systems in their work. The material is aimed at linguists or others engaged in language-related work who do not have a background in advanced mathematics or computer science. The curriculum progresses through the learning objective listed below.

1. Know terminology related to artificial intelligence and NLP (e.g. What is NLP and where does it fit in the field of AI?)

2. Understand the foundational statistical concepts underpinning machine learning

3. Distinguish between classification (supervised) and clustering (unsupervised)

4. Understand the role of features and the importance of feature selection in classical machine learning, and the importance of data representation or selection in deep learning

5. Grasp the differences between, and the reasons for using, precision, recall, and F1 measure versus accuracy

6. Learn what a classification report and confusion matrix are and how to read them from a model trained for a task related to basic linguistic analysis

7. Interpret the model's predictions on previously unannotated data

8. Improve the model's output with any of three steps:
    - correcting noisy training data
    - increasing training data by creating new examples or by correcting the model's annotations on previously unannotated data
    - customizing the machine learning model architecture

The material uses lectures and activities to convey concepts and guide participants through a MitL approach to language documentation and description task. It includes Python code that we used to preprocess data and train the NLP models. Other instructors may find the code helpful but will probably wish to adjust it to suit their context. The activities are of two types. The first are short activities usually in the form of games or worksheets that are intended to break up lectures and reinforce concepts. These can be done in groups or individually. The final activity is essentially the same as learning objective 8. It assumes participants can be grouped into teams of 2-6 members. For the final activity, the one-day version of the curriculum uses the same data for all teams. Details about this data is provided in the released material. The three-day version assumes teams will be formed before the workshop begins and each team will work on their own field data during the final activity. With this in mind, team leaders are encouraged to invite members who are knowledgeable about the language and the task.

In a workshop setting with more than two or three teams, we found it necessary to recruit "tech coaches" for each team. These are participants who have skills to download and run the workshop code. Tech coaches do not need to run the code for preprocessing data if the instructor can do this more complicated task beforehand. The tech coaches do not necessarily need to be familiar with the language.

The material was developed from stand-alone lectures and assignments in university classrooms which were gradually combined and redesigned for non-credit workshop settings aimed at faculty, graduate students, or others working with endangered languages. The material released with this paper are designed for all-day workshops either one or three days in length. The three-day version of the workshop aims to coach participants to apply NLP systems to their own data. Below we described how we covered the material in a university classroom in some detail because we did release curriculum for this setting and then outline more briefly how a one-day and three-day workshop can be conducted.

University Classroom. The earliest version of the combined material was piloted in a cross-listed graduate/undergraduate language documentation course. The course used the Nyagbo language (ISO: nyb) as a case study and the instructors spent one week teaching Nyagbo morphology. In another week, the instructors briefly introduced NLP (objectives 1-4 and 7). At the end of the week, they showed output of a morphological parser (segmentation and glossing) that had been trained on available Nyagbo documentary field data. The students formed groups and were assigned to improve the parser with the first two steps described in objective 8 above. Students could also fulfill the assignment by writing an error analysis on the test data. Each group worked independently. They were allowed to decide what steps to take but were encouraged to assign a group member to each of these three tasks. After two weeks, students submitted their new training data containing all corrections to the original annotations and all additional annotations. The instructor trained and tested the same architecture on the new training sets. The test data was not changed. In class, the instructor explained classification metrics (objectives 5-6) and showed the classification reports from each team's new data next to the original classification report. The reports were discussed together (objective 7).

1-day Workshop. The one-day version covers all eight objectives but in less depth. The material is designed to cover objectives 1–4 in the first 3-4 hours through lectures and short activities. Then after introducing the final activity (English POS tagging with MitL approach) and allowing participants to form groups, Objectives 6-8 are are best covered by walking the groups through each step of a first iteration of the MitL activity. This will take about 1 hour. After that, groups should work independently through as many training+re-annotation iterations as they can in the remaining time. The final 45-60 minutes can be reserved for discussion and reflective learning.

3-day Workshop. The three-day version of the workshop is designed for teams to spend half of each day covering objectives 1-5 and the other half

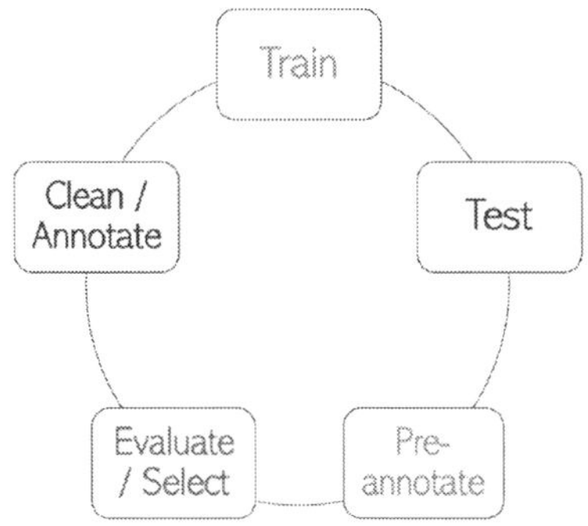

Figure 1: Machine-in-the-Loop approach to language documentation and description. A machine learning model is trained and tested for a NLP task on documentary data. The model is used to "pre-annotate" unannotated data. Linguists evaluate the pre-annotated data which is presented to them ranked according to some active learning selection strategy. The linguists then clean the initial training data or correct and add the pre-annotated data to the training data.

working through objectives 6-8 by applying a MiTL approach to their field data. Instructors may allow the teams to choose the NLP task for the MiTL activity, but it is recommended to limit the choice of tasks so that they suit the instructor's workload and are suitable to the participants' computing resources. We limited choices to POS tagging or morphological parsing.

4 The Machine-in-the-Loop Approach

The workshop curriculum centers around a Machine-in-the-Loop (MitL) approach comprising active learning cycles of training and annotation. The goal is to guide humans to new annotation that will have most impact towards gradually improving NLP performance so that the improved model offers useful assistance to the humans. We implemented re-active labeling (Lin et al., 2016) using least confidence uncertainty sampling (Lewis and Catlett, 1994; Culotta and McCallum, 2005). Other sampling strategies can be used by instructors, but uncertainty sampling is relatively easy to explain.

As implemented for the workshop, least confidence uncertainty sampling ranks the model's predicted annotations by the differences between the model's confidences for each predicted sequence. When using Conditional Random Fields (CRF), the model's confidence C is defined as its calculated probability P that unit x should be annotated with a particular class $\hat{y}$. Confidence for a predicted sequence is calculated by normalizing each unit probability by the number of units in the sequence. For POS tagging, units are words and sequences are sentences; for morphological parsing, units are morphemes and/or morpheme glosses and sequences are characters in a word. The same calculation of confidence can be used with other models, such as the Transformer, but probability can be substituted for the absolute value of the models' negative log likelihood for a unit.

$$C = \frac{P(\hat{y}|x)}{L}$$

The sequences and the predicted annotations are ranked from lowest to highest confidence scores and written to a plain text file without the scores. Since participants naturally begin at the top of a file, this ranking nudges them to start correcting the new annotations with examples that the model found most confusing.

The goal of the MitL activity in the three-day workshops is to provide AI assistance for basic language documentation tasks, specifically annotation (interlinerization), and thereby increase the amount and the quality annotated data in endangered languages. Where possible, the activity should be prepared before the workshop begins. Teams can choose their task, and if ethically sound, share their field data with the instructor two to six weeks before the workshop begins. The instructor can run the preprocessing code to separate the annotated and unannotated units (units causing problem for the code are removed to the unannotated corpus) and divide the annotated corpus into a 9/1 training/test split. An initial model can then be trained, tested, and then used to annotate unlabeled data. Ideally, participants bringing field data should first create gold standard labels by correcting the portion of the data withheld to serve as the test set. If this is all done before the workshop begins, participants can start the MitL activity (objective 8) on the first day by examining the initial model's classification report, confusion matrix, and predicted annotations. Then they can attempt to clean manually labeled training data, correct the model's annotations, or customize the model architecture of feature selection. At the end of each day or whenever teams feel ready, new models can be trained on the version of the training data.

5 Observations

We taught the material in all settings described in section 3, primarily to participants with higher education degrees primarily in linguistics or related social science fields. In all three settings, similar patterns of interaction with the MitL approach emerged. We feel that a description of these patterns may assist instructors who come from a computational background. We have no data to confirm these patterns quantitatively, but they match our broader experience as computational and quantitative linguists teaching in linguistic departments.[2]

We observed that linguists' interaction with the MitL approach tend to reflect their analytical training rather than statistical or engineering solutions. Given free choice of the sub-steps under objective 8, the linguists followed three stages. First, they remove noise in the manually annotated data by correcting mistakes and inconsistencies. Second, they revise their previous analytical decisions and change manual annotations accordingly. Third, they take strategic actions aimed to improve the representation of the training data. The first two stages held true across all settings, but the third one was primarily observed in the in our one three-day workshop. We include it because, based on our broader teaching experience, it seems likely to hold true generally for linguists newly introduced to NLP and MitL concepts, and so may be helpful for other instructors to look for.

First, clean data. Field data is inherently noisy, either due to the dynamic nature of linguistic analysis, or as a by-product of manual work. Given a choice between the tasks under objective 8, linguists showed a preference to clean training data. This held true even though the instructors emphasized the impact of data size on statistical models. Interestingly, research (Chen et al., 2022; Lin et al., 2016) suggests, given limited time, cleaning rather than adding more data is a wise choice.

Cleaning meant correcting typos and making glosses consistent (e.g. '1.sg' and 'I' $\rightarrow$ 1.SG). We noted that teams tended not to clean all data at once, but asked to retrain the model 2-5 times and leaned on the model's output to find mistakes for the next round of corrections. It seems they found that although language data can be cleaned without NLP assistance, the MitL approach helped them

[2] One reviewer noted these observations match their experience as well.

more quickly identify issues.

Second, reanalyze. As obvious mistakes in the training data were corrected, we observed the linguists started to lean more on the MitL approach, but not in the way we expected. They looked more closely at the model's predictions for the unlabeled data. Noting that some of the model's "mistakes" were due to isomorphism or other ambiguity, they asked questions about outliers and weighting in statistical modeling. We assumed they would focus on adding new annotated sequences to the training data. Instead, they shifted their focus to the analytical decisions which had governed their original annotation. Several mentioned how the model highlighted a tension between lumping versus splitting choices they had felt while analyzing and annotating the original data.

The linguists began reanalyzing their previous annotation choices. They used the highest listed sequences (ones with lowest confidence scores) in the computer-annotated file to guide their reanalysis. This indicates that they had grasped the concept of least confidence sampling. It seems they hypothesized that if they changed their entire annotation schema, either by adding new classes or lumping others and then bulk-edited the training data, this would solve with the model's "confusions". After one or two rounds, reanalysis resulted improvement and sometimes decreased performance. This led to conversations about how an MitL approach encourages iterative work just solving the next low-hanging fruit may be more effective than linear work that provides a comprehensive analysis.

Finally, strategize additional annotation. Once the original training data had been cleaned and the teams finished their reanalysis we observed the linguists really began to integrate the principles of statistical modeling that were covered during the lectures. Their questions and discussions turned to strategies for increasing annotated training data as much as possible. A notable pattern at this stage was they either did not fully grasp the impact of data size or were daunted by the task of providing enough new annotated data. Instead of bulk-editing, they tended to correct the model's annotations in small strategic efforts that seemed guided as much by their knowledge of the language as by the uncertainty sampling strategy. Then they would request for the model to be retrained so they could see the effect. For example, they might correct the machine annotations only on the first six (least confident) sequences or they might search for sentences with a rare part of speech. Sometimes the latter approach improved the model's performance on one class.

One group who had a member with Python programming skills and worked with a CRF for POS-tagging decided to experiment with the model architecture which was optimized for English. For example, because their language is more morphologically complex than English, they programmed the model to use the first and last six letters of a word as features, instead of the first and last four letters. This was the only example of participants attempting to customize the model, and they also seemed to prefer leveraging strategic knowledge of the language, rather than a statistical strategy (i.e. lots of annotation).

What's next? Participants progressed through these three stages independently. In general, they demonstrated understanding how noise and ambiguity present significant issues for statistical models with limited data. In the closing discussions, a repeated theme was the amount of annotation needed in order to make a significant impact would exceed their time limitations. This presented a chance to introduce "engineering" solutions not covered in the workshop materials, such as data hallucination and synthetic augmentation or cross-lingual transfer learning.

6 Conclusion

While teaching this material we observed that documentary and descriptive linguists bring their analytical strengths to the MitL approach. The material does not include formal assessments but we consider it successful because participants who brought their own data left with a better quality documentary corpus. A recent grant submitted by a workshop attendee to fund this workshop in another location indicates that the participants also assessed the material positively.

We conclude with specific recommenations. First, despite many successful remote collaborations in the post-pandemic age, we found that in-person events, removed from regular work, promote focused work and encourages social interaction that counteracts the intense schedule. Second, we recommend adding one day to the longer workshop schedule just to deal with anticipated and unanticipated issues (remote server not set up in time, flight delays, code bugs, forming teams, etc.).

Acknowledgements

The curriculum development was supported by the University of Florida and the "21st Century Tools for Indigenous Languages" Partnership (funded by grant #895-2019-1012 from the Social Sciences and Humanities Research Council of Canada [SSHRC] and the University of Alberta). We are very grateful to workshop participants and students who gave feedback on the curriculum and whose abilities and work exceeded our expectations!

References

Adrian Bridgwater. 2016. Machine Learning Needs A Human-In-The-Loop. *Forbes*.

Derek Chen, Samuel R. Bowman, and Zhou Yu. 2022. Clean or Annotate: How to Spend a Limited Data Collection Budget. In *Proceedings of the Third Workshop on Deep Learning for Low-Resource Natural Language Processing*, pages 152–168, Hybrid. Association for Computational Linguistics.

Aron Culotta and Andrew McCallum. 2005. Reducing Labeling Effort for Structured Prediction Tasks:. In *Proceedings, The Twentieth National Conference on Artificial Intelligence and the Seventeenth Innovative Applications of Artificial Intelligence Conference*, Pittsburgh, Pennsylvania, USA. American Association for Artificial Intelligence.

Long Duong. 2017. *Natural language processing for resource-poor languages*. Phd thesis, University of Melbourne, Melbourne, Australia.

Paul Felt. 2012. *Improving the Effectiveness of Machine-Assisted Annotation*. Ma thesis, Brigham Young University.

David D. Lewis and Jason Catlett. 1994. Heterogeneous Uncertainty Sampling for Supervised Learning. In William W. Cohen and Haym Hirsh, editors, *Machine Learning Proceedings 1994*, pages 148–156. Morgan Kaufmann, San Francisco (CA). Cite for uncertainty sampling.

Christopher Lin, M Mausam, and Daniel Weld. 2016. Re-Active Learning: Active Learning with Relabeling. *Proceedings of the AAAI Conference on Artificial Intelligence*, 30(1).

Sarah Moeller. 2021. *Integrating Machine Learning into Language Documentation and Description*. Ph.d., University of Colorado at Boulder, United States – Colorado.

Alexis Palmer, Taesun Moon, Jason Baldridge, Katrin Erk, Eric Campbell, and Telma Can. 2010. Computational strategies for reducing annotation effort in language documentation. *Linguistic Issues in Language Technology*, 3(4):1–42.

Alexis Mary Palmer. 2009. *Semi-automated annotation and active learning for language documentation*. Phd thesis, University of Texas at Austin.

Frank Seifart, Nicholas Evans, Harald Hammarström, and Stephen C. Levinson. 2018. Language documentation twenty-five years on. *Language*, 94(4):e324–e345.

Fei Xia, William D. Lewis, Michael Wayne Goodman, Glenn Slayden, Ryan Georgi, Joshua Crowgey, and Emily M. Bender. 2016. Enriching a massively multilingual database of interlinear glossed text. *Language Resources and Evaluation*, 50(2):321–349.

Shiyue Zhang, Ben Frey, and Mohit Bansal. 2022. How can NLP Help Revitalize Endangered Languages? A Case Study and Roadmap for the Cherokee Language. In *Proceedings of the 60th Annual Meeting of the Association for Computational Linguistics (Volume 1: Long Papers)*, pages 1529–1541, Dublin, Ireland. Association for Computational Linguistics.

Automatic Transcription of Grammaticality Judgements for Language Documentation

Éric Le Ferrand
Boston College
leferran@bc.edu

Emily Prud'hommeaux
Boston College
prudhome@bc.edu

Abstract

Descriptive linguistics is a sub-field of linguistics that involves the collection and annotation of language resources to describe linguistic phenomena. The transcription of these resources is often described as a tedious task, and Automatic Speech Recognition (ASR) has frequently been employed to support this process. However, the typical research approach to ASR in documentary linguistics often only captures a subset of the field's diverse reality. In this paper, we focus specifically on one type of data known as grammaticality judgment elicitation in the context of documenting Kréyòl Gwadloupéyen. We show that only a few minutes of speech is enough to fine-tune a model originally trained in French to transcribe segments in Kréyol.

1 Introduction

Under-resourced languages, characterized by insufficient data to train common statistical or neural models, stand in contrast to high-resource languages like English, French, and Mandarin. The EGIDS scale (Lewis and Simons, 2017) offers a more nuanced classification, assessing endangerment based on socio-political factors such as the number of speakers or support from public institutions. This scale can be used to assess a language's resource level and its ability to acquire linguistic resources. For instance, the presence of media representation in a language suggests a wealth of transcribed speech, while languages lacking media exposure or educational institutions typically possess limited data, often from descriptive linguistics efforts.

In the context of under-resourced languages falling below level 4 on the EGIDS scale, where a comprehensive educational system is lacking, attention has been directed towards advancing speech technologies. These innovations aim to assist linguists in overcoming the transcription bottleneck, thereby expediting the creation of new transcribed spoken resources. One potential procedural approach involves collecting a few hours of transcribed monolingual speech in the target language, training a model with this data, and subsequently employing the model to automatically transcribe new recordings. Despite the demonstrated effectiveness of such a workflow (Shi et al., 2021; Prud'hommeaux et al., 2021), it's crucial to acknowledge that monolingual data capture only a subset of the diverse recordings compiled by linguists in the field.

Grammaticality judgments constitute a form of interview commonly carried out in a shared language of the linguist and the speaker, involving one or more linguists engaging with one or more speakers to discuss grammatical structures in the target language. This dynamic interaction is inherently multilingual, featuring spontaneous speech from various contributors. In the context of the documentation of Kréyol Gwadeloupéyen (ISO-gcf), this paper aims to investigate the efficacy of cutting-edge speech recognition architectures in transcribing such recordings, even when confronted with severely limited available data.

2 Background

2.1 Research context

Kréyòl Gwadloupéyen originated within the colonial setting through the interaction of French colonists and African enslaved individuals in the region of the French West Indies (Prudent, 1999; Chaudenson, 2004). Kréyòl gwadloupéyen serves as the main means of everyday interaction for a substantial portion of Guadeloupe's population. In contrast, French is employed for official and formal purposes Creole languages typically borrow much of their vocabulary from the colonial language (the *lexifier*), while their grammatical structure diverges considerably from that of the lexifier. For instance,

Proceedings of the The Seventh Workshop on the Use of Computational Methods in the Study of Endangered Languages, pages 33–38
March 21-22, 2024 ©2024 Association for Computational Linguistics

in the following example, we can observe the similarity between the lexicon in Kréyol and French (sait/sav, creole/kréyol, parler/palé) and the difference in constructions.

(1) a. Jan pa sav palé kréyol
Jean NEG know speak creole
'Jean doesn't speak creole'

b. Jean ne sait pas parler créole
Jean NEG know NEG speak creole
'Jean doesn't speak creole'

It's worth noting that although the phonological systems in Kréyol and French share similarities, their writing systems exhibit substantial differences. Kréyol's writing system is relatively recent and reflects the language's pronunciation, whereas French retains artifacts from historical pronunciations.

In the NLP community, there is a common assumption that data collected during fieldwork is primarily limited to monolingual recordings in the target language, and the response to this assumption is to develop ASR models for transcribing this data. Two main purposes, however, lead researchers to record data in an endangered language: documentary linguistics and descriptive linguistics. While both disciplines involve the collection of language data, the methods used to gather that data and its eventual use differ depending on the field (Himmelmann, 1998). Documentary linguistics involves the collection of any material in the target language to document it, while descriptive linguistics involves the collection of any material (in the target language or not) that can be used to describe the language.

Recordings created in linguistic fieldwork typically fall into one of the following categories: monolingual recordings, usually comprised of narratives or elicited speech; interviews conducted in either the target language or a more widely spoken language like French or English; and "linguistic confirmations" which could include translations or grammaticality judgements. The latter involves interactions in which a native speaker is queried about the validity of sentence structures. Typically, these interactions occur in the shared language, with the segment to be assessed presented in the target language, as demonstrated in the following example:

Linguist	*i pousé mwen sa*, Can we say that?
Speaker	*i pousé mwen? i pousé mwen sa*
Linguist	does it sound a little bit weird?
Speaker	Wait, is there *mwen sa* in your sentence?

Note that this is the traditional code-switching context as the code-switched segments are systematically the core of the conversation and are introduced predictably (e.g. "Can you say X?", "Does Y sound correct to you").

2.2 Related work

Code-switching can be defined as the alternation between two language systems within the same discourse. This phenomenon is particularly common in the context of language contact (for instance Bentahila and Davies, 1983; Valenti, 2014). This phenomenon is particularly difficult to manage for ASR as most ASR systems are trained to be monolingual.

Two main approaches have been explored to address code-switching in ASR. The first one consists of identifying the language segments in each language with a language identification model and then applying their respective monolingual ASR models (Ahmed and Tan, 2012; Weiner et al., 2012). While this approach has shown poor performances for intrasentential code-switching (i.e., when the change of language system occurs within the same sentence), the identification of similar languages such as French and French-based Creoles presents an additional challenge (Scherrer et al., 2023). A second approach has been to train the ASR model directly on bilingual data with a joint acoustic and language model (Imseng et al., 2011; Li et al., 2011; Bhuvanagirir and Kopparapu, 2012; Yeh et al., 2010; Sivasankaran et al., 2018). Several corpora have been released for major languages to train this kind of model, including English-Chinese (Shen et al., 2011; Li et al., 2012), English-Hindi (Dey and Fung, 2014), and French-Arabic (Amazouz et al., 2018). The existence of large populations bilingual in these particular language pairs makes the collection of data easier than for endangered languages where we usually have access to only a few hours of transcribed speech.

The emergence of fine-tuning approaches using highly multilingual models such as Wav2Vec XLSR (Conneau et al., 2021) or Whisper (Radford et al., 2023) opened new opportunities for under-resourced languages whose data is not sufficient to train most state-of-the-art architectures. These new paths allowed more robust speech recognition systems for Indigenous, regional, and Creole languages (Le Ferrand et al., 2023; Macaire et al., 2022; Guillaume et al., 2022), where previous architectures would provide much higher error rates (Gupta and Boulianne, 2020b,a). Most of these previous studies approached these languages from a monolingual perspective with little space for multilingualism, code-switching, or empirical applications. While it is clear that highly multilingual models can be leveraged to transcribe under-resource languages with promising results, it is not clear if these models can be adapted to transcribe recordings in which a high-resource language contains many examples of code-switching in an under-resourced language.

In the field of documentary linguistics, the integration of ASR into the documentation workflow has been an enduring topic. Various approaches have been explored and have shown their efficiency in real-life scenarios. These approaches include the identification of spoken terms in a sparse transcription format (Le Ferrand et al., 2020; Bird, 2021) or the implementation of conventional ASR systems (Prud'hommeaux et al., 2021; Le Ferrand et al., 2023; Mitra et al., 2016).

3 Experiments

3.1 Data

As part of an NSF-funded student research program, a team of linguists went to Guadeloupe Island to document Kréyòl Gwadloupéyen in July 2022. During their trip, they were able to recruit language consultants. Most of the linguists involved in this project are English or Spanish speakers who also speak French with distinct accents, and they occasionally code-switch to English. Among the numerous recordings they collected, we have selected two that involve grammaticality judgments. The first recording features three speakers: two linguists and one native Kréyol speaker. The second recording involves two speakers: another linguist and another Kréyol speaker. Both recordings are primarily in French, with occasional interventions in English, and they contain segments in Kréyol that require verification. They focus on the same grammatical phenomena but use different examples. For instance, exploring the range of use of the preposition *pou*, the linguist in the first recording asked the validity of the sentence *i pousé sa pou mwen* ("he pushed it for me") while the linguist in the second recording used *i jèté sa pou mwen* ("he threw it for me").

The two recordings are 13 minutes and 20 minutes, respectively, with no overlapping speakers between the two recordings. The second recording is used for training and the first for testing. We will refer to this corpus as *CS* (Code-Switched) for the experiments in the next section.

To test the potential of monolingual data to transcribe grammaticality judgments, we incorporate a 70-minute-long corpus exclusively in Kréyol Gwadloupéyen. The audio recordings consist of spontaneous utterances about daily life topics from three male and three female speakers (Glaude, 2013).

3.2 Methods

For our task, we need an ASR model originally trained in French (or that includes French in the training data) and that can be fine-tuned to transcribe grammaticality judgements. Two main architectures are available: Wav2Vec (Conneau et al., 2021) and Whisper (Radford et al., 2023). For now, we use only Whisper as the Wav2Vec models available for French were not sufficiently large.

Whisper is an end-to-end encoder-decoder ASR system that relies on transformers. In a nutshell, the system takes 30s long audio segments and extracts log-Mel spectrograms. The resulting features are then passed into an encoder. The decoder is then trained to predict the corresponding transcription in an auto-regressive fashion. In other words, the transcription is generated one word at a time using the encoded input and the word previously transcribed.

We explore three configurations. The first is a traditional fine-tuning with our training set of grammaticality judgements (*CS* model). To determine whether the incorporation of monolingual data in Kréyol can boost the performance of the model, we train a second model on monolingual data in Kréyol and grammaticality judgements (*CS_mono* model) and a third model with only monolingual Kréyol data (*mono* model). Since the recordings are mostly in French, we also evaluate the model out of the box without any pretraining (*base*).

For all training, we use Whisper medium. We fine-tune it with the original hyperparamters [1] with only two changes. Because of memory limitations,

[1] https://huggingface.co/blog/fine-tune-whisper

we reduced the size of the training batch to 8 and increased the gradient accumulation to 2.

4 Results and discussion

	base	*CS*	*CS_mono*	*mono*
WER	50.98	40.85	40.53	79.78
CER	39.32	22.12	23.32	44.16

Table 1: WER and CER for the four models

.

	base	*CS*	*CS_mono*	*mono*
WER	98.96	40.15	46.58	65.66
CER	61.82	24.21	23.58	43.57

Table 2: WER and CER for the code-switched segments only.

oov rate	*CS*	*CS_mono*	*mono*
reference	62.16	35.13	47.29
predictions	14.68	3.8	7.69

Table 3: OOV rate for the three fine-tuned models.

We provide the overall Word Error Rate (WER) and Character Error Rate (CER) of all four models in Table 1. The first observation is that the initial model without fine-tuning (*base*) already performs relatively well. The reason is that most of the content of the recording is in French and we are only looking to adapt the model for code-switched segments. The model fine-tuned on only the code-switched dataset (*CS*) performs substantially better than the original model with an absolute WER decrease of 10%. These results are very encouraging considering the fact that only 20 minutes of speech has been used for the fine-tuning. The model fine-tuned with the code-switched data and the monolingual data together, *CS_mono*, does not show substantially better performances than the *CS* model. Finally fine-tuning only with monolingual data harms performance as it substantially modifies the objective of the model and transcribes everything in Kréyol.

For the second part of the evaluation we manually extract the code-switched segments from the transcriptions and perform the same evaluation on them (cf. Table 2). While the original model is not supposed to be robust at recognizing Kréyol, we notice that some segments were correctly transcribed. This can be explained by the similarity between French and Kréyol. The *CS* model performs noticeably better with about 60% of the Kréyol segments correctly transcribed. As before, the *CS_mono* model does not yield improvements over the *CS* model. Finally the monolingual model is not as robust as the *CS* model when transcribing the segments in Kréyol. This is perhaps because a language model is implicit in the auto-regressive generation of the transcription, meaning that the word order expected by the model is that of traditional Kréyol which differs substantially from the word order of the code-switched data.

The performance of the models given the minimal amount of data for fine-tuning suggests the ability of the models to infer the orthography of certain words. To explore this hypothesis, we calculated the out-of-vocabulary rate (OOV), which is the number of types in the test set that are not in the training set divided by the total number of types in the test set (see Table 3). Since most of the vocabulary in the corpus is French, we computed this rate only on the code-switched segments. Then, for each model we fine-tuned, we computed the number of OOVs correctly transcribed in the generated transcription out of all the tokens correctly transcribed (see Table 3)

The results suggest that when only the *CS* data is used for the fine-tuning, about 15% of the tokens correctly transcribed are OOVs. This number drops with the other models which suggests that the addition of monolingual data does not help during the training and using only *CS* data suffices to infer the orthography of unknown words. However, further analysis is necessary to confirm this trend.

Examples of transcriptions can be found in Table 4. We provide examples only from the original model and the *CS* model as it generally outperforms the others. A first observation is that the original model does not enforce a word order based on French but tries to provide French tokens that are close to the recordings (e.g. *je vais dire en cas content*: "I'm going to say in case happy"). For unknown words, it tries to make up a transcription based on French pronunciation rules (e.g. *kha*, *bai*, *moin* or *raï*). The *CS* model also tries to use known words when confronted with an OOV (*ti mwen/timoun*). Like the French model, it infers an orthography based on Kréyol pronunciation (*bo/ban*) or French pronunciation (e.g. *baï/bay*).

French model	*CS* model	Gold standard
enka raï blanc il y a deux choses	**an ka rayi blan** ah alors il y a deux choses	**an ka rayi blan** ah alors il y a deux choses
je vais dire **en cas content tu men amens**	vais dire **an ka contan ti mwen an mwen**	je vais dire **an ka conten timoun a mwen**
si je dis **un kha travail**	si je dis **an ka travayi**	si je dis **an ka travay**
pour moi et pour moi cest pas la même chose	**pour moi et ban mwen** cest pas la même	**pou mwen et ban mwen** cest pas la même chose
le verbe **bai** devient **bo** devant **moin**	le verbe **baï** devient **bo** devant **mwen**	le verbe **bay** devient **ban** devant **mwen**

Table 4: Examples of generated sentences. Code switched segments are bold

5 Conclusions

Here, we present the initial outcomes of our efforts to fine-tune a large speech recognition model for code-switching between two closely related languages: Kréyòl gwadloupéyen and its lexifier, French. Our focus is the specific scenario of grammaticality judgments, where linguists engage in conversations with native speakers in their shared language to evaluate the correctness of specific sentences in the target language.

The preliminary results illustrate that fine-tuning the Whisper model using just 20 minutes of speech substantially improves transcription quality. The refined model demonstrates increased resilience in transcribing noisy fieldwork data and accurately transcribes approximately 60% of the code-switched segments in our test set. This enhancement facilitates direct access to queries in the target language, which were consistently misinterpreted by the French model.

We present the findings of our initial experiments here, with more comprehensive details to be provided in future work. Subsequent experiments will involve comparing the Whisper model with alternative architectures, such as Wav2vec, and expanding the scope of experiments to encompass grammaticality judgments in other languages.

Acknowledgements

We would like to thank Dr. Fabiola Henri who agreed to share her data with us. We are also grateful for the work provided by the linguists on-site: Christian Jacobs, Erin Karnatz, Gideon Kortenhoven and José Pérez. Finally, we are grateful for the support of the Gwadeloupéyen speakers who agreed to be recorded and provide the grammaticality judgements used for this research. This material is based upon work supported by the National Science Foundation under Grant No. 1952568. Any opinions, findings, and conclusions or recommendations expressed in this material are those of the author(s) and do not necessarily reflect the views of the National Science Foundation.

References

Basem HA Ahmed and Tien-Ping Tan. 2012. Automatic speech recognition of code switching speech using 1-best rescoring. In *2012 International Conference on Asian Language Processing*, pages 137–140. IEEE.

Djegdjiga Amazouz, Martine Adda-Decker, and Lori Lamel. 2018. The french-algerian code-switching triggered audio corpus (facst). In *LREC 2018 11th edition of the Language Resources and Evaluation Conference,*.

Abdelali Bentahila and Eirlys E Davies. 1983. The syntax of arabic-french code-switching. *Lingua*, 59(4):301–330.

Kiran Bhuvanagirir and Sunil Kumar Kopparapu. 2012. Mixed language speech recognition without explicit identification of language. *American Journal of Signal Processing*, 2(5):92–97.

Steven Bird. 2021. Sparse transcription. *Computational Linguistics*, 46(4):713–744.

Robert Chaudenson. 2004. La créolisation: théorie, applications, implications. *La créolisation*, pages 1–480.

Alexis Conneau, Alexei Baevski, Ronan Collobert, Abdelrahman Mohamed, and Michael Auli. 2021. Unsupervised cross-lingual representation learning for speech recognition. *Proceedings of Interspeech 2021*.

Anik Dey and Pascale Fung. 2014. A hindi-english code-switching corpus. In *LREC*, pages 2410–2413.

Herby Glaude. 2013. Corpus créoloral. oai: crdo. vjf. cnrs. fr: crdo-gcf. *SFL Université Paris*.

Séverine Guillaume, Guillaume Wisniewski, Cécile Macaire, Guillaume Jacques, Alexis Michaud, Benjamin Galliot, Maximin Coavoux, Solange Rossato, Minh-Châu Nguyên, and Maxime Fily. 2022. Fine-tuning pre-trained models for automatic speech recognition, experiments on a fieldwork corpus of japhug (trans-himalayan family). In *Proceedings of the Fifth Workshop on the Use of Computational Methods in the Study of Endangered Languages*, pages 170–178.

Vishwa Gupta and Gilles Boulianne. 2020a. Automatic transcription challenges for inuktitut, a low-resource polysynthetic language. In *Proceedings of the Twelfth Language Resources and Evaluation Conference*, pages 2521–2527.

Vishwa Gupta and Gilles Boulianne. 2020b. Speech transcription challenges for resource constrained indigenous language cree. In *Proceedings of the 1st joint workshop on spoken language technologies for under-resourced languages (SLTU) and collaboration and computing for under-resourced languages (CCURL)*, pages 362–367.

Nikolaus P Himmelmann. 1998. *Documentary and descriptive linguistics*. Walter de Gruyter, Berlin/New York Berlin, New York.

David Imseng, Hervé Bourlard, Mathew Magimai Doss, and John Dines. 2011. Language dependent universal phoneme posterior estimation for mixed language speech recognition. In *2011 IEEE International Conference on Acoustics, Speech and Signal Processing (ICASSP)*, pages 5012–5015. IEEE.

Éric Le Ferrand, Fabiola Henri, Benjamin Lecouteux, and Emmanuel Schang. 2023. Application of speech processes for the documentation of kréyòl gwadloupéyen. In *The Second Workshop on NLP Applications to Field Linguistics (Field Matters)*, page 17.

Éric Le Ferrand, Steven Bird, and Laurent Besacier. 2020. Enabling interactive transcription in an indigenous community. In *28th International Conference on Computational Linguistics, COLING 2020*, pages 3422–3428. Association for Computational Linguistics (ACL).

M Paul Lewis and Gary F Simons. 2017. *Sustaining Language Use*. SIL International.

Ying Li, Pascale Fung, Ping Xu, and Yi Liu. 2011. Asymmetric acoustic modeling of mixed language speech. In *2011 IEEE International Conference on Acoustics, Speech and Signal Processing (ICASSP)*, pages 5004–5007. IEEE.

Ying Li, Yue Yu, and Pascale Fung. 2012. A mandarin-english code-switching corpus. In *LREC*, pages 2515–2519.

Cécile Macaire, Didier Schwab, Benjamin Lecouteux, and Emmanuel Schang. 2022. Automatic speech recognition and query by example for creole languages documentation. In *Findings of the Association for Computational Linguistics: ACL 2022*, pages 2512–2520.

Vikramjit Mitra, Andreas Kathol, Jonathan D Amith, and Rey Castillo García. 2016. Automatic speech transcription for low-resource languages-the case of yoloxóchitl mixtec (mexico). In *INTERSPEECH*, pages 3076–3080.

Lambert-Félix Prudent. 1999. Des baragouins à la langue antillaise. *Des Baragouins à la langue Antillaise*, pages 1–214.

Emily Prud'hommeaux, Robbie Jimerson, Richard Hatcher, and Karin Michelson. 2021. Automatic speech recognition for supporting endangered language documentation. *Language Documentation & Conservation*, 15:491–513.

Alec Radford, Jong Wook Kim, Tao Xu, Greg Brockman, Christine McLeavey, and Ilya Sutskever. 2023. Robust speech recognition via large-scale weak supervision. In *International Conference on Machine Learning*, pages 28492–28518. PMLR.

Yves Scherrer, Tommi Jauhiainen, Nikola Ljubešić, Preslav Nakov, Jörg Tiedemann, and Marcos Zampieri. 2023. Tenth workshop on nlp for similar languages, varieties and dialects (vardial 2023). In *Tenth Workshop on NLP for Similar Languages, Varieties and Dialects (VarDial 2023)*.

Han-Ping Shen, Chung-Hsien Wu, Yan-Ting Yang, and Chun-Shan Hsu. 2011. Cecos: A chinese-english code-switching speech database. In *2011 International Conference on Speech Database and Assessments (Oriental COCOSDA)*, pages 120–123.

Jiatong Shi, Jonathan D. Amith, Rey Castillo García, Esteban Guadalupe Sierra, Kevin Duh, and Shinji Watanabe. 2021. Leveraging end-to-end ASR for endangered language documentation: An empirical study on Yoloxóchitl Mixtec. In *Proceedings of the 16th Conference of the European Chapter of the Association for Computational Linguistics: Main Volume*, pages 1134–1145, Online. Association for Computational Linguistics.

Sunit Sivasankaran, Brij Mohan Lal Srivastava, Sunayana Sitaram, Kalika Bali, and Monojit Choudhury. 2018. Phone merging for code-switched speech recognition. In *Proceedings of the Third Workshop on Computational Approaches to Linguistic Code-Switching*, pages 11–19, Melbourne, Australia. Association for Computational Linguistics.

Eva Valenti. 2014. "nous autres c'est toujours bilingue anyways": Code-switching and linguistic displacement among bilingual montréal students. *American Review of Canadian Studies*, 44(3):279–292.

Jochen Weiner, Ngoc Thang Vu, Dominic Telaar, Florian Metze, Tanja Schultz, Dau-Cheng Lyu, Eng-Siong Chng, and Haizhou Li. 2012. Integration of language identification into a recognition system for spoken conversations containing code-switches. In *Spoken Language Technologies for Under-Resourced Languages*.

Ching Feng Yeh, Chao Yu Huang, Liang Che Sun, and Lin Shan Lee. 2010. An integrated framework for transcribing mandarin-english code-mixed lectures with improved acoustic and language modeling. In *2010 7th International Symposium on Chinese Spoken Language Processing*, pages 214–219. IEEE.

Fitting a Square Peg into a Round Hole: Creating a UniMorph dataset of Kanien'kéha Verbs

Anna Kazantseva and **Akwiratékha Martin**
National Research Council Canada
[anna.kazantseva, akwiratekha.martin]@nrc-cnrc.gc.ca

Karin Michelson and **Jean-Pierre Koenig**
University at Buffalo
The State University of New York
[kmich,jpkoenig]@buffalo.edu

Abstract

This paper describes efforts to annotate a dataset of verbs in the Iroquoian language Kanien'kéha (a.k.a. Mohawk) using the UniMorph schema (Batsuren et al., 2022a). The dataset is based on the output of a symbolic model - a hand-built verb conjugator. Morphological constituents of each verb are automatically annotated with UniMorph tags. Overall the process was smooth but some central features of the language did not fall neatly into the schema which resulted in a large number of custom tags and a somewhat *ad hoc* mapping process. We think the same difficulties are likely to arise for other Iroquoian languages and perhaps other North American language families. This paper describes our decision making process with respect to Kanien'kéha and reports preliminary results of morphological induction experiments using the dataset.

1 Introduction

It is generally believed that building language technology for morphologically rich languages benefits from knowing about morphology. Other things held constant, providing morphological information as a part of an NLP pipeline is likely to help, *e.g.* (Vania et al., 2018; Dehouck and Denis, 2018; Hofmann et al., 2021; Park et al., 2021). While there is no clear-cut definition of what makes a language morphologically rich, usually it refers to languages where words are composed of many parts. It certainly applies to most language families in North America (e.g. Algonquian, Iroquoian, Eskimo-Aleut, *etc.*)

Computational models of morphology are important also because mastering morphology is crucial when learning a morphologically rich language. Methods, techniques and aids that help students master morphology are helpful in speeding up the learning process (Renard, 2022).

The work described in this paper is a small step in this direction for Kanien'kéha, a.k.a. the Mohawk language. It started as a collaboration between the National Research Council Canada (further NRC) and a Kanien'kéha immersion school for adults, Onkwawénna Kentyóhkwa. The teachers at the school noticed that students in the immersion classes struggled most with mastering verbal morphology and often created hand-made 'verb conjugators' as study aids. The role of the NRC was to help build an interactive verb conjugator that was aligned with the school's curriculum. To the best of our knowledge this was the first computational model of a subset of Kanien'kéha grammar. However, we were unable to use any data driven methods because of the extreme paucity of textual data in Kanien'kéha.

One of the side effects of creating a symbolic language model was the creation of a large dataset of verbs (1,419K conjugations), complete with inflectional information and morphological segmentation. We have mapped this dataset into the UniMorph framework.

The motivation for this paper is two-fold. Firstly, the paper serves as a reference document for a new dataset for morphological induction in Kanien'kéha. The paper documents the dataset itself as well as the arbitrary decisions made during the labelling process. The second goal of this paper is to illustrate that such references are necessary when creating datasets for low-resource languages, especially less documented ones. We demonstrate several paradigms in the language that cannot be adequately described using the UniMorph framework without defining a large number of custom labels (e.g. pronominal system, aspect system, transitivity etc.). In some cases, existing UniMorph dimensions and features seem acceptable but upon closer inspection applying them would be misleading. These remarks are not meant as a criticism of UniMorph, but rather as suggestions for future updates of the schema. This is especially so since the same properties are common not only to all

Proceedings of the The Seventh Workshop on the Use of Computational Methods in the Study of Endangered Languages, pages 39–51

Iroquoian languages, but also to other language families in North America (e.g. Algonquian).

The main contribution of this work is the dataset[1]. The second contribution is preliminary results of morphological inflection experiments using this dataset. To the best of our knowledge, this is the first data-driven or corpus-based model of Kanien'kéha.

This paper is structured as follows. Section 2 places the work into existing research context. Section 3 provides a brief overview of the language. Section 4 gives an overview of UniMorph. Section 5 describes the initial data used for annotation. Section 6 is the main description of the new dataset and the decisions made. Section 7 briefly describes experiments and reports results. Sections 8 and 9 contain discussion and describe limitations of this work.

2 Related Work

Related work falls into two broad categories: linguistic and computational modelling of Kanien'kéha and research on computational models of morphology induction.

There is ample work in the field of Linguistics describing Kanien'kéha. Mithun (2000, 2005) provide thorough overviews of the language. Lounsbury (1953) describes the closest Iroquoian *sister* language - Oneida, and so do Michelson and Doxtator (2002). Beaty (1974) and Bonvillain (1973) are grammars of two dialects of Kanien'kéha. These resources describe the language as a system but we could not use them directly in computational modelling because of lack of both coverage and detail. A notable exception is Michelson (1983) which features a complete and detailed model of the stress system in Kanien'kéha; the symbolic model we have built is an implementation of this work.

Another type of descriptive work are educational materials: Maracle (2017); Martin (2023); Price et al. (2011). These are teaching textbooks and curriculum materials. As such they are complete, thorough and focus on the aspects of the language that are important for today's learners. We have used them extensively.

An important research hive for activity on computational models of morphology is the *Special Interest Group on Computational Morphology and Phonology* (*SIGMORPHON*). The annual shared task competitions (Nicolai et al., 2023) include morphological inflection. In 2023 the task was run on 26 languages across 9 language families. Systems that consistently perform better across languages are neural ones (e.g., Canby et al. 2020; Girrbach 2023). However for some languages a non-neural and rule-based systems designed specifically for those languages achieve best results (e.g., Kwak et al. 2023).

Within this context, our work is novel with respect to resources and research on computational modelling of Kanien'kéha. We have created the first large dataset of inflected verbs in Kanien'kéha that can be used in computational modelling. Our computational experiments at this point are basic - we use the SIGMORPHON neural character-level transformer baseline (Wu et al., 2021).

3 Kanien'kéha and Iroquoian Languages

Iroquoian languages are a group of approximately 17 historically documented languages situated in southeastern Canada (Ontario and Quebec) and northeastern US (New York State, but also in North Carolina and Oklahoma).

All spoken Iroquoian languages that still have first-language speakers (further *L1*) (Cherokee, Seneca, Cayuga, Onondaga, Oneida and Kanien'kéha) are endangered. Several others are either undergoing revitalization within communities or are considered sleeping languages. The majority of *L1* speakers are older than 75. However, in several communities a small number of new *L1* speakers are being raised by parents who are *L2* speakers.

Linguistically, Iroquoian languages can be divided into Southern Iroquoian and Northern Iroquoian branches. There is only one Southern Iroquoian language - Cherokee. The Northern branch of the Iroquoian language family contains all original Five Nations languages of the Haudenosaunee Confederacy. Many other Iroquoian languages are no longer spoken, with scant word lists available (e.g. Wyandot, Petun, Meherrin, Neutral, Wenro and Erie to name just a few) (Mithun, 2005).

Despite the current harsh linguistic reality, due to the effects of continued colonization and governments' efforts to linguistically and culturally destroy them, the language communities are very focused and interested in strengthening and reestablishing their ancestral languages. Many im-

[1]Due to the preference of the communities the dataset is not publicly available by default, however it is available upon request for research and educational purposes.

pressive and successful efforts are ongoing and evolving to fit their contemporary needs. The authors of the paper are only familiar with some of the communities and regret inevitable omissions. However, examples of thriving language schools are seen at Twatati Adult Oneida Immersion program for Oneida[2], Yawenda Project for Wendat[3] and Onkwawénna Kentyohkwa[4] and Kanien'kehá:ka Onkwawén:na Raotitióhkwa Language and Cultural Center for Kanien'kéha Ratiwennahní:rats Adult Language Immersion Program[5].

All Iroquoian languages are morphologically complex, with verbs being particularly elaborate. Verbs are composed of several parts, both prefixes and suffixes, as well as noun incorporation. Due to the languages' rich morphology, the linguistic practice of creating new words is deeply cultural, therefore restricting borrowing from other languages. Generally speaking, single-token verbs in an Iroquoian language correspond to simple clauses in English (however simpler verbs are possible too):

(1) *enhake'serehtakwatákwahse'*
en-hake-'sereht-a-kwatakw-a-hs-e'
will-he>me-car-link-fix-link-for-punctual
FUT-MSG>1SG-car-JR-fix-JR-BEN-PUNC

'he'll repair a car for me; he'll fix my car' (Kanien'kéha)

(2) *yusayenhohayaʔákhuʔ*
y-usa-ye-nhoh-a-yaʔak-hu-ʔ
there-again.did-she-door-link-hit-many-punc
TRANSL-REP.FACT-FI.A-door-JR-hit-
-DISTR-PUNC

'she knocked on the door again' (Oneida)

Example 1 and Example 2 are two unremarkable Kanien'kéha and Oneida verbs (Michelson et al., 2016, p.51) that correspond to simple clauses in English.

Since this work only focuses on verbal morphology, we will only discuss that part of speech from here on in. A minimal verb structure consists of a pronominal prefix, a verb stem and an aspectual suffix, which can be null. A verb stem can be simple or have a noun incorporated, as in Example 1.

[2]https://www.facebook.com/people/Twatati/100057069505224
[3]https://languewendat.com/en/ and (Lukaniec, 2018)
[4]https://onkwawenna.info/
[5]https://www.korkahnawake.org/kanienkha-ratiwennahnrats

Classificatory dimensions
Aktionsart
Animacy
Argument Marking
Aspect
Case
Comparison
Definiteness
Deixis
Evidentiality
Finiteness
Gender
Information Structure
Interrogativity
Language-specific features
Mood
Number
Part of Speech
Person
Polarity
Politeness
Possession
Switch-reference
Tense
Valency
Voice

Table 1: Classificatory dimensions in UniMorph

Additionally, a verb can also have pre-pronominal prefixes and the verb stem can include one or more prefixes or suffixes; these convey inflectional and derivational meanings.

4 UniMorph

The UniMorph project (Sylak-Glassman, 2016; Batsuren et al., 2022b) has two main parts: an annotation schema and an extensive collection of inflection tables for 182 languages, several dozens of them for endangered languages of the world. It also contains several datasets for morpheme segmentation and for derivational morphology.

The original goal of the project was to develop a language-independent schema that could adequately describe inflectional morphological breakdowns of words in any language. Currently in its 4.0 version, the UniMorph schema has been extended and improved but its skeleton remains unchanged.

The UniMorph schema contains 25 dimensions listed in Table 1. Each dimension has a number of possible features. For example, the features

Stem	Inflected form	UniMorph tags	Lang.
mercify	mercifies	V;PRS;3;SG	EN
mercify	mercifying	V;V.PTCP;PRS	EN
abalienare	abalienò	V;IND;PST;3;SG;PFV	IT
abbacare	abbacai	V;IND;PST;1;SG;PFV	IT

Table 2: Examples of words annotated using the UniMorph schema.

for the dimension *Animacy* are Animate, Human, Inanimate, Non-human. When default features are insufficient the annotators can also create language specific tags.

Table 4 shows examples of words annotated using UniMorph.

Using the UniMorph schema is not the only option. We could have devised our own set of tags as in Hämäläinen et al. (2021). We decided to opt for standardization possibly at the expense of specificity. This decision is due to the practical nature of our objectives. As the overarching goal is improving language technology for Kanien'kéha, choosing a widely used standard (UniMorph) seems more practical and more accessible for future users than devising our own.

5 The dataset

Kawennón:nis is an interactive verb conjugator for Kanien'kéha available online or locally. Currently two version of the software exist: one for the Ohswé:ken dialect (Ohswekèn:'a) and another for the Kahnawà:ke dialect (Kahnawa'kéha). This paper describes the dataset for Kahnawa'kéha.

This tool was designed as a teaching aid for students of immersion programs of Kanien'kéha and closely follows the curriculum. It allows the user to select one or more verb stems, one or more sets of pronominal prefixes and one or more tenses, and then outputs the corresponding conjugations. The tool has been designed in close collaboration with Onkwawénna Kentyóhkwaimmersion school. Following a user study and several consultations with teachers and students, a local artist was employed to design a culturally relevant interface.

The tool contains 662 verb stems and more are being added. It allows the user to choose one or more of the 12 available tense/aspect options, as well as apply negation and repetition. It does not contain derivational morphology, although we hope to add contained subsets in the future.

The complete output of the tool corresponds to inflectional tables for the 662 verbs within the modeled paradigms - 1,418,939 inflected forms. However because the dataset contains inflectional tables as opposed to intelligently created samples, there is a lot of redundancy (the size grows exponentially with the number of paradigms modeled).

Stress in Kanien'kéha is quite complex and is a major source of irregularities. We make available both the stressed and the unstressed versions on the dataset.

Extensive work has been done to ensure the quality of the dataset but as any computational model, it contains errors. 244 of the 662 inflection table files have been manually checked by an advanced L2 speaker who is an experienced teacher and linguist. As was mentioned in Section 3 there are very few L1 speakers of Kanien'kéha; what is even more important is that their time is better spent than checking conjugation tables. We realize that thorough evaluation is a weakness of this work but it is an unfortunate consequence of the capacity bottleneck.

6 UniMorph and Kanien'kéha

Our dataset contains only active verbs (as opposed to stative) and captures only foundational morphological paradigms. Therefore, only verb-related parts of the UniMorph schema are relevant to us. In this section we describe our efforts to align the properties of the language with the UniMorph schema. The process of mapping was not straightforward and arguably alternative choices could have been made. Yet, despite some difficulties we were able to automatically label our existing dataset, take advantage of the existing systems and train a model for morphological inflection in Kanien'kéha. Preliminary results are available in Section 7.

6.1 Valency and Voice-like features

Depending on the structure of their semantic arguments, there are three types of verbs in Kanien'kéha: two intransitive types, and one transitive. Intransitive verbs can be divided into two classes depending on the category of bound pronominal prefixes they take. Two types of pronominal prefixes are possible with intransitive verbs: *agent* prefixes and *patient* ones. The distribution of the prefixes typically has to do with the degree of control the actor has over the event.

(3) *ie'níkhons*
ie-'nikhon-hs
she/someone/they-sew-habitual
FI.A-sew-HAB

'she/they/someone sews or is sewing'

In Example 3 the actor (*she/someone/they*) is in control and the active pronominal prefix *ie-* (*she*) is used. If control is lacking or the actor is being acted upon, patient pronominal prefixes are used:

(4) *saho'nikónhrhen'*
s-wa-ro-'nikonhrhen-'
again-did-he-forget-punctual
REP-FACT-MSGP-forget-PUNC

'he forgot (again)'

In Example 4 the actor has less control over the event, hence the patient pronominal prefix *ro-* (*he/him*) is used. While the degree of control largely determines pronominal prefix preferences of a verb, it is not always the case and students must learn them for each verb. For instance, the verb *yo'ten* (*to work*) always takes patients pronominal prefixes:

(5) *enionkeniió'ten'*
en-ionkeni-io'ten-'
will-we-work-punctual
FUT-1DUP-work-PUNC

'we will work'

Also, patient pronominal prefixes are always used in certain tense/aspect combinations that emphasize the end result of an action:

(6) *wakatórion*
wak-atori-on
I-drive-stative
1SGP-drive-STAT

'I have driven (emphasis on the result)'

For transitive verbs when both participants in the event are animate, a separate set of pronominal prefixes is used to encode the relation between the participants, as in the following example:

(7) *taiethi'nikonhrakénnion*
t-a-iethi-'nikonhr-a-kenni-on
two-should-we>them-mind-link-challenge-stative
DUP-OPT-1INCL.NS>3NS-mind-JR-compete-STAT

'We should have convinced them.'

In Example 7 the transitive pronominal prefix *yethi-* is used, meaning *you-and-I/we-to-her/her/them*.

While there is a semantic distinction (based on the degree of control and the relationship between agents and patients), pronominal prefix preferences are sometimes lexicalized in intransitive cases. The three types of verbs are learned in the first lessons of Kanien'kéha and students need to memorize the type of pronominal prefixes each verb takes (some verbs can participate in constructions of more than one type).

These paradigms roughly correspond to two of the UniMorph dimensions: Valency (the transitive/intransitive distinction) and Voice (Active/Passive) distinction. However, we decided against using these default categories. The first reason is that even intransitive constructions such as those in Example 3 and Example 4 can be used with semantically transitive verbs - in those cases the pronominal prefix means *actor-to-it*. For instance, the verb *ie'níkhons* can mean *'She is sewing something'* (where the *'something'* is understood). So the distinction is not strictly in the number of semantic arguments. Secondly, the Voice dimension of UniMorph and Active/Passive distinction does not correspond to semantic differences of agent and patient pronominal prefixes and corresponding constructions. Voice alternations mark situations when the relationship between a verb and its core nominal arguments is altered. The distinction in Kanien'kéha is different; there is no true voice alternation in the language.

6.2 Pronominal prefix features

Verbs in Kanien'kéha require a bound pronoun to be grammatical. Bound pronouns are often referred to as *pronominal prefixes* and that is the terminology we use throughout this paper. The pronominal prefix signifies a relationship between an agent and a patient (e.g. *he-to-it*, *you and I-to-those two*, *it-to-me*). The pronominal system in Kanien'kéha is very complex and elaborate.

The Kanien'kéha pronominal system distinguishes person (*1st, 2nd, 3rd*) and number (singular, dual, plural). *1st* person dual and plural pronominal prefixes also mark for inclusivity of the listener (e.g. *teni-* (*you and I*) vs. *iakeni-* (*someone and I*)). There are three gender choices: masculine, feminine/indefinite (the indefinite pronominal prefix is identical to feminine across the pronominal prefix system) and feminine/zoic (referring to some female persons and animals).

Annotating person, number, gender and inclusivity categories within the UniMorph framework is straight-forward. The only thing worth noting is the distinction between the transitive and the quasi-intransitive verbs. Recall that intransitive verbs in Kanien'kéha can 1) truly take one semantic argument as in *teharáhtats* (*'he runs'*) or 2) they can denote a relationship between an animate and inanimate entity as in *wahahní:non'* (*'he bought (it, something)'*). For intransitive verbs we only annotate the agent (or the patient), but we do not explicitly annotate the implicit participant (*it*). For transitive pronominal prefixes we annotate both the agent and the patient.

6.3 Tense-related features

When looking at the verb conjugator Kawennón:nis and at the instructional texts for Kanien'kéha immersion courses we often see the term *tense*. Yet, the notion of tense in Kanien'kéha is quite different and the terminology is influenced by the fact that most teachers and students are L1 speakers of English rather than by the intrinsic semantics of Kanien'kéha.

Tense refers to the relationship between the time of utterance (TU) and topic time (TT) with other refinements possible (Reichenbach, 1947; Klein, 1994). However, in Kanien'kéha the meaning of tense is intertwined with the meaning of mood-related categories of *realis* and *irrealis*. So what we refer to as the past tense, in Kanien'kéha is closer to the marker of something having happened for sure; present time - happening at the time of utterance; future tenses refer to likely events in the future and optative constructions - to possible future events.

(8) *ie'níkhons*
ie-'nikhon-hs
she/someone/they-sew-habitual
FI.A-sew-HAB

'she sews it (either habitually or right now)'

(9) *enie'níkhon'*
en-ie-'nikhon-'
will-she/someone/they-sew-punctual
FUT-FI.A-sew-PUNC

'She will sew it (definitely)'

(10) *wa'e'níkhon'*
wa'-ie-nikhon-'
did-she/someone/they-sew-punctual
FACT-FI.A-sew-PUNC

'She sewed, she did sew it (it is a fact)'

(11) *aie'níkhon'*
a-ie '-nikhon-'
should-she/someone/they-sew-punctual
OPT-FI.A-sew-PUNC

'She should, might, or ought to sew it'

Our dataset contains two tenses that we label as past: 1) punctual factual and 2) habitual with former past.

Verbs with explicit markers of 'future' are labelled as future tense *(FUT)* and those with former past suffix *-kwe'* as past tense *(PST)*. We do not explicitly label what most students think of the present tense.

6.4 Aspect-related features

The situation with aspect is no less complicated. The notion of aspect is based on the relationship between Time of Situation (TSit) and Topic Time (TT) (Reichenbach, 1947; Klein, 1994). The UniMorph schema also defines aspect as the relationship between the time for which a claim is made (TT) and the time for which a situation actually held true (TSit) (Sylak-Glassman, 2016) (page 13).

Linguistic literature on Kanien'kéha (Beaty, 1974; Bonvillain, 1973; Price et al., 2011; Martin, 2023) varies somewhat in their labelling and the number of aspects. Recent work (Price et al., 2011; Martin, 2023) agrees on distinguishing three aspects: Imperfective (a.k.a. Habitual), Punctual (a.k.a. Perfective) and Stative, plus Imperative (which is marked by the absence of any aspectual information).

These categories are neither orthogonal nor parallel to the UniMorph labels which are *Imperfective, Perfective, Perfect, Progressive, Prospective, Iterative, Habitual.*

In Kanien'kéha, the Habitual aspect can denote three possible cases 1) Habitual occupation or profession 2) Daily recurring activity and 3) An event occurring at the moment of speech.

For example the verb *ie'níkhons* in Example 8 can be translated as 1) She is a seamstress 2) She sews (regularly) or 3) She is sewing right now.

We decided to label the Habitual aspect in Kanien'kéha using the UniMorph *Imperfective* label (*IPFV*), e.g. Example 8.

Punctual aspect can be combined with factual (Example 10), future (Example 9) or optative constructions (Example 11). It denotes actions that are viewed as complete events and approximately corresponds to *Perfective* aspect in UniMorph. We label constructions in punctual aspect as perfective using the UniMorph schema (*PFV*). Punctual factual constructions usually are translated as past tense, as in the Example 10 yet it is not truly a tense. Factual *wa'-* is a mood marker and the emphasis is on factuality and certainty, not tense (however, it is commonly translated as Simple Past into English).

Progressive meaning in Kanien'kéha is sometimes expressed with the habitual aspect, as in *ie'níkhons*: (*'she is sewing'*) in Example 8 and sometimes with the stative aspect, as in *wakatshenón:ni* (*'I am happy'*) in Example 12. There seems to be a correlation with the notions of accomplishment versus activity, but this varies so much that the distribution has to be learned for each verb. For Stative constructions, we define a language-specific label. (The stative also can convey the equivalent of the English perfect, as in Example 13, *tewaktà:on' 'I have stopped'*. We use the UniMorph label *Perfect* (*PFV*) for such cases.)

(12) *wakatshennón:ni*
wak-atshennonni-ø
I-happy-stative
1SGP-happy-STAT

'I am happy'

(13) *tewaktà:'on*
te-wak-t-a-'-on
two-I-stand-link-become-stative
DUP-1SGP-stand–JR-INCH-STAT

'I have stood up, I have stopped'

Two types of constructions that do not fit into the UniMorph dimensions are Perfect Progressive and Habitual Continuative constructions.

(14) *iako'nikhóntie'*
iako-'nikhón-ø-tie'
she-sew-stative-progressive
FI.P-sew-STAT-PROG

'She is sewing it (while moving along in space and or in time)'

(15) *enie'nikhónhseke'*
en-ie-'nikhón-hs-eke'
will-she-sew-habitual-continuative
FUT-FI.P-sew-HAB-CONT

'She will keep on sewing it'

The semantics of the Perfect Progressive in Kanien'kéha does not fit neatly into the aspectual hierarchy. For Perfect Progressive the semantic component of motion is as important as that of continuity, see Example 14. We define a language-specific feature for this type of constructions. Habitual continuative tenses (optative and future) emphasize events with duration, as in Example 15. Yet the markers seem to be formal elements that convey the usual semantics of habitual. We do not add a feature for these constructions.

6.5 Mood-related features

We annotate three possible feature values for the *Mood* dimension: *Imperative* (*IMP*) for commands, *Irrealis* (*IRR*) for optative constructions, and *Realis* (*REAL*) for past tense and factual constructions.

6.6 Finiteness features

In our annotation we annotate Perfect and Perfect Optative tenses as *Finite* (*FIN*). We do not explicitly mark *Nonfinite* constructions.

6.7 Deixis features

Deixis is a linguistic mechanism for referring to a location, entity or time within a given context. For instance, the use of words such as *this, that, here, then, etc.* are examples of deixis.

Kanien'kéha verbs can take on non-modal pre-pronominal prefixes that have deictic properties:

(16) *entkontáweia'te'*
en-t-kon-ataweia't-e'
will-here-they-enter-punctual
FUT-CIS-FZPLA-enter-PUNC

'they will come in, they will enter (here)'

(17) *ienkontáweia'te'*
i-en-kon-ataweia't-e'
there-will-they-enter-punctual
TRANS-FUT-FZPLA-enter-PUNC

'they will go in, they will enter (there)'

We define two language specific features to address such cislocative (Example 16) and translocative (Example 17) constructions.

The same morphological slot can be occupied by a number of other semantic prefixes that are not diectic in nature. Nevertheless, we list them in this section. The *TE* prefix is a dualic prefix that denotes various pair-wise relationships. The *NI* prefix is a partitive prefix that has several meanings: quantitative, intensity or location. There is also the *S* prefix denoting repetition. We defined three language specific tags to denote the meaning of these prefixes.

(18) *tesewakwáthon*
te-sewa-kwath-on
two-you-hem-stative
DUP-2PLP-hem-STAT

'you have hemmed it'

(19) *tho* *naieseniié:renke'*
tho n-aie-seni-ier-en-ke'
there partitive-should-you-do-st
partical PART-OPT-2DUP-do-STAT-CONT

'you should have done that'

Dataset	Accuracy	Edit distance
With stress	64.93	1.28
Unstresed	75.36	0.83

Table 3: Experimental results

(20) *ia'tesewakerihwaientà:se'*
ia'-te-se-wake-rihw-a-ient-a-'s-e'
there-two-again-I-issue-link
settle.on.ground-link-for-punctual
TRANS-DUP-REP-1SG-issue-
JR-put.down-JR-BEN-STAT

'I have decided again'

7 Experiments

For our experiments we apply the neural character-level transformer (Wu et al., 2021) that is used as a competitive baseline in SIGMORPHON competitions (Nicolai et al., 2023). We use the high-resource setting and the only parameter we change from default settings is the batch size, which we set to 1000[6].

The final version of the dataset contains 1,418,893 inflected verb forms. We split them into training, development and test sets in a 0.7 : 0.1 : 0.2 ratio. The splits are done at the level of individual verbs: the same verb does not appear in more than one split (and consequently none of the conjugated examples are overlapping either). The exception to this statement are verbs that can behave as both transitive and intransitive ones: in these cases while the stem is the same, the morphological preferences are different. Because of this we do not control that such verbs do not appear in training/development sets and test sets simultaneously.

The stress system is a major source of exceptions. In addition to placement of stress, it also determines variations in length and tone and whether some characters are omitted. Because of these challenges we create a second dataset without stress. To produce the dataset, we use the output of the symbolic model before stress rules are applied.

The results are shown in Table 3. As expected, the task of producing conjugations without stress is much easier: the system achieves 75.36% accuracy vs. 64.93% on the stressed dataset.

[6]This follows advice from Wu et al. (2021) who find that batch size plays a critical size for transformer-based models of morphology.

Preliminary error analysis suggests that indeed stress-related errors are common. However the biggest source of mistakes seems to be changes in verb stems related to aspect (habitual, punctual, stative and imperatives). This is supported by opinions of the speakers that aspectual endings are largely lexicalized with many exceptions from general loose rules. In the symbolic system used as the original source of data, four forms are given as input for each verb stem. The neural system learned how to generalize those forms, albeit imperfectly.

We hope to address these shortcomings in future work. Since stress in Kanien'kéha is determined from the end of the word, in right-to-left fashion, we expect that applying a right-to-left system such as that of Canby et al. (2020) may help. Also, we hope that learning generic rules about orthography in Kanien'kéha from an existing corpus may improve both stress and aspectual-class related errors.

8 Conclusions

We have described the first dataset for morphological induction for the Iroquoian language Kanien'kéha. Due to community preferences, the dataset is not publicly available by default but is available upon request for research and educational purposes.

While describing the dataset, we have demonstrated that the process of mapping ready morphologically segmented data into UniMorph is neither trivial nor always straight-forward. Some of the problematic categories, common to other Iroquoian languages, are tense, aspect, voice and mood. We have also reported first results of morphological induction experiments on this dataset.

In the future, we have practical and research directions to consider. We hope to use the results of experiments to speed up the circular process of improving the symbolic model, extending this dataset and hopefully eventually exceeding the precision of the symbolic model.

We also are exploring ways to improve performance on this dataset. One such avenue was mentioned in Section 7: using a learning model that considers both left-to-right and right-to-left input directions. We also would like to look into creating similar resources for related languages for which symbolic models already exist, *e.g.* Oneida (Lu, 2023) and Cherokee[7].

[7] https://www.yourgrandmotherscherokee.com

9 Limitations

This work is one small step in the direction of applying data-driven language technology to Kanien'kéha. As such, its limitations are plentiful.

The most obvious one is that the dataset covers only a subset of the language: only active verbs, and only foundational verbal paradigms. Despite the fact that verbs are the most complex and common part-of-speech in Kanien'kéha, the performance on this dataset may not generalize sufficiently well.

The second limitation is the precision of the dataset. The source of the dataset is a symbolic model built by hand and checked by hand. We have done our best (and continue to do so) to gradually check the correctness a large part of the conjugated forms (244 verbs have been manually checked). Yet, without a doubt some errors remain.

Another limitation is generalizing to other languages. The UniMorph repository contain a dataset for one more Iroquoian language - Seneca (Pimentel et al., 2021); it is even more limited in scope than ours. We would like to create datasets for related languages, but that is only possible for cases where there already exist high quality resources.

The fourth, perhaps most crucial limitation is in the applications of the dataset and of the experimental results. Kanien'kéha is an endangered language spoken by several hundred people across several communities. In this context it is crucial to check every step for whether a given technology or resource helps or hurts the vitality of the language, or has the potential to do so. It is not immediately clear how to use this resource especially given concerns about data governance and sovereignty. We intend to use our results to identify the most difficult verbs and create a feedback loop. This may or may not be helpful. We hope others may come up with better use cases.

Ethics Statement

When working with endangered languages ethical concerns are paramount. All Indigenous languages spoken in Canada have a history of language suppression, expropriation and, at times, misuse. In this historical context unhurried discussions with the language communities, genuine partnership in creating resources and software and informed consent are the bare minimum. It is not difficult to see that this requirement is likely to slow down the technical side. It is because of these concerns that we decided not to release the dataset by default but to make it available upon request.

Another ethical concern is how creation of a resource can affect the language - especially in situations where there are very few or no digital resources. For Kanien'kéha the writing system is fairly recent and the orthography is not always consistent. Creation of a resource can influence the standards of spelling - sometimes incorrectly so. This is especially dangerous in situations where few people are confident enough in their spelling to point out a mistake.

Acknowledgements

The authors of the paper would like to acknowledge extensive help and contributions of the personnel and of the students of Onkwawénna Kentyóhkwa immersion school, especially Owennatékha Brian Maracle, Karakwenhawi Zoe Hopkins, Rohahí:yo Jordan Brant, Jody Maracle, Ronkwe'tiyóhstha Josiah Maracle and Maura Abrams. We are grateful to Aidan Pine for his work on the server-side and GUI of Kawennón:nis and for multiple fruitful discussions. We also thank our colleagues Roland Kuhn and Patrick Littell for their help with this project.

References

Khuyagbaatar Batsuren, Omer Goldman, Salam Khalifa, Nizar Habash, Witold Kieraś, Gábor Bella, Brian Leonard, Garrett Nicolai, Kyle Gorman, Yustinus Ghanggo Ate, Maria Ryskina, Sabrina Mielke, Elena Budianskaya, Charbel El-Khaissi, Tiago Pimentel, Michael Gasser, William Abbott Lane, Mohit Raj, Matt Coler, Jaime Rafael Montoya Samame, Delio Siticonatzi Camaiteri, Esaú Zumaeta Rojas, Didier López Francis, Arturo Oncevay, Juan López Bautista, Gema Celeste Silva Villegas, Lucas Torroba Hennigen, Adam Ek, David Guriel, Peter Dirix, Jean-Philippe Bernardy, Andrey Scherbakov, Aziyana Bayyr-ool, Antonios Anastasopoulos, Roberto Zariquiey, Karina Sheifer, Sofya Ganieva, Hilaria Cruz, Ritván Karahóğa, Stella Markantonatou, George Pavlidis, Matvey Plugaryov, Elena Klyachko, Ali Salehi, Candy Angulo, Jatayu Baxi, Andrew Krizhanovsky, Natalia Krizhanovskaya, Elizabeth Salesky, Clara Vania, Sardana Ivanova, Jennifer White, Rowan Hall Maudslay, Josef Valvoda, Ran Zmigrod, Paula Czarnowska, Irene Nikkarinen, Aelita Salchak, Brijesh Bhatt, Christopher Straughn, Zoey Liu, Jonathan North Washington, Yuval Pinter, Duygu Ataman, Marcin Wolinski, Totok Suhardijanto, Anna Yablonskaya, Niklas Stoehr, Hossep Dolatian, Zahroh Nuriah, Shyam Ratan, Francis M. Tyers, Edoardo M. Ponti, Grant Aiton, Aryaman Arora, Richard J. Hatcher, Ritesh Kumar, Jeremiah Young, Daria Rodionova, Anastasia Yemelina, Taras Andrushko, Igor Marchenko, Polina Mashkovtseva, Alexandra Serova, Emily Prud'hommeaux, Maria Nepomniashchaya, Fausto Giunchiglia, Eleanor Chodroff, Mans Hulden, Miikka Silfverberg, Arya D. McCarthy, David Yarowsky, Ryan Cotterell, Reut Tsarfaty, and Ekaterina Vylomova. 2022a. UniMorph 4.0: Universal Morphology. In *Proceedings of the Thirteenth Language Resources and Evaluation Conference*, pages 840–855, Marseille, France. European Language Resources Association.

Khuyagbaatar Batsuren, Omer Goldman, Salam Khalifa, Nizar Habash, Witold Kieraś, Gábor Bella, Brian Leonard, Garrett Nicolai, Kyle Gorman, Yustinus Ghanggo Ate, Maria Ryskina, Sabrina Mielke, Elena Budianskaya, Charbel El-Khaissi, Tiago Pimentel, Michael Gasser, William Abbott Lane, Mohit Raj, Matt Coler, Jaime Rafael Montoya Samame, Delio Siticonatzi Camaiteri, Esaú Zumaeta Rojas, Didier López Francis, Arturo Oncevay, Juan López Bautista, Gema Celeste Silva Villegas, Lucas Torroba Hennigen, Adam Ek, David Guriel, Peter Dirix, Jean-Philippe Bernardy, Andrey Scherbakov, Aziyana Bayyr-ool, Antonios Anastasopoulos, Roberto Zariquiey, Karina Sheifer, Sofya Ganieva, Hilaria Cruz, Ritván Karahóğa, Stella Markantonatou, George Pavlidis, Matvey Plugaryov, Elena Klyachko, Ali Salehi, Candy Angulo, Jatayu Baxi, Andrew Krizhanovsky, Natalia Krizhanovskaya, Elizabeth Salesky, Clara Vania, Sardana Ivanova, Jennifer White, Rowan Hall Maudslay, Josef Valvoda, Ran Zmigrod, Paula Czarnowska, Irene Nikkarinen, Aelita Salchak, Brijesh Bhatt, Christopher Straughn, Zoey Liu, Jonathan North Washington, Yuval Pinter, Duygu Ataman, Marcin Wolinski, Totok Suhardijanto, Anna Yablonskaya, Niklas Stoehr, Hossep Dolatian, Zahroh Nuriah, Shyam Ratan, Francis M. Tyers, Edoardo M. Ponti, Grant Aiton, Aryaman Arora, Richard J. Hatcher, Ritesh Kumar, Jeremiah Young, Daria Rodionova, Anastasia Yemelina, Taras Andrushko, Igor Marchenko, Polina Mashkovtseva, Alexandra Serova, Emily Prud'hommeaux, Maria Nepomniashchaya, Fausto Giunchiglia, Eleanor Chodroff, Mans Hulden, Miikka Silfverberg, Arya D. McCarthy, David Yarowsky, Ryan Cotterell, Reut Tsarfaty, and Ekaterina Vylomova. 2022b. UniMorph 4.0: Universal Morphology. In *Proceedings of the Thirteenth Language Resources and Evaluation Conference*, pages 840–855, Marseille, France. European Language Resources Association.

John Beaty. 1974. *Mohawk Morphology*. Number 2 in Linguistic Series. Museum of Anthropology, University of Northern Colorado, Greeley, Colorado.

Nancy Bonvillain. 1973. *A Grammar of Akwesasne Mohawk*. Number 8 in Ethnology Division. National Museum of Man, Ottawa, Canada.

Marc E. Canby, Aidana Karipbayeva, Bryan Lunt, Sahand Mozaffari, Charlotte Yoder, and Julia Hockenmaier. 2020. University of illinois submission to the SIGMORPHON 2020 shared task 0: Typologically diverse morphological inflection. In *Proceedings of the 17th SIGMORPHON Workshop on Computational Research in Phonetics, Phonology, and Morphology, SIGMORPHON 2020, Online, July 10, 2020*, pages 137–145. Association for Computational Linguistics.

Mathieu Dehouck and Pascal Denis. 2018. A framework for understanding the role of morphology in Universal Dependency parsing. In *Proceedings of the 2018 Conference on Empirical Methods in Natural Language Processing*, pages 2864–2870, Brussels, Belgium. Association for Computational Linguistics.

Leander Girrbach. 2023. Tü-CL at SIGMORPHON 2023: Straight-through gradient estimation for hard attention. In *Proceedings of the 20th SIGMORPHON workshop on Computational Research in Phonetics, Phonology, and Morphology*, pages 171–185, Toronto, Canada. Association for Computational Linguistics.

Mika Hämäläinen, Niko Partanen, Jack Rueter, and Khalid Alnajjar. 2021. Neural morphology dataset and models for multiple languages, from the large to the endangered. In *Proceedings of the 23rd Nordic Conference on Computational Linguistics (NoDaLiDa)*, pages 166–177, Reykjavik, Iceland (Online). Linköping University Electronic Press, Sweden.

Valentin Hofmann, Janet Pierrehumbert, and Hinrich Schütze. 2021. Superbizarre is not superb: Derivational morphology improves BERT's interpretation of complex words. In *Proceedings of the 59th Annual Meeting of the Association for Computational Linguistics and the 11th International Joint Conference on Natural Language Processing (Volume 1: Long Papers)*, pages 3594–3608, Online. Association for Computational Linguistics.

Wolfgang Klein. 1994. *Time in Language*. Routeledge.

Alice Kwak, Michael Hammond, and Cheyenne Wing. 2023. Morphological reinflection with weighted finite-state transducers. In *Proceedings of the 20th SIGMORPHON workshop on Computational Research in Phonetics, Phonology, and Morphology*, pages 132–137, Toronto, Canada. Association for Computational Linguistics.

Floyd Lounsbury. 1953. *Oneida Verb Morphology*. Yale University Press.

Yanfei Lu. 2023. Empowering the oneida language revitalization: Development of an oneida verb conjugator.

Megan Lukaniec. 2018. *The elaboration of verbal structure: Wendat (Huron) verb morphology*. Ph.D. thesis, University of California, Santa Barbara.

Brian Maracle. 2017. *Onkwawenna Kentyohkwa 1st Year Adult Immersion Program 2017-18*. Onkwawenna Kentyohkwa, Ohsweken, ON, Canada. The book was co-written by several other staff members over the years. Brian Maracle is the author of the latest, 2017 edition.

Akwiratékha' Martin. 2023. *Tekawennahsonterónnion: Kanien'kéha Morphology*. Kanien'kehá:ka Onkwawén:na Raotitióhkwa Language and Cultural Center.

Karin Michelson and Mercy Doxtator. 2002. *Oneida-English/English Oneida Dictionary*. University of Toronto Press.

Karin Michelson, Norma Kennedy, and Mercy A. Doxtator. 2016. *Glimpses of Oneida Life*. University of Toronto Press.

Karin Eva Michelson. 1983. *A Comparative Study of Accent in the Five Nations Iroquoian Languages (Mohawk, Oneida, Onondaga, Cayuga, Seneca)*. Ph.D. thesis, Harvard University.

Marianne Mithun. 2000. *Noun and verb in Iroquoian languages: Multicategorisation from multiple criteria*, pages 397–420. De Gruyter Mouton, Berlin, New York.

Marianne Mithun. 2005. *"Routledge Encyclopedia of Linguistics"*, chapter "Mohawk and the Iroquoian languages". New York: Routledge.

Garrett Nicolai, Eleanor Chodroff, Frederic Mailhot, and Çağrı Çöltekin, editors. 2023. *Proceedings of the 20th SIGMORPHON workshop on Computational Research in Phonetics, Phonology, and Morphology*. Association for Computational Linguistics, Toronto, Canada.

Hyunji Hayley Park, Katherine J. Zhang, Coleman Haley, Kenneth Steimel, Han Liu, and Lane Schwartz. 2021. Morphology matters: A multilingual language modeling analysis. *Transactions of the Association for Computational Linguistics*, 9:261–276.

Tiago Pimentel, Maria Ryskina, Sabrina J. Mielke, Shijie Wu, Eleanor Chodroff, Brian Leonard, Garrett Nicolai, Yustinus Ghanggo Ate, Salam Khalifa, Nizar Habash, Charbel El-Khaissi, Omer Goldman, Michael Gasser, William Lane, Matt Coler, Arturo Oncevay, Jaime Rafael Montoya Samame, Gema Celeste Silva Villegas, Adam Ek, Jean-Philippe Bernardy, Andrey Shcherbakov, Aziyana Bayyr-ool, Karina Sheifer, Sofya Ganieva, Matvey Plugaryov, Elena Klyachko, Ali Salehi, Andrew Krizhanovsky, Natalia Krizhanovsky, Clara Vania, Sardana Ivanova, Aelita Salchak, Christopher Straughn, Zoey Liu, Jonathan North Washington, Duygu Ataman, Witold Kieraś, Marcin Woliński, Totok Suhardijanto, Niklas Stoehr, Zahroh Nuriah, Shyam Ratan, Francis M. Tyers, Edoardo M. Ponti, Grant Aiton, Richard J. Hatcher, Emily Prud'hommeaux, Ritesh Kumar, Mans Hulden, Botond Barta, Dorina Lakatos, Gábor Szolnok, Judit Ács, Mohit Raj, David Yarowsky, Ryan Cotterell, Ben Ambridge, and Ekaterina Vylomova. 2021. SIGMORPHON 2021 shared task on morphological reinflection: Generalization across languages. In *Proceedings of the 18th SIGMORPHON Workshop on Computational Research in Phonetics, Phonology, and Morphology*, pages 229–259, Online. Association for Computational Linguistics.

Catherine Price, Keith Lickers, and Karin Michelson. 2011. Native languages. a support document for the teaching of language patterns. oneida, cayuga, and mohawk. The Ontario Curriculum Grades 1 to 12. The Ontario Ministry of Education Resource Guide.

H. Reichenbach. 1947. *Elements of Symbolic Logic*. A Free Press paperback : philosophy. Macmillan Company.

Martin Renard. 2022. Revitalising kanyen'kéha on the grand river: A case study of indigenous language revitalisation and its theoretical implications. *Journal of Undergraduate Linguistics Association of Britain*, 1(2):32–64.

John Sylak-Glassman. 2016. The composition and use of the universal morphological feature schema (unimorph schema).

Clara Vania, Andreas Grivas, and Adam Lopez. 2018. What do character-level models learn about morphology? the case of dependency parsing. In *Proceedings of the 2018 Conference on Empirical Methods in Natural Language Processing*, pages 2573–2583, Brussels, Belgium. Association for Computational Linguistics.

Shijie Wu, Ryan Cotterell, and Mans Hulden. 2021. Applying the transformer to character-level transduction. In *Proceedings of the 16th Conference of the European Chapter of the Association for Computational Linguistics: Main Volume*, pages 1901–1907, Online. Association for Computational Linguistics.

A Acronyms Used in Linguistic Glosses

Acronym	Explanation
1	first person
2	second person
3	third person
A	agent
BEN	benefective
CIS	cislocative
CONT	continuative
DIST	distributive
DU	dual
DUP	duplicative
FACT	factual
FI	feminine indefinite
FUT	future
FZ	feminine zoic
HAB	habitual
INCH	inchoative
INCL	inclusive
JR	joiner vowel, link
M	masculine
NS	non-singular
OPT	optative
P	patient
PART	partative
PL	plural
PROG	progressive
PUNC	punctual aspect
REP	repetetive
SG	singular
STAT	stative
TRANSL	translocative

Table 4: List of acronyms used in linguistic glosses in the examples.

Data Mining and Extraction: the gold rush of AI on Indigenous Languages

Marie-Odile Junker
Carleton University

Abstract

The goal of this paper is to start a discussion on the topic of Data mining and Extraction of Indigenous Language data, describing recent events that took place within the Algonquian Dictionaries and Language Resources common infrastructure. We raise questions about ethics, social context, vulnerability, responsibility, and societal benefits and concerns in the age of generative AI.

1 Introduction

In 2023 Artificial Intelligence (AI) became the buzz word, the cool word that could be attached to anything, and so why not to Indigenous languages, their endangerment, and the savior role that generative AI could play to rescue those languages from disappearance. In practical term, though, AI needs data. And data about Indigenous languages is rare, and rarely of a quality that can be of use, due to lack of standardization of orthography, dialectal variation, attrition, generational differences, and the various ills of colonialism and imperialism that have affected Indigenous groups stability. In this chaotic mix, the work of long engaged groups into the health of their language has become the new gold for the AI machine. Such gold is exemplified by the Algonquian Dictionaries and Language Resources project. We describe three recent events of data mining and extraction of Indigenous language data, that took place within our common digital infrastructure. Our goal is to raise awareness towards the development of a code of conduct or best practices for generative AI development (or not) in the service of Indigenous languages.

2 The Algonquian Dictionaries and Language Resources Project

The Algonquian Dictionaries and Language Resources project has been building a common infrastructure with language websites and tools for more than 20 years in collaboration with various language groups of the Algonquian language family. This family of languages, structurally similar -- yet very different from Indo-European languages -- stretches from the Atlantic Ocean to the Rocky Mountains (see the linguistic atlas: atlas-ling.ca). All dictionaries supported by this common infrastructure were built directly with their original creators, consisting of linguists and community linguists, Indigenous content editors, etc. The project continues to focus on the creation or enhancement of existing dictionaries in order to make them viable for the long term in the digital economy, and aims to address the following needs:

- thematic multimedia dictionaries: research on categorization methods, knowledge graphs
- morpheme dictionaries with a historical perspective, dialectal relationships; applications for the creation of terminology, development of text parsers
- bilingual dictionaries: standardization of English and French keywords, issues of synonymy, homonymy and polysemy
- unilingual dictionaries: definitions in an Indigenous language, sound files
- connections between dictionaries, grammars and text corpora (oral, transcribed and written)

Proceedings of the The Seventh Workshop on the Use of Computational Methods in the Study of Endangered Languages, pages 52–57
March 21-22, 2024 ©2024 Association for Computational Linguistics

- pedagogical tools: online lessons for first- and second-language, resources for language teachers, training of Indigenous lexicographers

- search engines, syllabic convertors, and verb conjugation apps (with extensive documentation of inflectional morphology)

- database structure with multimedia integration and exports in multiple formats: books, apps, online

- documentation and conversational resources; addition of Algonquian dialects to the Linguistic Atlas: www.atlas-ling.ca

The atlas, started in 2005, currently contains 68 speakers, 25,108 sound files, 58 communities (20 languages, 47 dialects) on 21 topics of conversation (plus one of songs and stories).

The 12 different dictionaries currently supported are variously active. Some represent earlier stages of a particular language now severely endangered, or even reconstructed historical ones like the Proto-Algonquian dictionary, some (for whom the language is still spoken) have very active editorial teams who meet weekly to address users' questions and constantly improve the content. Most also contain a series of related language resources, like oral stories, book catalogue, lessons, terminology forum, modelled after the eastcree.org website started in 2000 in collaboration with the Cree School Board in Quebec, Canada. The data and the software developed reside on protected (in Canada) secure servers, with separate access (by language and by level) for each group of users.

The maintenance of these resources has always been problematic. It is because there was no capacity at the local, and no support at the governmental, level for the Algonquian languages, that the idea of a common infrastructure was developed. By pulling resources together, each group could take a turn at sustaining the whole; each funded project could pitch in to help the other ones. While these resources have always generated some interest outside the circle of the communities they were intended to serve (current average of over one million words searched annually in the dictionaries), there has been a recent surge of interest from Artificial Intelligence players and we have observed more and more data-mining events that have forced us to halt some work we were doing on search optimization, APIs availability, open-source practices and free open-access. In this paper, we disclose (anonymously[1]) three of these events that illustrate well the vulnerability of Indigenous groups in the face of AI. Our goal is to raise awareness towards the development of a code of conduct or best practices for AI development (or not) in the service of Indigenous languages.

3 The Good: Data mining with permission

This event took place between July and October 2023. The request came from a team of linguists in a European university, conducting research on morphological change, using AI for processing large data sets of as great a variety of languages as possible. Most of their research to date had been conducted on Indo European languages, and they wanted to include Algonquian languages to their dataset and research program, so as to avoid biases. For that, they needed access to conjugation guides[2] and the Proto-Algonquian dictionary. The questions they raised in their initial request were genuine and clear. For example: "Do you have the data in a .csv file? If not, are you OK with our data science consultant "scraping" the site? If we want to archive the database we build during this project, can we include this data (in a potentially open-source format, with appropriate citation of data sources)?" After several written exchanges and a zoom meeting they came up with an agreement proposal which we further edited together. It was quite restrictive and respectful of OCAP[3].

These European linguists submitted their data usage agreement to the Indigenous group. In light

[1] This paper is single authored to preserve anonymity of the stakeholders. It is the result of discussions with the Indigenous partners involved. All errors are mine.

[2] See for example: East Cree Verb Conjugation Guide (Southern dialect): `southern.verbs.eastcree.org/`; (Northern dialect): `northern.verbs.eastcree.org`; Innu Verb Conjugation Guide: `verbe.innu-aimun.ca`; Guide de conjugaison atikamekw: `verbes.atikamekw.ca`

[3] OCAP refers to the principles of (Canadian) First Nations ownership, control, access and possession (`https://fnigc.ca/`) - which assert that First Nations have control over the data collection processes, and that they own and control the way in which this information can be used.

of the next event (below), that group declined permission. The European linguists then announced they would respect that decision and leave Algonquian languages out of their research.

4 The Bad: Data extraction without permission

This event took place over more than a year, but was brought to our attention in March 2023, when a couple of students contacted the infrastructure administration / dictionary editors, announcing that their thesis director (Let's call him/her professor X) had a project about one of the Algonquian languages (Let's call it language Y) for machine learning and AI driven translation. These academics are not linguists, but computer scientists in the field of Natural Language Processing. Earlier, professor X had made several unsuccessful attempts to enlist into their research program organizations or Indigenous scholars active in language Y. Professor X was told that they were not interested in AI and machine translation, at the moment.

Like the previous group described above, the students of Professor X asked for .csv files of the data, and full access to language Y databases. When told they needed permission from the language group to get such data, the team forged ahead anyway, mining the entire dataset of trilingual examples of language Y dictionary; a feature not accessible as such to the public. They then ran their experiments on machine learning with the mined data. They presented a paper at a conference in October 2023, claiming collaboration with Indigenous group Y, and citing the source they had mined. This is where one of the Indigenous scholars and co-editors of dictionary Y, who was attending the conference, noticed. The Indigenous organizations concerned then co-signed a letter with the four editors of the dictionary, asking for deletion of the mined data from all repositories, corpora, backups, etc., as soon as possible and the removal of the term "collaboration" from their research program, along with a reminder of the principles of OCAP.

5 The Ugly: extracting their data and selling it back to the Indigenous people

The last example happened in the Winter and Spring of 2023. A private web designing company offered to an Indigenous institution to improve the look of an Oral Stories database that had been built in collaboration with the Algonquian language resources project in 2010-13. The person who signed the contract within the Indigenous organization was unaware of what the project consisted of and based their judgement on the looks of the site, not its structure (no awareness of the existence of back end and careful data organization). The private company scraped off the trilingual data (audio, text and video) from the public interface, and rebuilt the database incorrectly, with many mistakes, but a lovely look. They put the data on a commercial server, and nobody knows the exact terms of this server provider. They were paid a large sum of money, 10% of which would have probably been sufficient to simply update the site properly without messing up the data. This last example points to the vulnerability of the people and the organizations themselves in the face of convincing commercial entities.

6 Misunderstanding tools and potential further misuse

This somewhat anecdotal last case illustrates the degree to which the general public misunderstands Indigenous language tools and what their expectations have become. In late 2023, I was contacted by a social service in the prison system in Quebec to help them adapt a short Cri text into roman orthography, because "not all prisoners can read syllabics". They wanted to be inclusive with the 5 languages spoken in that prison. They had obtained the text from our syllabic convertors[4], mistaking it for an equivalent of Google Translate. It turned out that the text was purely a French text, converted into syllabics (Figure 1).

[4] Cree syllabics convertors (Jancewicz et al, 2014): `https://syllabics.atlas-ling.ca/`

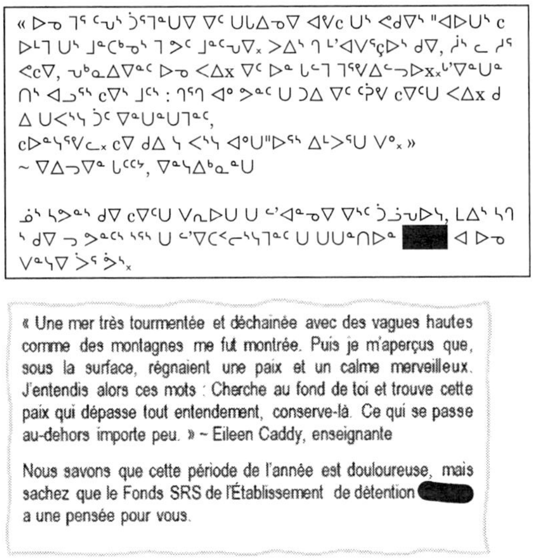

Figure 1: Cree Syllabic script on French text.

When I replied with explanations, they were truly incredulous; I do not know for how long they had been mistakenly using this tool to produce such "multilingual" messages. No wonder the Cree or Naskapi prisoners could not "read" or make sense of that syllabic text! Imagine what could happen when such data is scraped off the social media site of this organization and fed into the AI machine for further learning, thus compounding the confusion.

7 Discussion and Conclusion

The three events presented above are probably not the only ones that took place in 2023, as far as data mining and extraction is concerned on the Algonquian Dictionaries and Language Resources or the Linguistic Atlas. These are the ones for which we have solid proofs[5].

There is a huge economic imbalance at play here: the resources discussed, although freely available, are not supported, except by sporadic research grants to a few stable full-time academics[6], or by Indigenous organizations whose funding is usually unpredictable. Staff is hired on short-term or part-time contracts. Projects like ours wonder to whom we must "sell" ourselves next, in order for the language resources that we have worked so hard to develop, to survive. AI on the other hand, comes with lots of money, but none of the two above research cases discussed, offered any compensation[7]. Data available or extractible on the web is considered a free natural resource. But is it? Even if compensation was offered, how do we prevent downstream computational uses like models propagating mistakes in data? How are the models of generative AI going to feed back into the language and affect its (d)evolution? In a context of fragile language transmission, linguistic insecurity of younger speakers, and often severe endangerment, who can truly verify and validate the machine learning production? Who wants to? What kind of community-based important work is not going to be done if this is done instead? Whose agenda is controlling the field?

Many of these issues look like a new form of colonialism we could call "digital colonialism". While there has been some work by GIDA (the Global Indigenous Data Alliance) to address the ethics of Indigenous data and complement the FAIR (Findable - Accessible - Interoperable - Reusable) principles with the CARE (Collective Benefits - Authority to Control - Responsibility - Ethics) principles (Carrol et al., 2020, 2022) and Figure 2, we have not found (at the time of writing) any update on the GIDA site to help us deal specifically with the reality of Indigenous language data extraction.

[5] Meta released a paper about pre-trained Text-To-Speech systems including Canadian Indigenous languages, without stating that they obtained any permission and without evaluating the models with speakers. Since our databases contain lots of sound files, it is likely that they have been or will be mined like that for TTS research and development. See Pratap V. et.al (2023).

[6] These academics are usually in Linguistics or Language departments, an area way less funded, both in terms of academic positions and grants, than say, Computer Science and Engineering. While Inuktitut has some support due to its official status in Nunavut (Canada), there is no long-term governmental support for any Algonquian languages.

[7] The linguists of case one confirmed compensation for data had not been included in the research grant budget.

Figure 2: FAIR and CARE principles.

So, what might be some practical steps to address this current situation?

Protect the integrity of the data

While up to know the Algonquian project team has only been interested in anonymously tracking some human use of the Algonquian language resources to improve them, we recently asked our system administrator to implement analytics in order to inform our policies regarding bots. We have also started to post the following messages on top of all the dictionaries and conjugation apps credit pages: *Data-mining and scraping strictly prohibited.*

Our first attempt said "without permission" but we quickly realized we lacked time and human resources to handle requests for permissions and liaison with all the individual stakeholders.

Alert and inform all Indigenous and non-Indigenous stakeholders about the new reality of data-mining and generative AI

Most people have no idea what is happening with their own personal data, let alone what could happen to their language data. When contacted by people for projects some possible internal questions for Indigenous groups are:

- Who does this data belong to? Do I (as an individual) have a right to grant a permission to use it to someone? / Do I have the right to give it away? Who has this right?[8]
- Am I sufficiently skeptical about what is being offered for my language: are they using me for their own purpose, or to claim partnership?
- Do I have any control in this project? Did I define its goal, process? Do I/we need this? Or are they using me/us, paying me/us and I/we need the money?

When contacted by commercial entities to "update" or "modernize" their web resources, ask:

- How are you planning to retrieve the data? Can I provide it to you in proper form?
- Are you preserving all the functionalities of the site (front end, back end) for content updates?
- Where are you going to keep, store, distribute this data? Are you going to sell something to third parties?
- What programming tools, (open-?) source code are you going to use? And (since AI is increasingly used for code writing as well) how do you guarantee clean code?
- Do we get to keep the code?
- Who is going to provide updates and for how long?

When discovering data has been used without permission, do as the group in the second case did: ask for deletion of the mined data from all repositories, corpora, backups, etc. Demand a retraction and compensation? Explore legal avenues?

Some possible questions that genuinely respectful researchers should ask themselves:

- What can we offer in return?
- Do people need this or are we trying to convince them they do?
- What is my true goal/ purpose?
- Do I respect a "do no harm" principle?

The last three questions would also apply to the genuinely respectful commercial providers.

The ComputEL community of scholars should be engaging in this reflection and looking to contribute creative solutions. Let's not let the history of colonialism repeat itself! After the

[8] The Canadian government just completed (January 2024) a public consultation on generative AI and copyright, that will hopefully take into account Indigenous languages and cultures.

forests, the rivers, the soil, now the language? The challenge is upon us!

Acknowledgments

I am thankful to three anonymous reviewers for their suggestions on how improve my initial submission, to Te Taka Keegan for an earlier discussion of these problems with our team, to Delasie Torkornoo, and to my other colleagues and Indigenous partners who wish, at this point, to remain anonymous.

References

Jérémie Ambroise, Anne-Marie Baraby, Marie-Odile Junker, and Yvette Mollen (eds). 2023. Conjugaison des verbes innus (6th ed.). https://verbe.innu-aimun.ca

Marie-Odile Junker and Nicole Petiquay (eds). 2020. Conjugaison des verbes atikamekw (2nd ed.). https://verbes.atikamekw.atlas-ling.ca/

Marie-Odile Junker and Marguerite MacKenzie (eds). 2016. East Cree (Southern Dialect) Verb Conjugation (4th ed.). https://www.southern.verbs.eastcree.org/

Marie-Odile Junker and Marguerite MacKenzie (eds). 2020. East Cree (Northern Dialect) Verb Conjugation (5th ed.). https://www.northern.verbs.eastcree.org/

Stephanie Carroll, et al. 2020. The CARE Principles for Indigenous Data Governance. *Data Science Journal*, 19: XX, pp. 1–12. https://static1.squarespace.com/static/5d3799de845604000199cd24/t/6397b1aff7a6fb54defdf687/1670885815820/dsj-1158_carroll.pdf

Stephanie Carroll, Jewel Cummins, and Andrew Martinez. 2022. Indigenous Data Sovereignty and Governance. Global Indigenous Data Alliance. https://static1.squarespace.com/static/5d3799de845604000199cd24/t/640792a43ba5c11a1073bbc8/1678217895508/TheCAREPrinciples.pdf

Bill Jancewicz, Marie-Odile Junker and Delasie Torkornoo. *Cree Syllabics Convertor.* 2014-present https://syllabics.atlas-ling.ca/

(ISED Citizen Services Centre (Innovation, Science and Economic Development Canada). 2024. Consultation on Copyright in the Age of Generative Artificial Intelligence. https://ised-isde.canada.ca/site/strategic-policy-sector/en/marketplace-framework-policy/consultation-paper-consultation-copyright-age-generative-artificial-intelligence

Marie-Odile Junker, Marguerite MacKenzie, Nicole Rosen, J. Randolph Valentine and Arok Wolvengrey. (2005-present) *Algonquian Linguistic Atlas*. https://www.atlas-ling.ca/

Marie-Odile Junker (dir.) (2005-present) *Algonquian Dictionaries and Languages Resources Project*. https://www.algonquianlanguages.ca/

OCAP: Ownership, Control, Access and Possession. OCAP® is a registered trademark of the First Nations Information Governance Centre (FNIGC) in Canada. https://fnigc.ca/ocap-training/.

Vineel Pratap et al. (2023) Scaling Speech Technology to 1,000+ Languages. Preprint https://arxiv.org/pdf/2305.13516.pdf

Looking within the self: Investigating the Impact of Data Augmentation with Self-training on Automatic Speech Recognition for Hupa

Nitin Venkateswaran
University of Florida
venkateswaran.n@ufl.edu

Zoey Liu
University of Florida
liu.ying@ufl.edu

Abstract

We investigate the performance of state-of-the-art neural ASR systems in transcribing audio recordings for Hupa, a critically endangered language of the Hoopa Valley Tribe. We also explore the impact on ASR performance when augmenting a small dataset of gold-standard high-quality transcriptions with a) a larger dataset with transcriptions of lower quality, and b) model-generated transcriptions in a self-training approach. An evaluation of both data augmentation approaches shows that the self-training approach is competitive, producing better WER scores than models trained with no additional data and not lagging far behind models trained with additional lower quality manual transcriptions instead: the deterioration in WER score is just 4.85 points when all the additional data is used in experiments with the best performing system, Wav2Vec. These findings have encouraging implications on the use of ASR systems for transcription and language documentation efforts in the Hupa language.

1 Introduction

Automatic Speech Recognition (ASR) can assist with the manual process of transcribing audio recordings in low-resource and endangered languages, thereby facilitating language documentation efforts in these languages. With neural networks now dominating research in ASR (Baevski et al., 2020; Radford et al., 2023; Gulati et al., 2020), and with related efforts to build and release open-source neural-network based ASR frameworks (Wolf et al., 2020; Watanabe et al., 2018; Amodei et al., 2016), the possibilities for research on ASR for endangered languages have greatly increased; a researcher can now leverage one of the open-source ASR toolkits and apply it to their language of interest. Cross-lingual speech representations currently leveraged by state-of-the-art neural ASR systems (Babu et al., 2021; Conneau et al., 2020) also provide opportunities for knowledge transfer to endangered languages; commonalities across different speech representations can be leveraged to improve ASR performance.

The Hupa language from the Dene/Athabaskan language family is one such language that stands to benefit from these advances in ASR. Hupa is the ancestral language of the Hoopa Valley Tribe residing in Northern California. It is critically endangered with only a handful of first-language (L1) speakers and a number of second-language learners. Since the 1970s, the Hupa speech community has been actively engaged in documentation and reclamation work to preserve their language. ASR systems can be especially beneficial for Hupa, given that there may be low literacy levels among Hupa speakers and learners of the language who focus instead on oral proficiency; these low literacy levels may in turn hinder efforts to transcribe audio recordings.

However, the development of an ASR system for Hupa using supervised learning approaches faces a chicken-and-egg problem: high quality transcriptions are necessary to train a performant ASR system which can be leveraged in a manual transcription process to produce high quality transcriptions. Given the challenges with producing additional manual annotations, data augmentation approaches must instead be relied upon to generate the necessary data to train an ASR system.

In this study, we explore the efficacy of different ASR systems for Hupa, coupled with self-training, a data augmentation method that is favored in the literature due to its simplicity and elegance (Charniak, 1997; Zhang et al., 2022b). The general idea is to apply a trained model to unlabeled data, then combine the automatically annotated data with existing gold-standard training data to build a new model, to see whether the addition of model-generated annotations is helpful towards model performance. With this approach, here we seek to investigate if model-generated au-

Proceedings of the The Seventh Workshop on the Use of Computational Methods in the Study of Endangered Languages, pages 58–66
March 21-22, 2024

dio transcripts can be leveraged to improve acoustic model performance on gold-standard data with *high-quality* manual transcriptions. In addition, we compare the self-training approach to an alternative method, where we swap out the additional machine-produced transcripts in the training data with human-annotated data that has overall *lower transcription quality* (Section 3).

2 Related Work

ASR for endangered languages A number of studies use the popular ASR toolkit Kaldi (Povey et al., 2011) to probe how far simple deep neural networks can go when situated in severely resource-constrained settings with less than 10 hours of audio training data; these studies include languages such as Seneca (Jimerson and Prud'hommeaux, 2018), Cherokee (Zhang et al., 2022a) and Hupa (Liu et al., 2022), the last of which is closest to our work. Others apply more recent end-to-end architectures: for instance, Shi et al. (2021) explore models built from ESPnet (Watanabe et al., 2018) for Yoloxóchitl Mixtec, using more than 55h of conversational speech from more than 20 speakers.

In addition, others investigate augmentation methods applied on the acoustic signals to improve ASR performance for endangered languages. These include, but are not limited to, semi-supervised training and vocal tract length perturbation (Ragni et al., 2014), elastic spectral distortion methods (Kanda et al., 2013), creation of synthetic data using voice transformation and signal distortion (Thai et al., 2019) and transfer learning with data augmentation (Thai et al., 2020).

Self-training Some recent studies have begun to apply self-training, or "pseudo-labeling", for ASR, mostly focusing on English (Xu et al., 2021, 2020; Kahn et al., 2020). A few multilingual studies exist (Khurana et al., 2022; Lugosch et al., 2022), including investigations of cross-linguistic low-resource settings (Zhang et al., 2022b). For endangered languages, Bartelds et al. (2023) apply self-training to four minority languages, Gronings, West-Frisian, Besemah, and Nasal, each with 4h of acoustic training data to start with.

In comparison to previous approaches, our work uses the Wav2Vec 2.0 framework (Baevski et al., 2020), and generates transcripts from audio data in a self-training setting while leaving the audio intact. Self-training has not been widely applied to endangered languages with the exception of Bartelds et al. (2023), who do not include Hupa in their study; the amount of gold-standard high quality acoustic training data that we start out with is also quite small in comparison with their work (more details in Section 3).

3 The Hupa ASR Dataset

The audio data for Hupa is a result of continuous linguistic fieldwork since 2005. The spoken records are provided by Mrs. Verdena Parker, an L1 speaker of the language. The audio content is composed of different genres including descriptions of historical tribal events and stories and tales narrated by Mrs. Parker. The transcriptions of the audio files have been carried out by several linguistics researchers over the years with consultation from Mrs. Parker. Each transcript follows the practical orthography developed in Golla (1996), and is time aligned with annotation tools such as ELAN (Brugman and Russel, 2004).

Transcripts go through stages of manual verification to different extents, which are necessary since the recordings come from multiple fieldwork sessions across different years and are transcribed by different researchers. Some transcripts are checked more thoroughly than others, with more checks resulting in better transcription quality. Based solely on transcription quality, we divide the audio data and their corresponding transcripts into two datasets: the "fine" and the "coarse" datasets. The fine data has approximately 1h35m of audio with thoroughly checked transcriptions, and the coarse data has around 7h37m of audio with comparatively lower transcription quality.

4 Experiments

4.1 Training and data setup

We investigate two questions: the first question is whether adding the "coarse" data to the "fine" dataset for training results in better ASR performance than using just the "fine" dataset. We create partitions of the coarse dataset with different data sizes in each partition, to investigate the effect of augmenting data of different sizes on model performance; the data is randomly sampled into each partition. Three partitions are sampled with sizes being a) the same size as the fine dataset [1x], b) three times the size of the fine dataset [3x], and c) five times the size of the fine dataset [5x], which is roughly the same size as the full coarse dataset. Data from each partition is added to the training portion of the fine dataset (discussed below), and an ASR model is built for each partition. This overall setup lets us compare the performance of the partitions with each other as well as with a baseline consisting of just the fine dataset.

The second question is the impact on ASR performance of a self-training data augmentation approach using model-generated transcripts. An ASR model is first trained on the training portion of the fine dataset, and is then used to produce transcriptions from data in the coarse dataset, simulating the scenario when there are no transcriptions available. To facilitate comparisons, the coarse audio samples from the same partitions detailed in the previous setup are used to produce the transcriptions. Each partition containing model-generated transcriptions is then added to the training portion of the fine dataset, and an ASR model is built using each partition. This lets us directly compare results from using additional model-generated transcripts with results from using additional manually-transcribed coarse data, as well as with a baseline consisting of just the fine dataset.

To measure the quality of the model-generated transcripts as substitutes for the coarse transcripts, we calculate the word error rate (WER) scores of the generated transcripts using the coarse transcripts as references. Figure 1 in Appendix A.2 shows the box-plot distribution of WER scores: the average WER across transcripts is 38.15. To get another perspective, the Levenshtein edit distance is calculated between the coarse and model-generated transcripts to provide the number of character-level operations needed to convert one transcript to the other. The edit distance is normalized by the length of the coarse transcript, and reported as the number of operations per 100-character transcript. Figure 2 in Appendix A.2 shows the distribution of the normalized edit distance: the mean distance across all partitions is 8.58. In addition, Figure 3 in Appendix A.3 compares the distributions of token counts per transcript between the model-generated and coarse data; the distributions are quantitatively similar. Table 3 in the Appendix A.1 provides further comparisons, including type counts and average word length; while there are more types in the model-generated transcripts, the average word lengths are similar.

For evaluation, we use a random split approach: Liu et al. (2023) show random splits can yield reliable estimates of acoustic model performance, and that the WER from a single random split is comparable to that averaged from multiple random splits. Here we apply a single random split to the fine dataset, taking 20% as the test set which is used to evaluate ASR model performance across all experiments. The remaining 80% of the fine dataset is the training portion, used to train the baseline with no additional data. The coarse and model-generated transcripts from their respective partitions are added to the training portion of the fine dataset for the remaining experiments. Given the scarcity of training data, for hyper-parameter tuning we use 5-fold cross validation instead of a held-out development set. The WER and CER (character error rate) on the random test split are reported for all experiments.

4.2 Models

`Kaldi DNN` We use a hybrid fully connected deep neural network (DNN) from the Kaldi toolkit (Povey et al., 2011). Our implementations follow the default sequence training parameters from Karel's DNN recipe[1]. The model architecture has six hidden layers, each with 1024 hidden units. Previous studies (Morris et al., 2021; Morris, 2021) demonstrate that in resource-constrained scenarios, this DNN architecture is capable of yielding competitive performance compared to other neural models such as Whisper (Radford et al., 2023) and time delay neural networks (Peddinti et al., 2015). For decoding, we train trigram language models on the transcripts with Witten-Bell discounting (Witten and Bell, 1991), using the SRILM (Stolcke, 2002) toolkit. The training parameters for the DNN are present in Appendix A.5

`Wav2Vec2` We fine-tune the Wav2Vec XLS-R model with 2 billion parameters (2B), as studies have shown that models with more parameters perform better and are critical for better multi-lingual representations (Babu et al., 2021). Neither Hupa nor any of the other languages in the Athabaskan language family are among the languages used to pre-train the XLS-R models, implying that there is no transfer effect from using the pre-trained model. The XLS-R-2B architecture is based on the Wav2Vec 2.0 framework (Baevski et al., 2020). The training hyper-parameters are presented in Appendix A.5. The HuggingFace transformers library (Wolf et al., 2020) is used for the training setup. Our code for fine-tuning Wav2Vec is available.[2]

[1] `https://kaldi-asr.org/doc/dnn1.html`

[2] GitHub link: `https://github.com/ufcompling/asr_lm.git#hupa-asr-eval`

Model	Experiment Setup (Partition Size)	WER	Diff. w/ baseline	Diff. w/ best setup	CER
Kaldi DNN	Fine only (baseline)	42.79	–	(9.01)	14.72
	Fine + Coarse (1x)	39.29	3.5	(5.51)	12.54
	Fine + Coarse (3x)	35.73	7.06	(1.95)	11.10
	Fine + Coarse (5x)	**33.78**	9.01	–	10.26
	Fine + Model-generated (1x)	41.35	1.44	(7.57)	12.56
	Fine + Model-generated (3x)	38.45	4.34	(4.67)	10.74
	Fine + Model-generated (5x)	36.84	5.95	(3.06)	**9.98**
Wav2Vec2	Fine only (baseline)	29.49	–	(8.52)	6.41
	Fine + Coarse (1x)	24.87	4.62	(3.9)	5.77
	Fine + Coarse (3x)	22.25	7.24	(1.28)	5.15
	Fine + Coarse (5x)	**20.97**	8.52	–	**5.10**
	Fine + Model-generated (1x)	27.37	2.12	(6.4)	5.99
	Fine + Model-generated (3x)	26.82	2.67	(5.85)	6.16
	Fine + Model-generated (5x)	25.82	3.67	(4.85)	5.84

Table 1: WER and CER scores on the random test split, by model architecture and experiment setup. The best WER scores are from augmenting the fine dataset with the full coarse dataset (size 5x), and are highlighted in bold.

Model	Partition Size	Coarse WER	Model-generated WER	Diff
Kaldi DNN	1x	39.29	41.35	(2.06)
	3x	35.73	38.45	(2.72)
	5x	33.78	36.84	(3.06)
Wav2Vec2	1x	24.87	27.37	(2.5)
	3x	22.25	26.82	(4.57)
	5x	20.97	25.82	(4.85)

Table 2: Comparison of WER results on the random test split using additional coarse versus model-generated transcripts, across partition sizes and model architectures.

5 Results

It is clear from Table 1 that using any amount of additional data, whether from manually generated coarse transcripts or model-generated ones, improves the WER score over the baseline of using no additional data. Moreover, for both transcript types, using data from larger partition sizes leads to better acoustic model performance. These results are consistent across both Kaldi and Wav2Vec2. The best models are obtained by training on all the coarse transcripts from the size 5x partition together with the fine ones.

Comparing the two model architectures, Wav2Vec2 outperforms Kaldi across all experiments in terms of absolute WER. Both architectures are able to utilize both manually-transcribed and model-generated data to achieve improvements in WER, though the gains are slightly bigger with the former. Interestingly, Kaldi seems to better utilize the model-generated transcripts; looking at the best score with self-training normalized by the baseline, Kaldi shows an improvement of 13.91 percentage points over the baseline compared to 12.44 points for Wav2Vec2. These numbers suggest that Wav2Vec2 is possibly more sensitive to the noise present in model-generated transcripts.

While a self-training setup with model-generated transcripts under-performs versus training with additional coarse transcripts of the same size (Table 2), the differences in scores are not too large. The worst score difference is just 4.85 points for Wav2Vec2 in the size 5x partition when all the model-generated transcripts are used. Interestingly, the 1x partition results in a worsening of just 2.5 points, suggesting that it is possible to use smaller sets of model-generated transcripts to build an ASR system in the absence of any manual transcriptions. These findings suggest that it may be possible to effectively use self-trained ASR models for Hupa without needing large amounts of model-generated transcripts, which is a very encouraging find.

Lastly, the impact of using additional data from self-training versus manual annotation can be viewed from the perspective of an investigation of word types present in the transcriptions of each approach. Specifically, we look at the number of new word types introduced by each approach that are not present in the fine dataset; the coarse dataset from the 5x partition contains 5,521 new types not present in the fine dataset, versus 8,487 in the model-generated transcriptions. Given the similar number of tokens between the two, the model-generated transcripts have a higher type-token percentage of 17.71 when considering only new types (cf. 11.42 in the coarse transcripts), which seems to correlate with higher WER scores. However, of the 5,521 new types in the coarse transcripts, 2,516 (46%) are also found in the model-generated transcripts. This has implications for new vocabulary discovery in language documentation efforts for Hupa, as up to 46% of new words in the coarse dataset can be discovered through ASR transcriptions instead of solely through manual effort.

6 Conclusion and Future Work

We find that a self-training approach for Hupa ASR is able to produce transcriptions of better quality than one using no additional training data, as seen in the 3.67 point improvement in WER score; moreover, it does not fall far behind when compared to the best-performing setup of using all the additional human-transcribed coarse data (a 4.85 WER difference). Moreover, the availability of manually verified low-quality transcripts in the best performing setup should not be taken for granted; it is not uncommon, in the cases of indigenous and endangered languages, for the audio recordings to be sourced from just one speaker (see also Boulianne (2022)), and the resources needed to produce transcriptions from the audio may be very limited. With that in mind, we believe self-training to be a useful data augmentation method, at least in the initial stages of developing ASR systems for endangered languages when there is very little data available.

An important goal of developing ASR systems for endangered languages is to automate, fully or partially, the transcription of new fieldwork recordings; the automatic transcriptions can be manually corrected by speakers of the language, potentially removing the need to transcribe from scratch (Prud'hommeaux et al., 2021).

It would be interesting to study whether an ASR system trained on additional manually produced transcripts of any quality would be more beneficial to the transcription process than a system trained on additional model-generated transcripts using self-training; or in other words, can transcribers tolerate a 4.85 point degradation in WER score by using model-generated transcripts to train an ASR system, in exchange for not needing to manually produce transcriptions to improve that system? Additionally, would tools such as ELPIS (Foley et al., 2018) that take advantage of speech recognition technologies in their language documentation transcription workflows benefit from the integration of self-training or other data augmentation methods into existing pipelines? We leave these possibilities for future work.

Acknowledgements

We are grateful for the continuous support from the Hupa indigenous community. We thank Mrs. Verdena Parker for her generous and valuable input throughout the years, and Justin Spence for his work on language documentation efforts; this study has been made possible thanks to their work. In addition, we thank the anonymous reviewers for their helpful feedback.

References

Dario Amodei, Sundaram Ananthanarayanan, Rishita Anubhai, Jingliang Bai, Eric Battenberg, Carl Case, Jared Casper, Bryan Catanzaro, Qiang Cheng, Guoliang Chen, Jie Chen, Jingdong Chen, Zhijie Chen, Mike Chrzanowski, Adam Coates, Greg Diamos, Ke Ding, Niandong Du, Erich Elsen, Jesse Engel, Weiwei Fang, Linxi Fan, Christopher Fougner, Liang Gao, Caixia Gong, Awni Hannun, Tony Han, Lappi Vaino Johannes, Bing Jiang, Cai Ju, Billy Jun, Patrick LeGresley, Libby Lin, Junjie Liu, Yang Liu, Weigao Li, Xiangang Li, Dongpeng Ma, Sharan Narang, Andrew Ng, Sherjil Ozair, Yiping Peng, Ryan Prenger, Sheng Qian, Zongfeng Quan, Jonathan Raiman, Vinay Rao, Sanjeev Satheesh, David Seetapun, Shubho Sengupta, Kavya Srinet, Anuroop Sriram, Haiyuan Tang, Liliang Tang, Chong Wang, Jidong Wang, Kaifu Wang, Yi Wang, Zhijian Wang, Zhiqian Wang, Shuang Wu, Likai Wei, Bo Xiao, Wen Xie, Yan Xie, Dani Yogatama, Bin Yuan, Jun Zhan, and Zhenyao Zhu. 2016. Deep speech 2: End-to-end speech recognition in english and mandarin. In *Proceedings of the 33rd International Conference on International Conference on Machine Learning - Volume 48*, ICML'16, page 173–182. JMLR.org.

Arun Babu, Changhan Wang, Andros Tjandra, Kushal Lakhotia, Qiantong Xu, Naman Goyal, Kritika Singh, Patrick von Platen, Yatharth Saraf, Juan Pino, et al. 2021. Xls-r: Self-supervised cross-lingual speech representation learning at scale. *arXiv e-prints*, pages arXiv–2111.

Alexei Baevski, Henry Zhou, Abdel rahman Mohamed, and Michael Auli. 2020. wav2vec 2.0: A framework for self-supervised learning of speech representations. *ArXiv*, abs/2006.11477.

Martijn Bartelds, Nay San, Bradley McDonnell, Dan Jurafsky, and Martijn Wieling. 2023. Making more of little data: Improving low-resource automatic speech recognition using data augmentation. In *Proceedings of the 61st Annual Meeting of the Association for Computational Linguistics (Volume 1: Long Papers)*, pages 715–729, Toronto, Canada. Association for Computational Linguistics.

Gilles Boulianne. 2022. Phoneme transcription of endangered languages: an evaluation of recent ASR architectures in the single speaker scenario. In *Findings of the Association for Computational Linguistics: ACL 2022*, pages 2301–2308, Dublin, Ireland. Association for Computational Linguistics.

Hennie Brugman and Albert Russel. 2004. Annotating multi-media/multi-modal resources with ELAN. In *Proceedings of the Fourth International Conference on Language Resources and Evaluation (LREC'04)*, Lisbon, Portugal. European Language Resources Association (ELRA).

Eugene Charniak. 1997. Statistical parsing with a context-free grammar and word statistics. *AAAI/IAAI*, 2005(598-603):18.

Alexis Conneau, Alexei Baevski, Ronan Collobert, Abdel rahman Mohamed, and Michael Auli. 2020. Unsupervised cross-lingual representation learning for speech recognition. In *Interspeech*.

Ben Foley, Josh Arnold, Rolando Coto-Solano, Gautier Durantin, T. Mark Ellison, Daan van Esch, Scott Heath, František Kratochvíl, Zara Maxwell-Smith, David Nash, Ola Olsson, Mark Richards, Nay San, Hywel Stoakes, Nick Thieberger, and Janet Wiles. 2018. Building Speech Recognition Systems for Language Documentation: The CoEDL Endangered Language Pipeline and Inference System (ELPIS). In *Proc. 6th Workshop on Spoken Language Technologies for Under-Resourced Languages (SLTU 2018)*, pages 205–209.

Victor Golla. 1996. *Hupa Language Dictionary Second Edition*. Hoopa Valley Tribe.

Anmol Gulati, Chung-Cheng Chiu, James Qin, Jiahui Yu, Niki Parmar, Ruoming Pang, Shibo Wang, Wei Han, Yonghui Wu, Yu Zhang, and Zhengdong Zhang, editors. 2020. *Conformer: Convolution-augmented Transformer for Speech Recognition*.

Robbie Jimerson and Emily Prud'hommeaux. 2018. ASR for documenting acutely under-resourced indigenous languages. In *Proceedings of the Eleventh International Conference on Language Resources and Evaluation (LREC 2018)*, Miyazaki, Japan. European Language Resources Association (ELRA).

Jacob Kahn, Ann Lee, and Awni Hannun. 2020. Self-training for end-to-end speech recognition. In *ICASSP 2020 - 2020 IEEE International Conference on Acoustics, Speech and Signal Processing (ICASSP)*, pages 7084–7088.

Naoyuki Kanda, Ryu Takeda, and Yasunari Obuchi. 2013. Elastic spectral distortion for low resource speech recognition with deep neural networks. In *2013 IEEE Workshop on Automatic Speech Recognition and Understanding*, pages 309–314.

Sameer Khurana, Antoine Laurent, and James Glass. 2022. Magic dust for cross-lingual adaptation of monolingual wav2vec-2.0. In *ICASSP 2022 - 2022 IEEE International Conference on Acoustics, Speech and Signal Processing (ICASSP)*, pages 6647–6651.

Zoey Liu, Justin Spence, and Emily Prud'hommeaux. 2022. Enhancing documentation of Hupa with automatic speech recognition. In *Proceedings of the Fifth Workshop on the Use of Computational Methods in the Study of Endangered Languages*, pages 187–192, Dublin, Ireland. Association for Computational Linguistics.

Zoey Liu, Justin Spence, and Emily Prud'hommeaux. 2023. Investigating data partitioning strategies for crosslinguistic low-resource ASR evaluation. In *Proceedings of the 17th Conference of the European Chapter of the Association for Computational Linguistics*, pages 123–131, Dubrovnik, Croatia. Association for Computational Linguistics.

Loren Lugosch, Tatiana Likhomanenko, Gabriel Synnaeve, and Ronan Collobert. 2022. Pseudo-labeling for massively multilingual speech recognition. In *ICASSP 2022 - 2022 IEEE International Conference on Acoustics, Speech and Signal Processing (ICASSP)*, pages 7687–7691.

Ethan Morris. 2021. Automatic Speech Recognition for Low-Resource and Morphologically Complex Languages. Master's thesis, Rochester Institute of Technology.

Ethan Morris, Robert Jimerson, and Emily Prud'hommeaux. 2021. One size does not fit all in resource-constrained ASR. In *The Annual Conference of the International Speech Communication Association (Interspeech)*, pages 4354–4358.

Vijayaditya Peddinti, Daniel Povey, and Sanjeev Khudanpur. 2015. A time delay neural network architecture for efficient modeling of long temporal contexts. In *Proc. Interspeech 2015*, pages 3214–3218.

Daniel Povey, Arnab Ghoshal, Gilles Boulianne, Lukas Burget, Ondrej Glembek, Nagendra Goel, Mirko Hannemann, Petr Motlicek, Yanmin Qian, Petr Schwarz, et al. 2011. The Kaldi speech recognition toolkit. In *IEEE 2011 workshop on automatic speech recognition and understanding*, CONF. IEEE Signal Processing Society.

Emily Prud'hommeaux, Robbie Jimerson, Richard Hatcher, and Karin Michelson. 2021. Automatic speech recognition for supporting endangered language documentation. *Language Documentation and Conservation*, 15:491–513.

Alec Radford, Jong Wook Kim, Tao Xu, Greg Brockman, Christine McLeavey, and Ilya Sutskever. 2023. Robust speech recognition via large-scale weak supervision. In *International Conference on Machine Learning*, pages 28492–28518. PMLR.

Anton Ragni, Kate Knill, Shakti Prasad Rath, and Mark John Francis Gales. 2014. Data augmentation for low resource languages. In *Interspeech*.

Jiatong Shi, Jonathan D. Amith, Rey Castillo García, Esteban Guadalupe Sierra, Kevin Duh, and Shinji Watanabe. 2021. Leveraging end-to-end ASR for endangered language documentation: An empirical study on Yoloxóchitl Mixtec. In *Proceedings of the 16th Conference of the European Chapter of the Association for Computational Linguistics: Main Volume*, pages 1134–1145, Online. Association for Computational Linguistics.

Andreas Stolcke. 2002. SRILM-an extensible language modeling toolkit. In *Seventh international conference on spoken language processing*.

Bao Thai, Robert Jimerson, Dominic Arcoraci, Emily Prud'hommeaux, and Raymond Ptucha. 2019. Synthetic data augmentation for improving low-resource ASR. In *2019 IEEE Western New York Image and Signal Processing Workshop (WNYISPW)*, pages 1–9. IEEE.

Bao Thai, Robert Jimerson, Raymond Ptucha, and Emily Prud'hommeaux. 2020. Fully convolutional ASR for less-resourced endangered languages. In *Proceedings of the 1st Joint Workshop on Spoken Language Technologies for Under-resourced languages (SLTU) and Collaboration and Computing for Under-Resourced Languages (CCURL)*, pages 126–130, Marseille, France. European Language Resources association.

Shinji Watanabe, Takaaki Hori, Shigeki Karita, Tomoki Hayashi, Jiro Nishitoba, Yuya Unno, Nelson Enrique Yalta Soplin, Jahn Heymann, Matthew Wiesner, Nanxin Chen, Adithya Renduchintala, and Tsubasa Ochiai. 2018. ESPnet: End-to-End Speech Processing Toolkit. In *Proceedings of Interspeech*, pages 2207–2211.

Ian H Witten and Timothy C Bell. 1991. The zero-frequency problem: Estimating the probabilities of novel events in adaptive text compression. *Ieee transactions on information theory*, 37(4):1085–1094.

Thomas Wolf, Lysandre Debut, Victor Sanh, Julien Chaumond, Clement Delangue, Anthony Moi, Pierric Cistac, Tim Rault, Remi Louf, Morgan Funtowicz, Joe Davison, Sam Shleifer, Patrick von Platen, Clara Ma, Yacine Jernite, Julien Plu, Canwen Xu, Teven Le Scao, Sylvain Gugger, Mariama Drame, Quentin Lhoest, and Alexander Rush. 2020. Transformers: State-of-the-art natural language processing. In *Proceedings of the 2020 Conference on Empirical Methods in Natural Language Processing: System Demonstrations*, pages 38–45, Online. Association for Computational Linguistics.

Qiantong Xu, Alexei Baevski, Tatiana Likhomanenko, Paden Tomasello, Alexis Conneau, Ronan Collobert, Gabriel Synnaeve, and Michael Auli. 2021. Self-training and pre-training are complementary for speech recognition. In *ICASSP 2021 - 2021 IEEE International Conference on Acoustics, Speech and Signal Processing (ICASSP)*, pages 3030–3034.

Qiantong Xu, Tatiana Likhomanenko, Jacob Kahn, Awni Hannun, Gabriel Synnaeve, and Ronan Collobert. 2020. Iterative Pseudo-Labeling for Speech Recognition. In *Proc. Interspeech 2020*, pages 1006–1010.

Shiyue Zhang, Ben Frey, and Mohit Bansal. 2022a. How can NLP help revitalize endangered languages? a case study and roadmap for the Cherokee language. In *Proceedings of the 60th Annual Meeting of the Association for Computational Linguistics (Volume 1: Long Papers)*, pages 1529–1541, Dublin, Ireland. Association for Computational Linguistics.

Zi-Qiang Zhang, Yan Song, Ming-Hui Wu, Xin Fang, Ian McLoughlin, and Li-Rong Dai. 2022b. Cross-lingual self-training to learn multilingual representation for low-resource speech recognition. *Circuits, Systems, and Signal Processing*, 41(12):6827–6843.

A Appendix

A.1 Partition statistics for all transcripts

Table 3 details the statistics of the training and test partitions for the different experimental setups.

A.2 WER & edit distance distributions

Figure 1 shows the box-plot distribution of WER scores between coarse and model-generated transcript types. Figure 2 shows the normalized edit distance distribution between coarse and model-generated transcript types.

A.3 Distribution of token counts

Figure 3 shows the distributions of token counts per transcript between coarse and model-generated transcript types.

A.4 Distribution of word length

Figure 4 shows the distribution of word length across all manually annotated texts.

A.5 Model training hyper-parameters

Table 4 and Table 5 show the hyper-parameters used to train Wav2Vec2 and Kaldi.

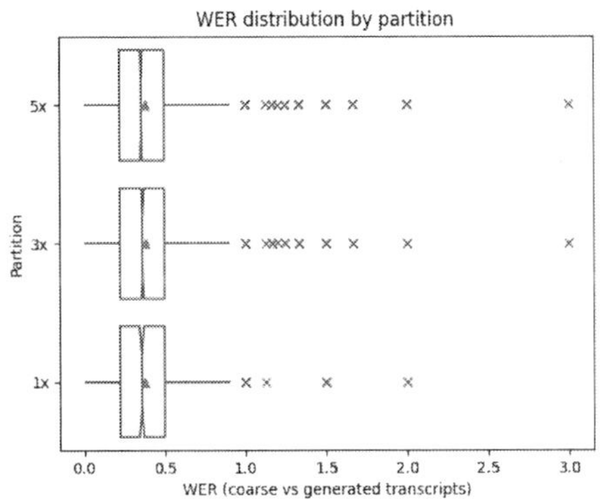

Figure 1: WER scores for coarse versus model-generated transcripts by partition. The mean WER scores for the 5x, 3x and 1x partitions are 0.3819, 0.3848, 0.3779 respectively.

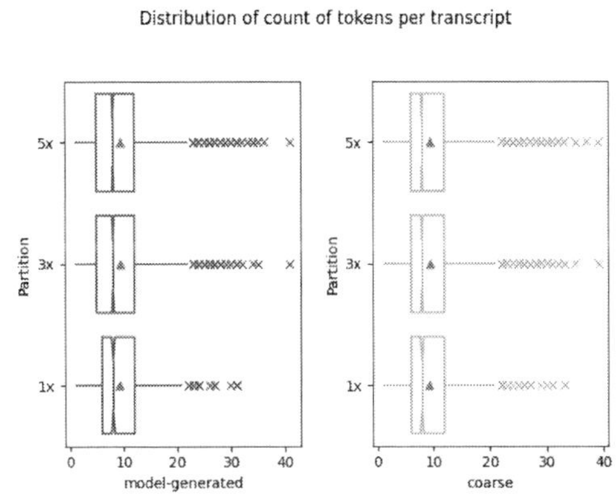

Figure 3: Distribution of token count per transcript, grouped by partition. The distributions appear quantitatively similar across model-generated and coarse transcripts.

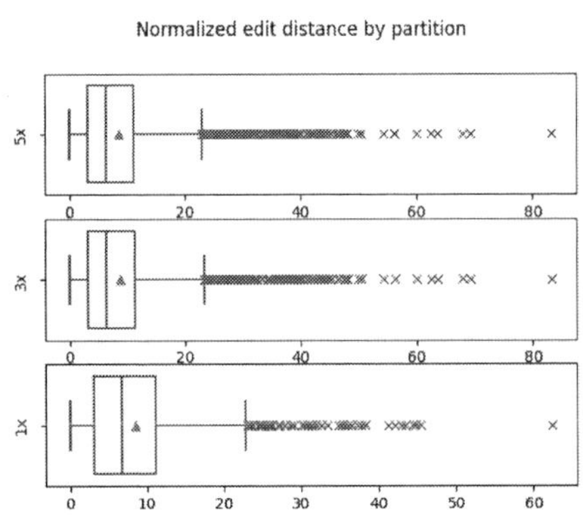

Figure 2: Distribution of normalized edit distances for the 5x, 3x and 1x partitions between the coarse transcripts and the model generated transcripts; the distances are normalized by the length of the coarse transcript and reported as edits per 100-character transcript. The mean normalized edit distances for the 5x, 3x and 1x partitions are 8.51, 8.73 and 8.47 respectively.

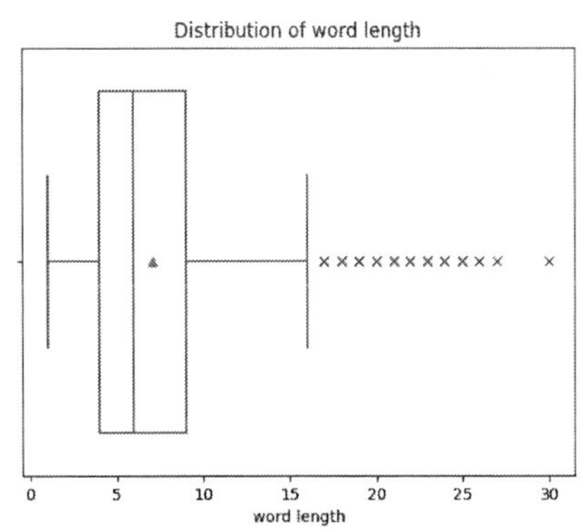

Figure 4: Distribution of word length across all manually-annotated texts. The mean word length is 7.05.

Experiment setup (Partition Size)	Duration	Token count	Type count	Avg. tokens per sentence	Avg. word length (chars)
Fine only (baseline)	1h 16m	7,438	2,028	9.15	7.22
Fine + Coarse (1x)	2h 52m	16,126	3,649	9.26	7.09
Fine + Coarse (3x)	6h 1m	32,828	5,889	9.32	7.04
Fine + Coarse (5x)	9h 12m	48,342	7,549	9.34	7.03
Fine + Model-generated (1x)	2h 52m	16,041	4,255	9.21	7.12
Fine + Model-generated (3x)	6h 1m	32,557	7,774	9.24	7.10
Fine + Model-generated (5x)	9h 12m	47,922	10,515	9.26	7.09
Test Split	19m	1,797	754	8.81	7.42

Table 3: Statistics about the train-test split across fine, coarse, and model-generated transcripts.

Parameter	Value
Number of Epochs	60
Training Batch Size	4
Evaluation Batch Size	8
Warmup Size	0 (no warmup)
Gradient Accumulation Size	2
Learning Rate	3e-5

Table 4: Parameters used to train Wav2Vec XLS-R-2B.

Parameter	Value
Hidden layers	4
Hidden dim	1024
Learning Rate	0.08

Table 5: Parameters used to train Kaldi DNN.

Creating Digital Learning and Reference Resources for Southern Michif

Heather Souter, Olivia Sammons
Prairies to Woodlands
Indigenous Revitialization Circle
{hsouter,osammons}@p2wilr.org

David Huggins-Daines
Independent Researcher
dhd@ecolingui.ca

Abstract

Minority and Indigenous languages are often under-documented and under-resourced. Where such resources do exist, particularly in the form of legacy materials, they are often inaccessible to learners and educators involved in revitalization efforts, whether due to the limitations of their original formats or the structure of their contents. Digitizing such resources and making them available on a variety of platforms is one step in overcoming these barriers. This is a major undertaking which requires significant expertise at the intersection of documentary linguistics, computational linguistics, and software development, and must be done while walking alongside speakers and language specialists in the community. We discuss the particular strategies and challenges involved in the development of one such resource, and make recommendations for future projects with a similar goal of mobilizing legacy language resources.

1 Introduction

Michif, ma-laañg-inaan, katawashishin[1] (Heather Souter). Southern Michif (ISO 639-3: crg; hereafter "Michif"), is one of three language varieties spoken by the Métis (Bakker, 1997; Sammons, 2019). It is a contact language combining elements from Algonquian languages—Plains Cree and the Saulteaux dialect of Ojibwe—with Métis French. Michif has traditionally been spoken in small, diasporic communities across western Canada and the northern United States, mainly on the Prairies. Reliable census data regarding the current number of Michif speakers are unavailable, largely due to ambiguity around the use of the label "Michif", However, Southern Michif speakers and community members who are actively involved in community-based language revitalization informally estimate that there are likely fewer than 100 speakers today (Chew et al., 2023). Intergenerational transmission of the language has ceased, and all but one or two mother-tongue speakers are over 70 years of age. Despite growing revitalization activities in Métis communities in western Canada, few print and digital resources based on best practices in lexicography, language documentation, and second language acquisition are available to support those efforts.

The primary aim of this project was to digitize and make accessible an out-of-print Michif dictionary (Laverdure et al., 1983), while also developing local capacity in technologies for Indigenous language documentation and revitalization. With the assistance of Michif first-language speakers, community-based language workers, project partners, and computational linguists, we have developed the Michif Talking Dictionary,[2] a digital spoken version of this important print resource. This dictionary is now available as a progressive web application, adapted to a wide variety of screen sizes, as shown in Figure 1. The application does not require an Internet connection to search and browse once accessed. Its source code, along with the code used to process the text and annotated speech data for the dictionary, is publicly available under an open-source license.[3]

Another major goal of this project was to develop capacity through the training of emerging Métis community linguists, language workers, and scholars in the areas of audio recording, application of speech technologies, and annotation. Between September 2019 and May 2021, one workshop on recording and five workshops on annotation were held in Brandon, Manitoba, Ottawa, Ontario, and online via Zoom.[4]

The original book, *The Michif Dictionary: Tur-*

[1] Michif, our language, is beautiful.

[2] https://dictionary.michif.org/

[3] https://github.com/p2wilrc/mtd-michif/

[4] After the outbreak of COVID-19 and resulting restrictions on travel and gathering.

Proceedings of the The Seventh Workshop on the Use of Computational Methods in the Study of Endangered Languages, pages 67–75
March 21-22, 2024 ©2024 Association for Computational Linguistics

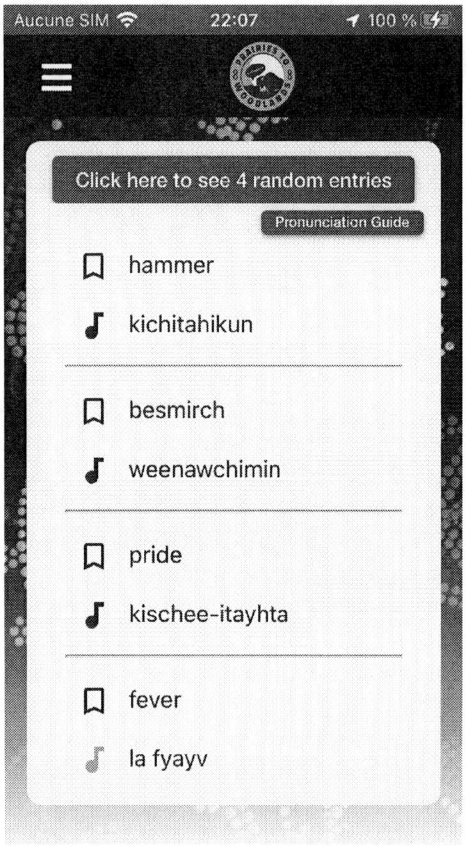

Figure 1: Mobile dictionary on iPhone SE

tle Mountain Chippewa Cree, is recognized for its valuable contribution to Michif language documentation. However this now out-of-print resource is largely inaccessible to learners of Michif unless purchased used at a high price, and is rarely available for purchase. While other Michif dictionaries that include audio from native speakers have been published and made available in electronic format (e.g., Rosen et al., 2016; Gabriel Dumont Institute, 2012), both of which are based primarily on Michif as it is spoken in Manitoba and Saskatchewan), this dictionary is exceptional in its degree of coverage of lexical items and example sentences. In addition, many important linguistic studies of Michif (e.g. Bakker, 1997), as well as the lexical resources mentioned above, have relied to varying degrees on the contents of the original Turtle Mountain Dictionary as one of their primary sources. The Turtle Mountain Dictionary is also an important historical resource, as many Métis community members in Canada have kinship ties to Belcourt, ND, where the dictionary was created, and because it includes the speech of an under-represented dialect of Michif. For all of these reasons, multiple Elders and community members identified the creation of an electronic edition of this dictionary as a priority, as it is viewed as a resource that is much too valuable to remain inaccessible, but should rather be put into the hands of Michif language learners and educators.

Permission was granted by Turtle Mountain Community College, the dictionary's copyright holder, to the project team to create a digital version of the dictionary for online, offline, and mobile use. This "new" version retains all of the original content, but will also allow for the inclusion audio recordings of headwords and example sentences, as well as further enrichment in the eventual addition of alternate orthographies and grammatical information for lexical entries.

2 Recording

For the dictionary, 181 hours of high-quality audio recordings were collected from four separate speakers. One speaker, Verna DeMontigny, recorded the entire dictionary from cover to cover, while others recorded selected portions of it. Thus, all entries have been recorded by at least one speaker, with some entries being recorded by two or more speakers.

As shown in Table 1, multiple Michif varieties are represented in these recordings. It was particularly important for the Belcourt, ND variety to be represented here, as the original creators of the dictionary spoke this variety.

All the recordings, backed up regularly on multiple hard drives and on Dropbox, were named according to a consistent file-naming process. Metadata for each session, such as speaker name, location, and covered pages of the dictionary, was tracked and shared among team members via a Google spreadsheet. As we will discuss below, the management of metadata was one of several challenges we faced in the production of the dictionary; for example, the information in this spreadsheet ultimately diverged from that contained in the annotation files. In our discussion of these challenges we hope to identify pitfalls and propose solutions for other groups involved in a similar endeavour. In this case, in the absence of a content management system for the recordings, this problem could have been partially mitigated with the "data validation" feature, similar to the use of controlled vocabularies in ELAN.

Speaker	Michif Variety	Hours Recorded
Verna DeMontigny	The Corner, Manitoba	143h14m34.45
Sandra R. Houle	Belcourt, North Dakota	12h40m47.14
Albert Parisien	Belcourt, North Dakota	15h31m40.16
Connie Henry	Boggy Creek, Manitoba	10h00m00.97
	TOTAL	181h27m02.72

Table 1: Dictionary recording hours by speaker

3 Annotation

All audio recordings were annotated using ELAN (Wittenburg et al., 2006) to produce time-aligned transcripts. First, each recording was segmented into pause-delimited utterances automatically using a Deep Neural Network (DNN) voice activity detection service that was developed within the VESTA-ELAN project by the Centre de Recherche Informatique de Montréal (Gupta and Boulianne, 2022). This auto-segmentation saved an immeasurable amount of time in the annotation process.

To support remote annotators with heterogeneous Internet connections and computer hardware, hosting of the annotations was switched to Google Drive from Dropbox. As per the requirements of earlier versions of ELAN, it was necessary to provide WAV files to visualize waveforms, which were critical for annotators to be able to see and correct the automatic segmentation. However, dissemination of the 'master' WAV files was a challenge, given their large size. To address this, we first down-sampled the original audio from 48 kHz, 24-bit WAV into two different formats: (1) high-quality MP3 files (44.1kHz, 16-bit, 128kbps), which were used for playback; and (2) low-quality WAV files (8kHz, 8-bit), which were provided only for waveform visualization in ELAN, and were never used in playback. This approach made it feasible to share the entire audio collection with annotators over a cloud-based service, enabling them to both listen to high-quality versions of the audio and to display the corresponding waveforms in ELAN. The master recordings were maintained separately and later used as the source of the audio that was included in the dictionary.

The paper dictionary was scanned and converted to text using the Tesseract 4 optical character recognition engine. An ELAN template was created with tiers for English headwords, Michif definitions, and example sentences, and these were then integrated from the OCR text of the dictionary into these transcripts by a team of Indigenous and non-Indigenous language workers who contributed to the project as paid contract employees, volunteers, and, in one case, as a student in a for-credit independent study course in applied linguistics.

In most cases, the speakers recorded multiple instances of each word and example sentence. The annotators were therefore instructed to select the best recording for "export" to the talking dictionary. Due to the slow and careful speaking style used, the example sentences and definitions were frequently split into multiple segments, which had to be reassembled in the construction of the talking dictionary. Annotators were also instructed to adjust the boundaries of these segments to ensure that no words were cut off. In some cases, it was necessary to splice together different instances in order to obtain an audio clip without false starts or mispronunciations.

Because of the dialect variation which exists in Southern Michif, as well as the fact that the recordings were made nearly 40 years after the creation of the print dictionary, the speakers often diverge from the original text, or in some cases, provide a corrected version of a dictionary entry. Annotators were thus instructed to flag partial matches as well as novel forms. In the initial version of the the talking dictionary, we have attempted to remain faithful to the original text as much as possible, with the exception of typos and misspellings. A revised version is in development which will present these variant and corrected forms along with relevant grammatical information.

Manual review and corrections of the text of the dictionary was performed by 14 undergraduate students as part of a Community Service-Learning project in an Indigenous Languages of Canada course in winter 2021. Students in this course used Transkribus Lite, a web-based interface to functions of the Transkribus transcription platform (Kahle et al., 2017), to identify and address errors in the computer-readable text of the dictionary that were introduced by the previously applied OCR methods (e.g., correcting misspelled words, entering words or lines that were present on the page but missed by the OCR software, etc.). Errors were found and corrected on a total of 1600 lines of text, or 8.5% of the dictionary. However, there remained a large number of systematic OCR errors, such as ambiguity between `l`, `1`, and `I`, which were corrected semi-automatically in the dictionary build.

Since different parts of the project were conducted simultaneously, technical issues arose from the ordering of this work. For instance, the post-correction of the dictionary text took place *after* the start of the annotation process, resulting in a divergence between the text in the ELAN annotations and the text dictionary. Likewise, while the dictionary entries from the original OCR output were separated into definitions and examples when creating the ELAN files, and sometimes also corrected by the annotators afterwards, these modifications were not synchronized or linked in any way to the dictionary text. Because it was infeasible to correct these discrepancies manually, it was necessary to develop a complex data extraction process using heuristic matching algorithms to align dictionary text and annotations.

4 Dictionary Construction

The electronic dictionary was produced using a customized version of the MotherTongues (Littell et al., 2017) platform. This well-documented open-source tool provides Web and mobile applications with a flexible and configurable approximate search feature, shown in Figure 2, along with a tool to automate the conversion of dictionaries from a variety of formats including spreadsheets, XML, and JSON files. Compared to tools such as FLEx (Beier and Michael, 2022), it supports a very restricted set of lexicographical data, but no such data exists in the original dictionary in any case. This is a common situation for community-developed resources, and the relatively lightweight nature of MotherTongues allows for the creation of dictionaries with a minimum of technical expertise. That said, the absence of grammatical information in the Michif Talking Dictionary limits its usefulness for language learners, and we hope to address this in a subsequent revision.

As detailed in sections 2 and 3, there were four separate sources of information used to produce the talking dictionary:

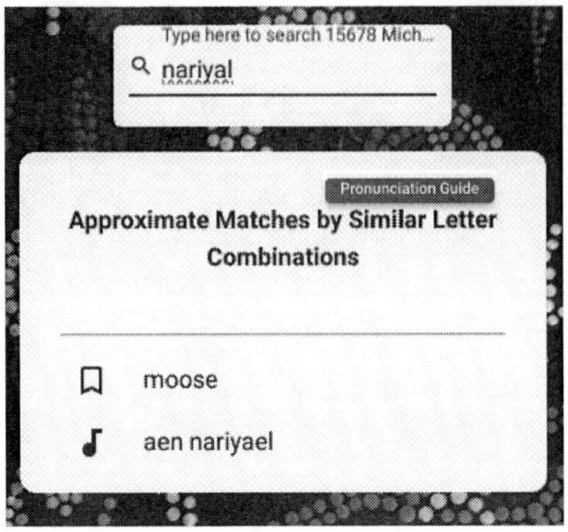

Figure 2: Approximate Search

1. The corrected OCR dictionary text.
2. The original recordings.
3. The metadata spreadsheet identifying the speaker, date and location of each recording along with the pages of the dictionary covered and any comments on audio quality.
4. The ELAN files containing speech segments and aligned lexical entries and examples for each recording.

Unfortunately, the need to rapidly organize a distributed annotation effort, turnover of key personnel, and other difficulties arising from the COVID-19 pandemic led to widespread inconsistencies within and between these data sources. The initial version of the talking dictionary reflected these inconsistencies; the audio was widely misattributed, mismatched with the text, and of poor quality as it was mistakenly taken from the low-quality files used for visualization rather than the original master recordings. In the absence of a content management system adapted to this task, it is imperative that the project manager work in close collaboration with technical resources to identify and correct these problems. It would be useful to continuously build and deploy the electronic version of the dictionary, and to track any integration problems, from the beginning of the annotation process.

The first priority when building the dictionary was thus the reconstruction of the metadata and retrieval of the original audio files. As well, while the post-correction of the OCR output resulted in a fairly consistently formatted text faithful to the original print version, the organization of the entries in this text created numerous problems when converting them to a structured format for presentation.

Among other things, this required the development of a language identification system, detailed in Section 4.1.

Finally, after extracting structured text from the dictionary entries, a subsequent matching was performed against the ELAN annotations to identify and extract the corresponding audio segments. Because of the divergence between original and post-corrected text, as well as the fact that annotators frequently (but inconsistently) corrected the text in the annotations, this required a multi-stage heuristic strategy in order to maximise the audio coverage, detailed in Section 4.2.

Because of the extensive recording and annotation efforts detailed in Section 2, there are often recordings of multiple speakers for both Michif definitions and example sentences. This level of complexity in the dictionary entries was not supported by the current version of MotherTongues at the time. We therefore extended both the dictionary builder and the Web user interface to support it, using a more flexible JSON-based input format.[5]

In order to quantify progress in improving the conversion workflow, 100 random entries were sampled and manually converted to this format, and the performance of the system evaluated using precision and recall over definitions and examples. Along with the audio coverage, this F1 score was also recorded and tracked for each weekly build of the dictionary during the development process.

4.1 Entry Extraction

The text of the Turtle Mountain Dictionary consists of 350 pages of Michif lexical entries and example sentences, organized into 9,181 English headwords followed by one or more Michif definitions and associated example sentences in English and Michif. We use "definitions" to describe these because they are not necessarily Michif lexical entries; in many cases, they give a *description* of the English word rather than the actual term used in Michif. For example, the definition for *zucchini*, shown in Figure 3, literally means 'a type of pumpkin', while the example sentence simply uses *zucchini*. [6] Likewise, the defintion of *zinnia* literally means 'flowers of all sorts of colours'. No lexical information such as part of speech, verb class, order, or gender is provided in the original text.

```
zucchini en sort di sitroouy; I
like zucchini cooked any way.
Niweehkishpwow zucchini pikou
ishi ay-ishikeeshishoust.
```

```
zinnia lee flueur tout sort di
kouleur.
```

Figure 3: Examples of descriptive definitions

reflect `wawshaynikayw, wawshayshkoutayw, nanawkatawayistamihk, kanaw katawayhtem;` *The mirror reflects the light.* `Wawshaynikayw le meerway. Wawshayshkoutayw li meerway.` *He'll reflect on his past actions.* `Kananawkatawayistam tawnshi aykitahkamikishit. Kanawkatawayhtem kawpaytootahk.`

Figure 4: Entry structure *(English in italic)*

Though the text of the dictionary entries have a relatively consistent structure, the English example sentences and their Michif translations are not attached to the corresponding Michif definitions or consistently ordered. In general, they are organized in pairs of English and Michif texts. However, these pairs may contain varying numbers of sentences, which in turn may correspond to one or more examples. For example, in Figure 4, there are four Michif definitions and two English example sentences, each of which has two different corresponding Michif examples. The extraction process must therefore:

1. Identify and separate the headword and the individual definitions.
2. Separate English and Michif example texts.
3. Create pairs of English and corresponding Michif examples.
4. Match Michif example texts to the corresponding definition words.

In the majority of cases the dictionary text follows one of two straightforward patterns; either

[5] Our modifications will be included in the next release of MotherTongues but are also available at `https://github.com/p2wilrc/mothertongues/`

[6] *zucchini* is also commonly used in Québec French instead of the standard *courgette*.

English and Michif examples alternate, or a single English example is followed by multiple Michif example sentences, one for each definition. In some cases, the individual examples also consist of multiple sentences.

To split the text into sentences, we used the `PySBD` library (Sadvilkar and Neumann, 2020), which required some post-processing to compensate for inconsistencies in how punctuation and abbreviations were used in the original dictionary. The initial version of the dictionary used the off-the-shelf `langid.py` library (Lui and Baldwin, 2012) to identify "not English" sentences as presumably Michif. This performed poorly, because obviously, Michif is not present in the `langid.py` model, but also because the orthography used in the Turtle Mountain Dictionary was specifically designed to resemble English (Laverdure et al., 1983).

Instead, we created a binary classifier for English versus Michif, using `fastText` (Bojanowski et al., 2017) with 5-gram subword features, making the assumption that the English headwords are valid English and the Michif definitions are valid Michif. We manually created a development set consisting of 1250 Michif and and 1239 English example sentences to evaluate the performance of these models, obtaining 99.4% accuracy, compared to 84.3% for the original `langid.py` based approach. Because any error is unacceptable in the final dictionary, we maintain a separate list of "overrides" to correct any errors found in testing. Likewise, we keep a list of "uncorrectable" dictionary entries with manually extracted definitions and examples where the original text cannot be parsed.

Once the English and Michif sentences have been identified and pairs of examples created, they are scored against the Michif definitions using the minimum Levenshtein distance between the definition and any subsequence of the example, with whitespace and punctuation removed. In some rare cases, this leads to incorrect matches due to the fact that the definitions are fully-inflected forms rather than lemmas and may not match the forms used in the examples. It may be useful to implement and evaluate a lemmatizer to improve the example matching.

4.2 Annotation Matching

As mentioned in Section 2, the original recordings contain 181 hours of audio. Of these, there are 105 hours of speech, which were annotated to identify the 18 hours of speech corresponding to the Michif dictionary entries and examples. This number is considerably smaller than the total amount of speech, as all entries and examples were read multiple times, with the best reading selected for the dictionary. There are also numerous discussions between the speaker and the linguist regarding the text. After extracting the structure of the dictionary entries, we process the annotation files using `pympi-ling` (Lubbers and Torreira, 2013-2021), collecting all the tiers for an aligned annotation in a single "Span" and matching these spans to entries in the dictionary.

To compensate for the variable correction of OCR errors in the ELAN files, we perform a severe normalization of the text before matching annotations, collapsing various ambiguous characters or sequences (for example, `w/vv`, `t/f`, as well as the ones noted previously). In addition, we neutralize common spelling variations in the Michif text such as `ou/oo`. In some cases, the text is reduplicated in the annotations, so we check and repair this as well.

Finally, although we used a controlled vocabulary for the type of annotations, the difference between definitions and examples is not at all clear in the original dictionary, so they are often misannotated. In the case where this misannotation is unambiguous, we were able to repair these automatically with a Python script, but in some cases this was not possible. For this reason, the matching algorithm collects as many annotations as possible, matching on both the English and Michif text, then ordering by match and annotation type as well as normalized Levenshtein distance.

A significant challenge for the audio matching is reassembling the multiple fragments of an example which were split by voice activity detection. Annotators were instructed to select only one instance of any definition or example for a given speaker, and to use annotation types for the subsequent fragments, but this is not done consistently. In the case where an audio clip is to be spliced together from multiple instances, the original fragments are sometimes out of order in the recording, and while this is indicated by annotator notes, it is done in free text rather than with a controlled vocabulary, requiring heuristics and in many cases manual corrections to the annotator notes in order to get the correct ordering in the output. We discuss the detection and correction of these errors in the next section.

5 Verification and Re-Annotation

In testing the talking dictionary, it became obvious that many audio entries were incomplete or mismatched to the text. Given the scale of the recordings and annotations and the limited resources available, we attempted to use force-alignment to detect these problems, similarly to how the Festvox system (Anumanchipalli et al., 2011) excludes incorrectly labeled prompts to avoid egregious errors in unit-selection synthesis. Of course, no pre-trained acoustic models exist for Michif. Using the "universal" grapheme-to-phoneme technique from Pine et al. (2022), we create an approximate phonetic transcription of the Michif text, then use the same alignment technique as Littell et al. (2022) with a narrow beam search, flagging examples that fail to align for review. To streamline the workflow, we collect the audio clips on an HTML page, shown in Figure 5, which we package with the relevant ELAN annotation files and preference (`.pfsx`) files which direct ELAN to open directly on the annotation to be reviewed.

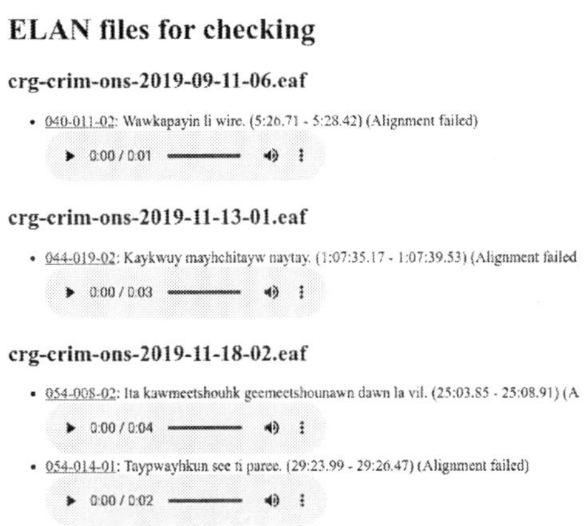

Figure 5: HTML page for reannotation

Since false positives are not problematic (we can simply listen to them to determine that they are correct), a weak alignment model of this sort is quite effective, allowing us to detect and correct several hundred annotations which could not be fixed by the automated processes described in Section 4.2, generally in cases where one segment of an example that was split by VAD was not properly labeled by the annotators. An unintended side benefit of this verification is that it gives us word-level time alignments for the example sentences. We therefore extended the MotherTongues system to include a "read-along" style highlighting of each word when listening to the examples in the talking dictionary, as shown in Figure 6.

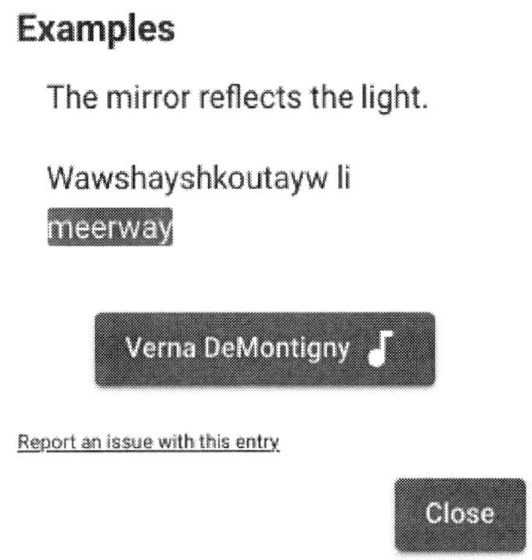

Figure 6: Read-along highlighting

6 Conclusions

Some of the technical difficulties we had to overcome in creating this resource stem from organizational difficulties exacerbated by the COVID-19 pandemic. Others may simply be inherent to a large-scale, widely distributed and heterogeneous data collection and annotation effort. For future projects of this scale, it is crucial to endure that metadata is continuously validated and to avoid, at all costs, duplicating it across multiple unsynchronized data sources. It is equally important to involve a variety of perspectives in the design of the data collection and processing workflows, including members of the speech community, documentary and computational linguists, and to allow for iterative improvements to these processes.

When structured data is created as part of the data collection and annotation process, this data should be considered authoritative and maintained as such. If created from an unstructured data source (such as the OCR output of the paper dictionary), there should either be a robust process to pull changes and corrections from this original data source into the structured data, or the original unstructured data should be archived and left alone. This may require careful consideration of the dependencies between different steps in the process to avoid duplicate or conflicting efforts.

Some of these issues could be avoided with sufficient and appropriate tooling. In particular, while

ELAN is a robust and highly useful tool for annotation, it is difficult to integrate with external sources of metadata, distributed filesystems, or version control systems. While ELAN is highly extensible, with numerous third-party plug-ins and add-ons, it inherently operates at a single-file level, making it cumbersome to perform tasks involving individual annotations across a large number of EAF files. This could potentially be achieved by adding an API to ELAN which would allow it to be controlled by an external content management system.

Overall, this project has resulted in a resource that will be of long-term use in Michif language teaching, revitalization, and study. The dictionary application is now not only accessible to a wide range of users, but is also searchable, and the recorded Michif pronunciations of the headwords and example sentences will be extremely valuable for learners. Moreover, a total of 16 Métis team members were trained in language documentation and Indigenous language technologies, developing local capacity. In particular, the annotators involved in this project developed technical skills while also gaining valuable exposure to the Michif language. They will be able to carry this experience and knowledge with them as they continue their language journeys and contribute to future language revitalization initiatives.

Acknowledgements

This work would not have been possible without the participation of Verna DeMontigny, who not only recorded every single page of the dictionary, but also provided invaluable expertise as a native Michif speaker, educator, and Elder. Thank you also to the other Michif speakers who lent their voices to the dictionary: Connie Henry, Albert Parisien, Sr., and the late Sandra Houle. This work would equally have been impossible without the contribution of Turtle Mountain Community College, who graciously gave permission to use the original dictionary text. Samantha Cornelius and Janelle Zazalak coordinated the annotation effort, while Jacob Collard and Fineen Davis implemented the initial processing of the OCR text and annotations for MotherTongues. Tiara Opissinow provided essential assistance with project management and reannotation. David Delorme-Forsman also assisted the reannotation effort. Christopher Cox and students in the School of Linguistics and Language Studies at Carleton University contributed to the digitization and OCR correction processes, while Gilles Boulianne of the CRIM aided greatly with the ELAN-VESTA annotation process. We are extremely grateful to the National Research Council for supporting the project, and especially to Roland Kuhn for his support, patience, and enthusiasm. Kihchi-marsii!

References

Gopala Krishna Anumanchipalli, Kishore Prahallad, and Alan W Black. 2011. Festvox: Tools for creation and analyses of large speech corpora. In *Workshop on Very Large Scale Phonetics Research, UPenn, Philadelphia*, volume 70.

Peter Bakker. 1997. *A Language of Our Own : The Genesis of Michif, the Mixed Cree-French Language of the Canadian Metis*. Oxford University Press, Oxford & New York.

Christine Beier and Lev Michael. 2022. Managing Lexicography Data: A Practical, Principled Approach Using FLEx (FieldWorks Language Explorer). In Andrea L. Berez-Kroeker, Bradley McDonnell, Eve Koller, and Lauren B. Collister, editors, *The Open Handbook of Linguistic Data Management*, page 301–314. The MIT Press.

Piotr Bojanowski, Edouard Grave, Armand Joulin, and Tomas Mikolov. 2017. Enriching word vectors with subword information. *Transactions of the Association for Computational Linguistics*, 5:135–146.

Kari A.B. Chew, Sara Child, Jackie Dormer, Alexa Little, Olivia Sammons, and Heather Souter. 2023. Creating Online Indigenous Language Courses as Decolonizing Praxis. *The Canadian Modern Language Review*, 79(3):181–203.

Gabriel Dumont Institute. 2012. Michif Dictionary and Phrase Primer. `https://www.metismuseum.ca/michif_dictionary.php`. Accessed: 2024-01-31.

Vishwa Gupta and Gilles Boulianne. 2022. CRIM's Speech Recognition System for OpenASR21 Evaluation with Conformer and Voice Activity Detector Embeddings. In *International Conference on Speech and Computer*, pages 238–251. Springer.

Philip Kahle, Sebastian Colutto, Günter Hackl, and Günter Mühlberger. 2017. Transkribus-a service platform for transcription, recognition and retrieval of historical documents. In *2017 14th IAPR International Conference on Document Analysis and Recognition (ICDAR)*, volume 4, pages 19–24. IEEE.

Patline Laverdure, Ida Rose Allard, and John C. Crawford. 1983. *The Michif Dictionary: Turtle Mountain Chippewa Cree*. Pemmican Publications, Winnipeg.

Patrick Littell, Eric Joanis, Aidan Pine, Marc Tessier, David Huggins Daines, and Delasie Torkornoo. 2022. ReadAlong studio: Practical zero-shot text-speech alignment for indigenous language audiobooks. In *Proceedings of the 1st Annual Meeting of the ELRA/ISCA Special Interest Group on Under-Resourced Languages*, pages 23–32, Marseille, France. European Language Resources Association.

Patrick Littell, Aidan Pine, and Henry Davis. 2017. Waldayu and waldayu mobile: Modern digital dictionary interfaces for endangered languages. In *Proceedings of the 2nd Workshop on the Use of Computational Methods in the Study of Endangered Languages*, pages 141–150, Honolulu. Association for Computational Linguistics.

Mart Lubbers and Francisco Torreira. 2013-2021. pympi-ling: a Python module for processing ELANs EAF and Praats TextGrid annotation files. `https://pypi.python.org/pypi/pympi-ling`. Version 1.70.

Marco Lui and Timothy Baldwin. 2012. langid.py: An off-the-shelf language identification tool. In *Proceedings of the ACL 2012 System Demonstrations*, pages 25–30, Jeju Island, Korea. Association for Computational Linguistics.

Aidan Pine, Patrick William Littell, Eric Joanis, David Huggins-Daines, Christopher Cox, Fineen Davis, Eddie Antonio Santos, Shankhalika Srikanth, Delasie Torkornoo, and Sabrina Yu. 2022. G_i2P_i rule-based, index-preserving grapheme-to-phoneme transformations. In *Proceedings of the Fifth Workshop on the Use of Computational Methods in the Study of Endangered Languages*, pages 52–60, Dublin, Ireland. Association for Computational Linguistics.

Nicole Rosen, Marie-Odile Junker, Delasie Torkornoo, and Andrei Belcin. 2016. Michif Online Dictionary. `https://dictionary.michif.atlas-ling.ca/`. Accessed: 2024-01-31.

Nipun Sadvilkar and Mark Neumann. 2020. PySBD: Pragmatic sentence boundary disambiguation. In *Proceedings of Second Workshop for NLP Open Source Software (NLP-OSS)*, pages 110–114, Online. Association for Computational Linguistics.

Olivia Sammons. 2019. *Nominal Classification in Michif.* Ph.D. thesis, University of Alberta.

Peter Wittenburg, Hennie Brugman, Albert Russel, Alex Klassmann, and Han Sloetjes. 2006. ELAN: a professional framework for multimodality research. In *Proceedings of the Fifth International Conference on Language Resources and Evaluation (LREC'06)*, Genoa, Italy. European Language Resources Association (ELRA).

MunTTS: A Text-to-Speech System for Mundari

Varun Gumma[♠] **Rishav Hada**[♠] **Aditya Yadavalli**[◇]
Pamir Gogoi[♡*] **Ishani Mondal**[♣*] **Vivek Seshadri**[♠◇] **Kalika Bali**[♠]
[♠]Microsoft Corporation [◇]Karya Inc. [♡]Project VANI [♣]University of Maryland
varun230999@gmail.com, kalikab@microsoft.com

Abstract

We present MunTTS, an end-to-end text-to-speech (TTS) system specifically for Mundari, a low-resource Indian language of the Austo-Asiatic family. Our work addresses the gap in linguistic technology for underrepresented languages by collecting and processing data to build a speech synthesis system. We begin our study by gathering a substantial dataset of Mundari text and speech and train end-to-end speech models. We also delve into the methods used for training our models, ensuring they are efficient and effective despite the data constraints. We evaluate our system with native speakers and objective metrics, demonstrating its potential as a tool for preserving and promoting the Mundari language in the digital age[1].

1 Introduction

India is home to approximately 1652 languages and 22 official languages written in different scripts (Prakash and Murthy, 2023; Gala et al., 2023). Many of these languages are classified as low-resource, as native speakers are moving towards dominant languages that are supported by modern-day technologies (Bali et al., 2019).

According to a UNESCO report, India ranks fourth in the list of critically endangered languages with 41 languages (Kwan, 2022). If a language becomes extinct we lose out a large part of the culture. Motivated by these factors, many communities have self-initiated data collection and partnered with tech organizations to build technologies for their language (Diddee et al., 2022).

Text-to-speech (TTS) systems have been gaining a lot of importance as a vital language technology due to their applications in education, navigation, accessibility, voice assistants etc. (Kumar et al., 2023). However, the development of TTS systems for low-resource languages has several challenges (Pine et al., 2022). Firstly, training current-day TTS systems requires many hours of audio recordings and corresponding text transcriptions which is resource-intensive. Secondly, carefully curating the training data such that it covers the phonetic complexity of the given language requires expert input. This becomes a problem especially when the available data is already scarce. Thirdly, the availability of native speakers who are familiar with technology and can do audio recordings in a high-quality studio setup. Fourthly, availability of enough native speakers, who could systematically evaluate these systems for subjective metrics. Lastly, getting high-quality audio recordings can be very expensive. Overcoming these challenges requires not only technical expertise to extract the most out of limited resources but also significant on-field operational efficiency to collect the right quality and quantity of data. No such data collection is possible without the active participation of the community and other stakeholders.

In this work, we build a TTS system for Mundari. Mundari is an Austro-Asiatic language spoken by Munda tribes in the eastern Indian states of Jharkhand, Odisha, and West Bengal. According to the 2011 India census, there are ≈1M native speakers of this language (2011, Archived from the original on 6 March 2021). Mundari is mainly written in the dominant script of the region where it is spoken, viz. Devanagari, Odia, and Bangla. In this study, we worked with the Mundari spoken in Jharkhand and written in the Devanagari script.

We collected audio recordings for 15,656 unique sentences in Mundari. Our Mundari speech corpus consists of high-quality 26,868 audio recordings in male and female voices consisting of 27.51 hours. The average duration of the recordings in our dataset is 3.7 seconds, and the average sentence length is 8.4 words. Using this data we train three TTS systems: Variational Inference with adversarial learning for end-to-end (E2E) Text-to-Speech

*Work done when the author was at Microsoft

[1]Artifacts available at https://aka.ms/MUN-TTS

Proceedings of the The Seventh Workshop on the Use of Computational Methods in the Study of Endangered Languages, pages 76–82
March 21-22, 2024 ©2024 Association for Computational Linguistics

(VITS) with 22KHz sampling rate (VITS-22K), VITS with 44KHz sampling rate (VITS-44K) and fine-tune XTTS v2 as well. We have audio samples from each of these systems evaluated by native speakers for subjective metrics. VITS-44K gives the best overall performance with MOS = 3.69 $\pm$ 1.18.

2 Related Works

- **Neural Speech Synthesis:** The field of neural speech synthesis has experienced a series of transformative developments. WaveNet (van den Oord et al., 2016), utilized a convolutional neural network for raw audio waveform generation, marking a shift from previous heuristic synthesis methods. Tacotron (Wang et al., 2017) further advanced the field with its end-to-end text-to-speech synthesis, streamlining the synthesis process. Tacotron 2 (Shen et al., 2018) built upon this by incorporating WaveNet as a vocoder, enhancing speech quality. Parallel WaveGAN (Yamamoto et al., 2020) introduced a generative adversarial network approach for faster waveform generation. FastSpeech (Ren et al., 2019) and FastSpeech 2 (Ren et al., 2021) utilized feed-forward networks for faster speech generation and enhanced control over speech attributes. VITS (Kim et al., 2021) combined variational autoencoders (Kingma and Welling, 2019) with GANs (Goodfellow et al., 2014) in an end-to-end structure, enabling more expressive speech synthesis. Lastly, XTTS (Coqui, 2023) provided cross-lingual text-to-speech capabilities, representing a notable advancement towards adaptable speech synthesis systems. We refer the readers to Tan et al. (2021) for a comprehensive survey of neural text-to-speech.

- **Relevant TTS systems:** In recent times, there has been a shift towards TTS models for low-resource languages, especially for Indian languages. EkStep Foundation (2021) put forth the first open-source monolingual neural systems for 9 Indic languages using a Glow-TTS + HiFi-GAN combination. Prakash and Murthy (2020) advance it by releasing multilingual TTS models within the same family using a multilingual character map (Prakash et al., 2019) and common label set (Prakash et al., 2019) for Tacotron2 + WaveGlow. Kumar et al. (2023) extend the language coverage to 13 by including 3 low-resource languages, Rajasthani, Bodo, and Manipuri. They also conduct a thorough analysis of different Non-Autoregressive (NAR), flow-based, and end-to-end models in a multi-speaker and multilingual setting and find that single-language models are preferable. Globally, Pratap et al. (2023) expand the text-to-speech coverage to 1017 languages by training individual end-to-end VITS models for each language. However, none of them have developed a dedicated, high-quality, multi-speaker TTS for an extremely low-resource language. In this paper, we present our experiences in developing a high-quality, multi-speaker TTS model for such a language – Mundari.

3 Data

Multiple steps were involved in the data collection process. First, the text data was obtained by translating a Hindi corpus of 100,000 sentences obtained from the Karya database. Karya[2] is a data services organization that takes requests from clients and breaks down these complex requests into simple microtasks that users with little to no digital literacy can perform.

We randomly selected 20,000 of these sentences and manually translated them to Mundari. The translated Mundari sentences were expressed using the Devanagari script. The translators were instructed to prefer fluency of the sentences over faithfulness of the translations wherever they had to make a choice. The translated sentences were then validated for appropriateness by native speakers. This text corpus was then used as the final dataset for recording one male and one female speaker. The male and female speaker was selected from a pool of 12 speakers (6 male and 6 female), who were asked to complete a reading task online. After they submitted the speech samples, the speakers were then evaluated by native speakers and given a score for their reading efficiency and pronunciation. Based on these scores, 3 male and 3 female speakers were shortlisted, and finally, from these 6 speakers, 1 male and 1 female speaker was selected after analyzing some voice quality features. The speakers, i.e., the voice artists, were instructed to record the sentences shown to them without any false starts, filled pauses, hiccups, or any other mistakes. All the recordings are done in a

[2]https://karya.in/

Data	Train	Val	Test
Avg. Sentence Length	8.48	8.57	8.44
Total Duration (in hours)	24.76	1.379	1.375
Male			
Num of Recordings	6302	350	350
Avg. Duration (in seconds)	3.85	3.80	3.88
Total Duration (in hours)	6.74	0.37	0.38
Female			
Num of Recordings	17,879	993	994
Avg. Duration (in seconds)	3.62	3.67	3.62
Total Duration (in hours)	18.02	1.01	0.998

Table 1: Dataset Metrics for the Mundari speech dataset.

studio-quality room with a microphone connected to the Karya crowdsourcing application for the convenience of collecting the data. The recordings' sampling rate is 44.1 KHz with 32 bits per sample.

Finally, the curated text used to collect recordings contains 15,656 unique sentences. The average sentence length in the collected text corpus is 8.4 words. Some duplication of sentences across speakers yields a total of 26,868 sentences and recordings in our final dataset. Around 74% of the recordings in our dataset feature a female speaker, while the remaining 26% are attributed to a male speaker. We notice that the female recordings are, on average, slightly shorter than male recordings – females' being 3.62 seconds compared to males' 3.85 seconds. We present more details in Table 1.

4 Experiments

4.1 Pre-Processing

The source sentences were normalized by collapsing repeated punctuations, exclamations, and spaces. Next, all kinds of brackets were removed and newline and tab characters were substituted with spaces. The `indic_nlp_library`[3] was used to further normalize the Devanagari text and appropriately space words with "matras". The dataset was split into train (95%), dev (5%), and test (5%) sets by stratifying on the number of speakers. The exact number of data points per split is available in Table 1.

4.2 Models

We train E2E TTS models using the `coqui-ai`[4] framework. These include a VITS model (Kim et al., 2021) trained from scratch, and a finetuned XTTS v2. Additionally, we also evaluated the zero-short performance of the pretrained XTTS v2 model and MMS-UNR Mundari model[5][6] from Facebook's Massively Multilingual Speech project (Pratap et al., 2023). Since the data curated is of very high-quality and sampled at 44.1KHz, we trained our VITS models with 44.1KHz data and standard 22.05KHz sub-sampled data. The latter was also used for finetuning the XTTS v2 model.

Here, we suggest the usage of single E2E models, as they are found to be significantly faster than two-stage models (Kim et al., 2021) and are optimal for deployment and efficient real-time usage.

4.3 Training Strategies

Both variants of the VITS models were trained with an elevated learning rate of $5e$-4 for the generator and discriminator, batch size of 128, and default ExponentialLR scheduler and AdamW (Loshchilov and Hutter, 2019) optimizer. As for the XTTS v2 finetuning, a significantly lower learning rate of $5e$-6 was used with a batch size of 256, and AdamW with a weight_decay of $1e$-2 was preferred as the optimizer along with a MultiStepLR Scheduler.

All our models were trained, and evaluated on a single A100 80GB GPU and were trained for 2500 epochs and converged within 5 days. A speaker-weighted sampler was also incorporated during the training/finetuning procedure to handle the speaker imbalance on our dataset. The models were checkpointed after every epoch based on the `loss_1` of the dev set and the best model checkpoint was used for evaluation.

5 Results and Discussions

5.1 Post-Processing

We use `ffmpeg` for rudimentary band-pass filtering and noise reduction on synthesized speech. To evaluate the XTTS v2 models, we provide one speaker reference audio from the dev set for conditioning and voice-cloning. Note that, the same reference audio was used for all the test examples for that speaker, and it was manually chosen to be a longer text and speech pair.

[3]`https://github.com/VarunGumma/indic_nlp_library`

[4]`https://github.com/coqui-ai/TTS`

[5]`https://huggingface.co/facebook/mms-tts-unr`

[6]To evaluate the MMS-UNR model, we transliterate our text from Devanagiri to Odia script using `indic_nlp_library`

Model	Full $n = 100$	Male $n = 26$	Female $n = 74$
gt-22k	4.62±0.68	4.59±0.65	4.63±0.69
gt-44k	4.58±0.70	4.47±0.79	4.62±0.66
mms	0.79 ± 1.02	0.79 ± 1.02	–
vits-22k‡	3.04 ± 1.29	2.65 ± 1.34	3.18 ± 1.25
vits-44k†	3.69 ± 1.18	3.39 ± 1.25	3.79 ± 1.13
xtts-finetuned	0.05 ± 0.30	0.13 ± 0.52	0.02 ± 0.16
xtts-pretrained	2.20 ± 1.32	2.10 ± 1.36	2.23 ± 1.31

Table 2: MOS values for ground truth and various models. The best and second-best scores are represented by † and ‡ respectively. (*gt* = ground truth)

5.2 Subjective Metrics

We use the Mean-Opinion-Score (MOS) as the subjective metric for which 100 data points are randomly subsampled from the test set (with speaker stratification). Audio samples generated by various models for this set were sent for human evaluations to native speakers. The task was set up on the Karya platform, and each sample was rated on a scale of 1 to 5 with 0.5 points increments. As discussed earlier, for low-resource languages it is often difficult to find raters for subjective evaluation of the speech samples. In our case, each sample is rated 5 annotators. Using these ratings, we calculate the MOS for the ground truth (both 22.05 KHz and 44.1 KHz) and various models. In total, there were 7 variations for each text sample. Each sample was rated independently, so different variations of a sample were not directly compared. Raters were instructed to use headphones and rate the naturalness of the speech, considering factors such as prosody, intonation, and overall fluency. Detailed instructions are shown in Figure 1. Table 2 shows a comparison of the MOS values for the ground truth and the various models. We can see that the VITS-44K model performs the closest to ground truth. We also noticed a huge gap between the VITS model and the other models we studied. Interestingly, the MOS values for XTTS v2 became much worse on finetuning than using it in a zero-shot setup.

5.3 Objective Metrics

Mel-Cepstral Distortion (MCD) (Kubichek, 1993) is an objective measure used to quantify the difference between two sets of Mel-frequency cepstral coefficients and is useful in evaluating the performance of speech synthesis systems as it provides a numerical indication of how closely the synthesized speech matches the target or reference speech

Model	Full $n = 1344$	Male $n = 350$	Female $n = 996$
mms	15.13±4.19	15.13±4.19	–
vits-22k‡	9.45±3.71	10.03±4.05	9.24±3.56
vits-44k†	7.60±3.99	7.27±3.08	7.72±4.25
xtts-finetuned	13.65±5.92	10.73±5.33	14.69±5.77
xtts-pretrained	15.80±7.03	13.89±5.87	16.48±7.27

Table 3: MCD scores. The best and second-best scores are represented by † and ‡ respectively.

in terms of spectral characteristics.

For all the models, we compute the MCD scores with dynamic-time wrapping and weighted by speech length with respect to the ground truth subsampled to the sampling rate of the generated speech, if required. We present those in Table 3. Similar to the MOS scores, VITS-44K achieves the lowest error, followed by VITS-22K. Despite XTTS v2 employing speaker conditioning, the scores the significantly worse compared to the best model, VITS-44K.

XTTS v2 does not natively support Mundari but is pretrained with Hindi, which shares the same characters and pronunciations. Spot-checking some of the audios of the models revealed that the vanilla pretrained XTTS v2 had long pauses between words and made it sound unnatural. However, it captured the intonation and pronunciation well due to its voice-cloning capabilities. The process of finetuning the model resulted in a notable degradation in performance, leading to the generation of nonsensical outputs despite successful convergence. This might due to the catastrophic forgetting induced by the finetuning. We also observed that XTTS v2, which is based on GPT2 (Radford et al., 2019), generated phantom speech in many cases similar to hallucinations in Large Language Models. This phenomenon manifested as the introduction of random Hindi words and gibberish towards the end of the sentence.

6 Conclusion

In this work, we develop a TTS system for a low-resource language, Mundari, a low-resource language spoken by $\approx$ 1M people in India. We also analyze existing models for this language and evaluate popular multilingual and multi-speaker models by finetuning them. We show that the VITS-44K model achieves a mean MOS score of 3.69 and is evaluated as the best among the ones compared by native speakers. We release our model publicly and

You are given a piece of text in Mundari with its corresponding audio recording. **Your task is to evaluate the naturalness of synthesized speech.** Rate each speech sample on a scale of 1 to 5.

Instructions:

1. **Rating Scale:**
   - **1:** Bad
   - **2:** Fair
   - **3:** Good
   - **4:** Excellent
   - **5:** Outstanding
2. **Task:**
   - Listen to each speech sample carefully.
   - Focus on the **naturalness** of the speech, considering factors such as prosody, intonation, and overall fluency.
3. **Rating Process:**
   - Assign a rating to each sample based on your perception of naturalness.
   - Utilize the entire scale, including the 0.5 increments, to provide a nuanced assessment.
4. **Listening Conditions:**
   - Use headphones for a more accurate assessment.
   - Ensure a quiet environment to minimize external disturbances.

Figure 1: MOS guidelines provided to the annotators.

hope this research further promotes the development of speech systems for endangered and low-resource languages, aiding in bridging the digital divide in India.

7 Limitations

- Our primary emphasis in this study centers on E2E TTS, deliberately excluding the consideration of combinations involving Acoustic models and Vocoders, as observed in prior works (EkStep Foundation, 2021; Prakash and Murthy, 2020; Kumar et al., 2023). The motivation behind this choice is the intention to construct a simple unified system for speech synthesis, designed for straightforward deployment and ease of use by the general public.

- We explicitly recognize the inherent bias in the speaker distribution employed for our study. The challenge of recruiting native proficient speakers, capable of dedicating extended hours and effort to the recording process, contributed to a noticeable synthesis disparity, particularly evident in the diminished quality of male speech synthesis outputs.

8 Ethical Considerations

We use the framework by Bender and Friedman (2018) to discuss the ethical considerations for our work.

- **Institutional Review:** All aspects of this research were reviewed and approved by Karya.

- **Data:** Our data is collected in multiple steps as described in section 3. We first source the Hindi sentences and manually translate them to Mundari. Specific guidelines for translations were provided. These Mundari sentences were then recorded in a studio by 2 speakers.

- **Speaker Demographic:** We recruited 2 speakers to record the audio. Their payment was set after deliberation and contracts were signed. Speakers were paid INR 8 per recording. The average duration of a sample is $\approx$ 3.7 seconds.

- **Annotator Demographics:** Annotators for MOS rating were recruited through an external annotator services company. All annotators were native speakers of the language. The pay was INR 2 per sample, with an average sample length of $\approx$ 3.7 seconds.

- **Annotation Guidelines:** We draw inspiration from the community standards set for similar tasks. These guidelines were created following best practices after careful research. Annotators were asked to rate the speech samples on naturalness. A detailed explanation was given for the task. Annotator's identity was hidden from the authors to limit any bias.

- **Methods:** In this study, using our Mundari speech dataset, we trained 2 models: VITS-22K and VITS-44K, and finetuned the XTTS v2 model. We release the models for the benefit of the Mundari and the research community.

9 Acknowledgements

We sincerely thank the voice artists, Roshan and Meenakshi, for lending us their voices to create the speech dataset. We also extend our gratitude to Prof. Bornini Lahiri and Prof. Dripta Piplai from IIT Kharagpur for their advice on data collection and processing. Finally, we thank Praveen SV (Ph.D. Student, IIT Madras) and Gokul Karthik (MLE, Technology Innovation Institute) for their walk-throughs of IndicTTS[7] and Coqui.

References

India Census 2011. Archived from the original on 6 March 2021. Statement 1: Abstract of speakers' strength of languages and mother tongues – 2011. Office of the Registrar General & Census Commissioner, India.

Kalika Bali, Monojit Choudhury, Sunayana Sitaram, and Vivek Seshadri. 2019. Ellora: Enabling low resource languages with technology. In *Proceedings of the 1st International Conference on Language Technologies for All*, pages 160–163, Paris, France. European Language Resources Association (ELRA).

Emily M. Bender and Batya Friedman. 2018. Data statements for natural language processing: Toward mitigating system bias and enabling better science. *Transactions of the Association for Computational Linguistics*, 6:587–604.

Coqui. 2023. XTTS Models - Coqui Documentation. Accessed: 2023-12-14.

Harshita Diddee, Kalika Bali, Monojit Choudhury, and Namrata Mukhija. 2022. The six conundrums of building and deploying language technologies for social good. In *Proceedings of the 5th ACM SIGCAS/SIGCHI Conference on Computing and Sustainable Societies*, COMPASS '22, page 12–19, New York, NY, USA. Association for Computing Machinery.

EkStep Foundation. 2021. Vakyansh: Open source speech recognition. Accessed: 2023-12-14.

Jay Gala, Pranjal A Chitale, A K Raghavan, Varun Gumma, Sumanth Doddapaneni, Aswanth Kumar M, Janki Atul Nawale, Anupama Sujatha, Ratish Puduppully, Vivek Raghavan, Pratyush Kumar, Mitesh M Khapra, Raj Dabre, and Anoop Kunchukuttan. 2023. Indictrans2: Towards high-quality and accessible machine translation models for all 22 scheduled indian languages. *Transactions on Machine Learning Research*.

Ian Goodfellow, Jean Pouget-Abadie, Mehdi Mirza, Bing Xu, David Warde-Farley, Sherjil Ozair, Aaron Courville, and Yoshua Bengio. 2014. Generative adversarial nets. In *Advances in Neural Information Processing Systems*, volume 27. Curran Associates, Inc.

Jaehyeon Kim, Jungil Kong, and Juhee Son. 2021. Conditional variational autoencoder with adversarial learning for end-to-end text-to-speech. In *Proceedings of the 38th International Conference on Machine Learning*, volume 139 of *Proceedings of Machine Learning Research*, pages 5530–5540. PMLR.

Diederik P. Kingma and Max Welling. 2019.

R. Kubichek. 1993. Mel-cepstral distance measure for objective speech quality assessment. In *Proceedings of IEEE Pacific Rim Conference on Communications Computers and Signal Processing*, volume 1, pages 125–128 vol.1.

Gokul Karthik Kumar, Praveen S V, Pratyush Kumar, Mitesh M. Khapra, and Karthik Nandakumar. 2023. Towards building text-to-speech systems for the next billion users. In *ICASSP 2023 - 2023 IEEE International Conference on Acoustics, Speech and Signal Processing (ICASSP)*, pages 1–5.

Michael Kwan. 2022. On the edge: Critically endangered languages in top countries. Taken from: UNESCO Atlas of the world's languages in danger 2010.

Ilya Loshchilov and Frank Hutter. 2019. Decoupled weight decay regularization. In *International Conference on Learning Representations*.

Aidan Pine, Dan Wells, Nathan Brinklow, Patrick Littell, and Korin Richmond. 2022. Requirements and motivations of low-resource speech synthesis for language revitalization. In *Proceedings of the 60th Annual Meeting of the Association for Computational Linguistics (Volume 1: Long Papers)*, pages 7346–7359, Dublin, Ireland. Association for Computational Linguistics.

Anusha Prakash, Anju Leela Thomas, S. Umesh, and Hema A Murthy. 2019. Building Multilingual End-to-End Speech Synthesisers for Indian Languages. In *Proc. 10th ISCA Workshop on Speech Synthesis (SSW 10)*, pages 194–199.

Anusha Prakash and Hema A. Murthy. 2020. Generic Indic Text-to-Speech Synthesisers with Rapid Adaptation in an End-to-End Framework. In *Proc. Interspeech 2020*, pages 2962–2966.

Anusha Prakash and Hema A. Murthy. 2023. Exploring the role of language families for building indic speech synthesisers. *IEEE/ACM Transactions on Audio, Speech, and Language Processing*, 31:734–747.

[7]https://github.com/AI4Bharat/Indic-TTS

Vineel Pratap, Andros Tjandra, Bowen Shi, Paden Tomasello, Arun Babu, Sayani Kundu, Ali Elkahky, Zhaoheng Ni, Apoorv Vyas, Maryam Fazel-Zarandi, Alexei Baevski, Yossi Adi, Xiaohui Zhang, Wei-Ning Hsu, Alexis Conneau, and Michael Auli. 2023. Scaling speech technology to 1,000+ languages. *arXiv*.

Alec Radford, Jeff Wu, Rewon Child, David Luan, Dario Amodei, and Ilya Sutskever. 2019. Language models are unsupervised multitask learners.

Yi Ren, Chenxu Hu, Xu Tan, Tao Qin, Sheng Zhao, Zhou Zhao, and Tie-Yan Liu. 2021. Fastspeech 2: Fast and high-quality end-to-end text to speech. In *International Conference on Learning Representations*.

Yi Ren, Yangjun Ruan, Xu Tan, Tao Qin, Sheng Zhao, Zhou Zhao, and Tie-Yan Liu. 2019. Fastspeech: Fast, robust and controllable text to speech. In *Advances in Neural Information Processing Systems*, volume 32. Curran Associates, Inc.

Jonathan Shen, Ruoming Pang, Ron J. Weiss, Mike Schuster, Navdeep Jaitly, Zongheng Yang, Zhifeng Chen, Yu Zhang, Yuxuan Wang, Rj Skerrv-Ryan, Rif A. Saurous, Yannis Agiomvrgiannakis, and Yonghui Wu. 2018. Natural tts synthesis by conditioning wavenet on mel spectrogram predictions. In *2018 IEEE International Conference on Acoustics, Speech and Signal Processing (ICASSP)*, pages 4779–4783.

Xu Tan, Tao Qin, Frank Soong, and Tie-Yan Liu. 2021. A survey on neural speech synthesis.

Aaron van den Oord, Sander Dieleman, Heiga Zen, Karen Simonyan, Oriol Vinyals, Alex Graves, Nal Kalchbrenner, Andrew Senior, and Koray Kavukcuoglu. 2016. Wavenet: A generative model for raw audio.

Yuxuan Wang, R.J. Skerry-Ryan, Daisy Stanton, Yonghui Wu, Ron J. Weiss, Navdeep Jaitly, Zongheng Yang, Ying Xiao, Zhifeng Chen, Samy Bengio, Quoc Le, Yannis Agiomyrgiannakis, Rob Clark, and Rif A. Saurous. 2017. Tacotron: Towards End-to-End Speech Synthesis. In *Proc. Interspeech 2017*, pages 4006–4010.

Ryuichi Yamamoto, Eunwoo Song, and Jae-Min Kim. 2020. Parallel wavegan: A fast waveform generation model based on generative adversarial networks with multi-resolution spectrogram. In *ICASSP 2020 - 2020 IEEE International Conference on Acoustics, Speech and Signal Processing (ICASSP)*, pages 6199–6203.

End-to-End Speech Recognition for Endangered Languages of Nepal

Marieke Meelen
University of Cambridge
Cambridge, UK
mm986@cam.ac.uk

Alexander O'Neill
SOAS, University of London
London, UK
ao34@soas.ac.uk

Rolando Coto-Solano
Dartmouth College
New Hampshire, United States
rolando.a.coto.solano@dartmouth.edu

Abstract

This paper presents three experiments to test the most effective and efficient ASR pipeline to facilitate the documentation and preservation of endangered languages, which are often extremely low-resourced. With data from two languages in Nepal —Dzardzongke and Newar— we show that model improvements are different for different masses of data, and that transfer learning as well as a range of modifications (e.g. normalising amplitude and pitch) can be effective, but that a consistently-standardised orthography as NLP input and post-training dictionary corrections improve results even more.

1 Introduction

Of the 120+ distinct languages identified in the 2011 Nepali census, at least 60 are endangered due to socio-political unrest, globalisation and environmental challenges. The 2015 earthquake and the global pandemic have had devastating effects on the tourist industry, which formed the major source of income for the country. Long-lasting consequences include the increased migration away from the rural areas where many endangered languages are spoken towards Kathmandu and other areas where the Nepali language is dominant, as well as international destinations for education and employment. The loss of these languages also means the loss of unique cultural and religious identifiers. Given this, there is a clear need for methods and tools to preserve linguistic and cultural diversity.

A well-known challenge in language preservation, however, is the transcription bottleneck (Shi et al., 2021): transcribing one minute of audio requires at least an average of 40+ minutes (Durantin et al., 2017). The transcription process is furthermore severely hindered by the fact that many endangered languages do not have written traditions or standardised orthographies. While advanced automatic speech-recognition (ASR) tools are available, they are often ineffective for these extremely low-resource languages (Foley et al., 2018), due to the lack of good-quality training data.

In this paper we present results from three experiments aimed at creating ASR models for the endangered languages of Nepal: (a) Training models for two extremely low-resourced languages, Dzardzongke (South Mustang Tibetan) and Kathmandu Valley Newar, (b) testing the effectiveness of transfer learning for Dzardzongke from the related Standard Tibetan language, and (c) testing other techniques that are useful to enhance low-resource ASR such as sound and output manipulation, to measure their effectiveness on datasets of different sizes.

1.1 Languages

Dzardzongke or South Mustang Tibetan (SMT) is a severely endangered language spoken by maximum ca. 1200 people in a small number of villages in Mustang, Nepal. Most speakers of Dzardzongke are fluent in Nepali and Seke as well, and Dzardzongke is not used in writing or education, putting it in a very precarious situation. The difficult socio-economic situation in the aftermath of the 2015 earthquake and global pandemic is having a disastrous effect on the local language and unique pre-Buddhist Bon cultural tradition.

Newar, or Nepāl Bhāṣā, is a "definitely endangered" language (Moseley, 2010), with about 846,557 native speakers out of a population of about 1,321,933 ethnic Newars (Central Bureau of Statistics (Nepal), 2012). Newars live in 63 of the 77 districts of Nepal but are the indigenous inhabitants of the Kathmandu Valley, where they are centred and now make up a sizeable minority (Kansakar, 1999). While ethnic Newars mostly use Newar amongst themselves and in private, al-

Proceedings of the The Seventh Workshop on the Use of Computational Methods in the Study of Endangered Languages, pages 83–93

most all Newars use Nepali in public domains (Kansakar et al., 2011). Newar has been grouped into five geographical groupings, each including various dialects (Shakya, 2019). Our work in this paper utilised recordings from Lalitpur, Kritipur, and Kathmandu Newar, which, while they belong to the same geographical grouping (Kathmandu Valley Newar), are distinct dialects. In addition, we utilised historical recordings from Bhaktapur, which is from a distinct geographical grouping.

Speakers of both Dzardzongke and Newar are keen to preserve their language and cultural traditions and would therefore greatly benefit from the development of tools that can facilitate this preservation.

1.2 ASR for Low-Resource Languages

As mentioned in the previous section, the problem of the transcription bottleneck presents serious issues to language documentation. The ASR technology to perform this task is not new (Besacier et al., 2014), but it traditionally only achieved good results on large corpora. Recent years have seen work on end-to-end transcription of low-resource languages (Prud'hommeaux et al., 2021; Coto-Solano et al., 2022). These are made possible by the emergence of models that are pre-trained with acoustic data from other languages. These offer a robust acoustic model from their previous knowledge of multiple high-resource languages. Presently there is work beyond the high-resource languages, bootstrapping available data from low-resource languages to enhance both the acoustics and the textual output. Some techniques involve training with data from text-to-speech systems (Bartelds et al., 2023), and augmenting the data with other written sources such as dictionaries and word lists (Hjortnaes et al., 2020; Arkhangelskiy, 2021), as well as manipulating the transcription of the input (Coto-Solano, 2021).

One way to leverage data from other languages is to apply transfer learning. Transfer learning is a technique that uses knowledge from one language to improve the results of another with lower resources. It is a common technique in NLP fields like Machine Translation, where the model is trained on high-resource languages, and it is then fine-tuned on languages with fewer resources (Zoph et al., 2016; Kocmi and Bojar, 2018). This approach is useful when there are similarities between the source and target languages, be they genetic, typological or orthographic. Usually, a greater overlap in vocabulary between the high and low-resource languages leads to higher gains (Nguyen and Chiang, 2017; Dabre et al., 2017). However, this overlap is not necessary for models to benefit from transfer learning. In the case of ASR, models can pre-train on data from languages that are unrelated to the target, and even then the acoustic model section will see gains in performance (Bansal et al., 2019).

There are simple transformations that can help the model learn from the data. For example, researchers have found that manipulating acoustic characteristics like amplitude (Mitra et al., 2012) and pitch (Yadav and Pradhan, 2021) can lead to lower error rates.

2 Methodology

In this section we discuss our data collection and ASR pipeline, followed by a description of our experiments.

2.1 Data collection

The data for Dzardzongke was collected in August 2022 in a range of villages in Mustang.[1] We collected over 20 hours of interviews, conversations, as well as descriptions of rituals, traditional activities, and, finally read narratives in controlled environments. 251 minutes (4 hrs 11 minutes) are fully transcribed; over half of which containing read narratives by one near-native male speaker and the rest a mixture of conversational data from native speakers (2 male; 1 female, all 55+ years old). As Dzardzongke does not have any written history, we developed an orthography in collaboration with the local community. Unlike Standard Tibetan, this is a romanised script, which is not only more intuitive for native speakers who never learnt to read Tibetan, but also much more suited to the phonotactics of the language, yielding a straightforward mapping of sounds to graphemes. This enhances results of ASR models based on Wav2Vec2, as many of the languages in the pre-training set are written using the Roman alphabet. In total, the transcriptions contain 32,598 words in 5498 utterances, for an average of 5.9 words per utterance. There are 4664 unique words in the Dzardzongke transcriptions. The utterances are an average of 2.7 seconds long.

[1]All Dzardzongke audio-visual materials are available on ELAR `http://hdl.handle.net/2196/70707494-ag7d-4hf2-ag77-fe21` (Meelen and Ramble, 2023).

The data for Newar comes from a combination of sources. 86 minutes of Kathmandu Newar were recorded in 2019 in a diaspora setting using read materials, the texts of which were later adapted for use with ASR.[2] 30 minutes of Bhaktapur Newar were used from historical recordings provided on a CC license by the CNRS's Pangloss project (Michailovsky and Sharma, 1968). The remaining data was collected in Nepal during fieldwork from August to November 2022. We collected 10 hours and 25 minutes of interviews, speeches, and spontaneous conversation, of which 185 minutes were fully transcribed and adapted for use with ASR. These were transcribed using the romanised IAST transliteration, which allows for one-to-one representation of and conversion to Devanagari, the script used for contemporary Newar. In addition to using data from four distinct dialects, this dataset includes data from two female speakers from Bhaktapur, yielding a combined total of 294 minutes (4 hrs 54 minutes) of transcribed data. The transcriptions contain 38,360 words in 4815 utterances, for an average of 8.0 words per utterance. The recordings are an average of 3.7 seconds long (1 second longer than our Dzardzongke recordings). There are 8038 unique words in the Newar transcriptions. Together, these factors mean that our Newar data would be a more significant challenge for training an ASR model.

2.2 ASR Training

We used Wav2Vec2 (Baevski et al., 2020) to train the models. First, we trained separate models for each language. We used different time partitions to measure the progress of the word error rate (WER) and the character error rate (CER) as the volume of data increases. We believe that these results could be valuable to other researchers in the area of extremely low-resource ASR, as they would give them an approximate idea how much data they would need to get the results they are aiming for. For both languages we randomly selected files until we reached partitions of [5, 10, 15, 30, 45, 60, 90, 120, 180] minutes. For Dzardzongke we also used a model trained on 251 minutes, the maximum amount of data available. For Newar, we also trained models of 240 and 294 minutes, the last one of which included all of the data available. For each of these, we randomly shuffled the dataset and distributed the available files into train/valid/test splits of 80%, 10%, 10%. We repeated this procedure ten times for the models without any input or output modifications. We trained on each of these and then retrieved the resulting model with the lowest WER validation values from the earliest possible checkpoint before overfitting. This model was then used to get the median CER and WER from the test set. The charts and tables below report the average values of the median over the 10 repetitions.

Wav2Vec2 uses multilingual quantisation to get better performance when transcribing sounds, and these might be to our advantage. The models presented here are "monolingual" in that the fine-tuning was done on only one of the languages (Dzardzongke or Newar), but the models are initialised from the highly multilingual XLSR-wav2vec2 base model, which includes data from 128 different languages. We used the instantiation in the Hugging Face (2024) libraries with their default parameters.[3]

2.3 Transfer Learning

Since Dzardzongke is related to Standard Spoken Tibetan, and the latter has a large amount of training data and an ASR model available, it is worth exploring the option of transfer learning from the higher-resourced language to the lower-resourced one. Although there are some distinct differences in vocabulary and morphosyntax, Standard Tibetan phonology is very similar to Dzardzongke. Unlike Dzardzongke, Standard Tibetan is widely spoken, not just in Tibet, but mainly in the Tibetan diaspora communities all over the world.

For the transfer-learning experiments, we trained our own small Standard Tibetan model based on 7 hours of training data, and also used a ready-made model based on 550 hours of training data, made available by OpenPecha.[4] Both models were later fine-tuned in the same way, by converting the Tibetan Unicode to Dzardzongke Romanised script output. These Standard Tibetan datasets contain a large variety of recordings, ranging from conversational data from media outlets (both TV and radio mainly based in Dharamsala, India) to Tibetan audiobooks and speeches from members of the Tibetan community.

[2]This is freely available on Zenodo https://zenodo.org/records/10611827.

[3]The hyperparameters, as well as the best performing models, can be downloaded from http://github.com/rolandocoto/nepali-asr.

[4]https://huggingface.co/datasets/openpecha/tibetan-voice-550

The test procedure is very similar to the one for the monolingual ASR models described above. We randomly selected audio files and put them in time partitions of [5, 10, 15, 30, 45, 60, 90, 120, 180, 251] minutes for Dzardzongke, and [5, 10, 15, 30, 45, 60, 90, 120, 180, 240, 294] minutes for Newar. We made five samplings for each of these time points (where we randomly selected from the entire pool of files for each language), and split them into 80%, 10% and 10% for the train/valid/test sets. From each training run we extracted the median CER and WER values for the best-performing model and calculated the average across the five different runs.

Standard Tibetan is written in a different script, however. Therefore, we also developed conversion rules to change the Standard Tibetan script to the newly-developed romanised Dzardzongke orthography. Since Newar is linguistically much further removed from Tibetan and there were no other datasets available for languages closer to Newar, we limited the transfer-learning experiments to Dzardzongke only for now.

2.4 Signal and output transformations

We performed several manipulations of the input wave files and the output transcriptions to improve our results.

Three of them included modifying the acoustic properties of the input audio files. In one subexperiment we normalised the amplitude (Mitra et al., 2012). We modified the audio files so that their peak would correspond to 70dB. These were then used to train a new monolingual model for each of the languages. The second modification was normalising the pitch, which has been observed to help with ASR in some populations, for example children (Shahnawazuddin et al., 2017). We changed the median pitch of all of the wave files to 151Hz. These new recordings were used to make another, separate model, so that we could compare these modifications to the performance with the unmodified wave files. For the third modification we included noise (Braun and Gamper, 2022), in particular pink noise, at a volume of 45dB. Pink noise has a more realistic and irregular distribution, compared to other types of synthetic noise, and could potentially make the system more robust in learning human speech. All of these modifications were carried out using the algorithms in the *Praat Vocal Toolkit* (Corretge, 2012).

The evaluation for these was performed in a similar way to the experiments above. Therefore, the results between the "no modification" condition and modifications are directly comparable. The error reporting is identical to the experiments above (average of the median WER and CER for all available test sets).

The final modification was the 'Dictionary word correction' performed on the output. When dealing with low-resource languages many non-words can be produced, which can ultimately undermine readability. In order to compensate for this, we introduced a series of simple modifications to the output. We used Norvig's (2021) unigram statistical spelling corrector but introduced one modification: if (i) the source and the ASR hypothesis transcription have the same number of words, and (ii) the word in source_i is not the same as the word in hypothesis_i, then we will assume that the word hypothesis_i is a spelling mistake and it will be changed to a different, existing word. This is meant to minimise the disruption on the output that standard statistical spell checking can introduce. We used the random shuffles from the monolingual models in section 2.2 and corrected their outputs here to make the spell checking results directly comparable to the "no modification" results.

3 Results

3.1 ASR Training

Table 1 shows the results of training monolingual models for each of the languages, when the models are trained for 30, 60 and 120 minutes of data. It also shows the models trained with the maximum amount of data for each language. Dzardzongke data achieved lower error rates despite having less data: WER=34 for 251 minutes, compared to WER=50 for the 294 minutes of Newar.

As Figure 1 shows, the character error rates drops relatively rapidly as the volume of data increases. The error for models trained on 5 minutes of data is CER=25 for Dzardzongke and CER=38 for Newar. Models trained on 60 minutes of data have half of this error (CER=11 for Dzardzongke and CER=18 for Newar), and subsequent models have smaller reductions: CER=8 and CER=12 for Dzardzongke and Newar respectively when training on all available data. The WER also follows a similar pattern, albeit with a slower reduction. When trained on 5 minutes, the Dzardzongke models have an average of WER=70, and the Newar

		CER				WER			
		30	60	120	Max	30	60	120	Max
Dzardzongke	No recording or output modifications	13	11	9	8	50	44	38	34
	Transfer from Tibetan (7 hrs)	13	10	8	**7**	50	42	35	33
	Transfer from Tibetan (550 hrs)	12	9	8	**7**	49	39	35	33
Dzardzongke	Normalise amplitude	11	9	8	**7**	48	41	37	33
	Normalise pitch	13	10	9	**7**	52	43	39	33
	Pink noise	14	13	9	8	50	46	43	33
	Word correction	14	11	9	8	46	41	34	**32**
Newar	No recording or output modifications	25	18	16	**12**	74	63	59	**50**
	Normalise amplitude	19	16	16	**12**	64	57	54	**50**
	Normalise pitch	22	17	18	14	67	67	60	**50**
	Pink noise	20	17	16	13	67	67	57	**50**
	Word correction	40	20	17	14	77	61	55	**50**

Table 1: Average error rates for ASR models of Dzardzongke (max 251 mins) and Newar (max 294 mins).

models WER=94. Models trained on 60 minutes have approximately 65% of the error (WER=44 and WER=63). The errors are halved by the time the models are trained with all the available data (WER=34 for Dzardzongke and WER=50 for Newar).

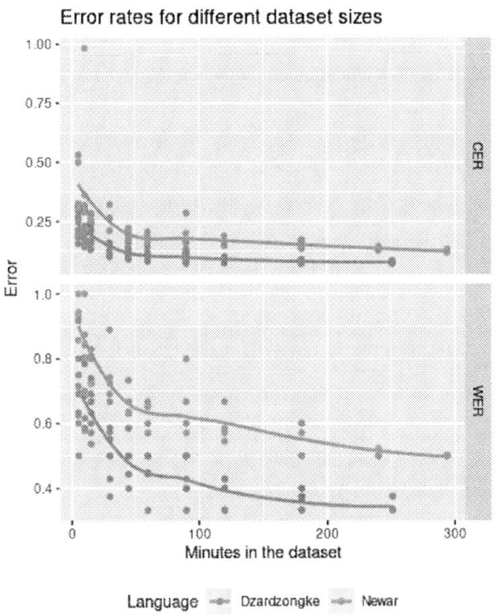

Figure 1: Character and word error rates for ASR training in Dzardzongke and Newar, by the minutes in the combined train-eval-test sets.

It is noteworthy that there is a wider gap between the languages in the word error rate. When using all available data the difference in character error between the two languages is ΔCER=4, but the difference in word error rate is ΔWER=16. This might be because of the architecture of Wav2Vec2. Given that it uses quantisation based on phones from numerous languages, it has more information about the sounds of human languages in a straightforward romanised representation, which is closer to the orthography that was developed especially for Dzardzongke than the non-standardised transcriptions found in the diverse Newar varieties.

3.2 Transfer Learning results

Table 1 also shows the performance of the transfer learning experiments, where Standard Tibetan models were used as a basis to enhance the results for the related Dzardzongke language. When trained on all available data, there is only a small gain: the WER is reduced by one unit for both of the transfer models (WER=34 for no transfer; WER=33 for 7 or 550 hours of Tibetan). The CER is also reduced by one (CER=8 for no transfer; CER=7 for 7 or 550 hours of Tibetan).

Figure 2 shows the difference in error rates when trained with different amounts of data. The gains from transfer learning are greater when the model has fewer minutes of the target language available. For example, when training on 60 minutes of data, the model transferring from 550 hours of Tibetan has a WER=39, 5 units lower than the WER for the model without transfer (WER=44). The model transferring from 7 hours of Tibetan has more modest gains (ΔWER=2 points; WER=42), but it also improves results. Even when you only have two hours of data the gains are still present: the transfer models had WER=35 compared to WER=38 without transfer. As mentioned above, these gains begin to disappear as the data in the target language increases.

3.3 Signal and output transformations

The second and third sections of Table 1 show the average results for the signal and output transformations performed on the Dzardzongke and Newar

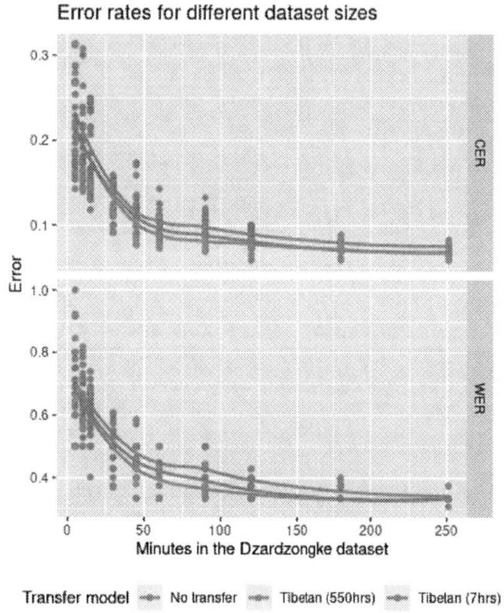

Figure 2: Transfer learning from two Tibetan models.

models. When training on all the data, applying the word correction to the output of the Dzardzongke monolingual (i.e. non-transfer-learning) model provides improvements in word error rate (WER=32). As for CER, normalising the amplitude and the pitch provided a small improvement for Dzardzongke (WER=7, compared to WER=8 without modifications). None of the modifications improved the results of the Newar model trained with all its data; they all reached a WER=50, and normalising the amplitude produced the same CER results as making no modifications (CER=12).

Figure 3 shows the result of the transformations done on datasets of different sizes. In the case of Dzardzongke, there is virtually no difference between the conditions when it comes to CER performance. Normalising the amplitude produces gains of approximately ΔCER=2 (e.g. at 30 and 60 minutes of total data), but normalising the pitch does not lead to improvements. Adding (pink) background noise and correcting the words can make the CER worse.

Some of the modifications do have a positive impact on the WER of Dzardzongke. For example, applying the word corrections to the 30 minute datasets improves the results by ΔWER=4 (46, compared to WER=50 for the non-corrected version). These gains diminish as data increases, but they are still present. When the dataset has 60 minutes, the gain is ΔWER=3 (41, compared to WER=44 for non-corrected), and when the dataset has 2 hours of audio, the gain is ΔWER=4 (34, compared to WER=38 for non-corrected). Normalising the amplitude also produced improvements (e.g. ΔWER=1∼2), but normalising the pitch and adding noise can produce increases in error rates.

The modifications produce more improvements in the Newar data. As for the CER, all the modifications of the audio improved the error rates to some degree, with normalisation in amplitude being the one that reduced the error the most (ΔWER=2∼6). Normalising the amplitude also produced gains in the WER. When training on 30 minutes, there was a gain of ΔWER=10 (64, compared to 74 for non-modified audio). The improvements from amplitude normalisation became smaller when training on 60 minutes (ΔWER=6) and on two hours of data (ΔWER=5), and they finally disappear when training on the maximum amount of data. Adding pink noise also leads to some improvements (ΔCER=0∼5, ΔWER=2∼7), but normalising the pitch can lead to increases in error rates. Unlike Dzardzongke, applying word corrections does not consistently improve the CER and WER of Newar. When training on 30 minutes of data, the error increases (ΔCER=-15, ΔWER=-3), but when training on 60 and 90 minutes of data, there are some improvements in the WER (ΔWER=2∼4), but not in the CER (ΔCER=-1∼-3).

In summary, normalising the amplitude of the signal seems to uniformly decrease the error rates, while applying word corrections can lead to WER reduction for Dzardzongke in particular.

3.4 Transcription results

The first part of Table 2 shows four transcription results for Dzardzongke. Example (1) contains a number of phonetic difficulties, like the similarity between the velar and palatal nasal in front of high vowels (*nyí* vs *ngi*) and the difference between high and low tone (indicated by an acute accent, e.g. *léparak* vs *leparak*). Finally, it shows that rare personal names can be difficult to transcribe. These difficulties can be remedied by adding more monolingual data, as shown by the improved error rates comparing the 5 vs 251 min models (ΔCER=4; ΔWER=24). Example (2) shows similar improvements in a more challenging utterance from a conversation in a noisy environment, whose WER can be improved even further using the spell checking on the output. This does not work for the highly

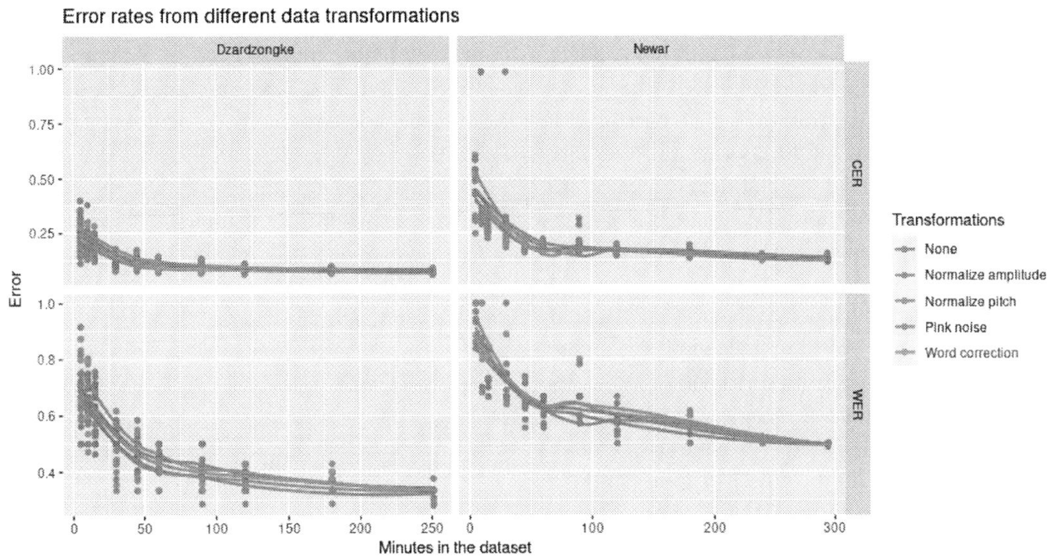

Figure 3: Transformations of input and output of Dzardzongke and Newar models.

	Dzardzongke controlled near-native narrative		
1. [smt-041-296]	"When 2 (more) came, Ódrong-Gepo arrived at the end"		
Target transcription	*nyí ongna ódrong gepo katsa ru dzangi léparak*	CER	WER
5 mins	*ngi o nga odrong gepo katsa ru dzangi leparak*	13	62
251 mins	*nyi onga ódrong gepo katsa ru dzangi leparak*	**7**	**38**
	Dzardzongke native conversation in noisy environment		
2. [smt-005-896]	"Then all of a sudden, having gone outside,"		
Target transcription	*da japtsowe phita la sori*	CER	WER
5 mins	*ta jzapdi phital sori óo*	48	100
251 mins	*da zaptsi phitala sori*	**20**	60
251 mins + Dict	*da lapti phita sori*	32	**40**
	Dzardzongke very bad CER and WER		
3. [smt-005-587]	"...the girl I like ..."		
Target transcription	*... ngi sempa ... theken bomo*	CER	WER
251 mins + transfer	*de sempi ta nyikure nyi sempa te bomo*	110	150
	Dzardzongke very good CER and WER		
4. [smt-037-390]	"Look, I only have 150 rupees at the moment"	CER	WER
251 mins + transfer	*nga la danda ale gya dang ngápcu mana me* = target	**0**	**0**
	Lalitpur Newar		
5. [ltp-016-2526]	"...a preacher of the Dharma..."		
Target	*dharmabhānaka*	CER	WER
294 mins	*dharma bhānaka*	8	200
	Kritipur Newar		
6. [VM-VM2-157]	"First of all,"		
Target	*dakale nhāpā*	CER	WER
294 mins	*dakal nhāpāṃ*	17	100
294 mins + Dict	*dakale nhāpāṃ*	**8**	**50**
	Bhaktapur Newar very bad CER and WER		
7. [HD-HD-260]	"Now, that's not the case. You..."		
Target	*āḥ thva athe makhu chiṃ*	CER	WER
294 mins	*aāmaka thvāṅā ānikāṃ thātheyake naypiṃ yaṅ āḥ thaḥre makhu chiṃ*	178	160
	Lalitpur Newar very good CER and WER		
8. [ltp-016-3930]	"You deigned to say to me, 'O son of good family,..."'	CER	WER
294 mins	*vasapolapiṃsaṃ jita dhayā bijyāta he kulaputra* = target	**0**	**0**

Table 2: ASR results from various experiments for Dzardzongke and different varieties of Newar

infrequent *japtsowe* 'all of a sudden', whose orthography exceptionally differs significantly from pronunciation [japtsi] (almost captured by the model).

Finally, (3) and (4) respectively show representative examples of very bad and very good transcriptions. The wave file for example (3) actually contains noise at the start and middle of the utterance, leading to the ellipsis for missed words in the target transcription (which were automatically filtered out as punctuation during training). The best Dzardzongke model (max + 550 hrs transfer) actually does a very reasonable job, but the error rates are very high due to the incomplete original transcription. To improve overall results, utterances with incomplete transcriptions due to noise etc. should therefore be filtered out before the training to avoid skewing the overall error rates. Example (4) on the other hand is from a narrative in a controlled, quiet environment and is one of many such examples for which the best model yields perfect transcriptions. Although many of these zero-error transcriptions come from these narrative, controlled recordings, the model is already robust enough to generalise beyond this one speaker as shown by results from the noisy, conversational recordings like (2).

Table 2 also highlights the success and difficulty we encountered with Newar and some examples of why our WER is misleading when evaluating this model's quality. Example (5), for instance, whose target was *dharmabhānaka* was recognised as *dharma bhānaka*. While the CER=8 was good, it had an extra word than the source, resulting in WER=200. However, inconsistent spacing in Newar orthography means the result is legitimate; thus, we can qualitatively assign this a true CER and WER of 0. This issue consistently resulted in a high WER for Newar when in fact the result was qualitatively acceptable.

Word separation and a unigram-based probabilistic calculation for the spell checking meant that our corrected outputs were less optimal than we would have liked. However, Kritipur Newar (6) is an example of a success of spelling correction, where the target was *dakale nhāpā* was initially recognised incorrectly as *dakal nhāpāṃ*, but the automatic correction changed this to *dakale nhāpāṃ*. While the resulting WER=50 is expected, as the second word in the source was *nhāpā*, again, the flexibility of Newar orthography means that *nhāpāṃ* is both a standard and acceptable variant of *nhāpā*. Therefore, we could qualitatively assign this example a true CER and WER of 0.

Example (7) is taken from a public performance recording, where the target only shows the speaker's speech, but the ASR model also identified the speech of an audience member. As with the incomplete Dzardzongke transcription of example (3), this utterance should either be removed or completed before training.

In (8), finally, we see an example of how this ASR model could perfectly recognise complicated and relatively lengthy speech. If one considers that the first two Newar examples are also qualitatively perfect, these examples demonstrate that with the careful selection of training data, one can develop optimal ASR models for low-resource languages without too much difficulty.

4 Discussion

From the results of all three experiments it becomes apparent that modifications are most useful up to around 90 minutes of 'monolingual' transcriptions. Transfer learning in particular proved more effective at this stage than sound modifications, although the size of the Standard Tibetan datasets mattered less than expected.[5]

The Newar dataset exhibits a broad heterogeneity, encompassing a wide range of sources, whereas the Dzardzongke data originates from a more specific geographical area with more data from one speaker, and, on average, shorter utterances, which could explain the higher Newar WER of 50 (vs Dzardzongke 32). Additionally, the Newar collection primarily features literary works, including readings of literature, theatrical performances, and discourses on religious or literary subjects that do not generalise well to more casual conversations that are also part of the same dataset.

Post-training corrections based on probabilistic spell checking from existing monolingual transcriptions is marginally effective for improving WER in Dzardzongke, but would be more effective especially for recordings on new topics if a more comprehensive corpus were available.

For Newar, the lack of standardised, romanised spelling leads to higher word (but not character) error rates, but as shown in the previous section, these are not necessarily representative of actual qualitative errors in transcription.

For both languages, as well as the Standard Tibetan datasets, an in-depth analysis of transcriptions results reveals the importance of a well-balanced, varied dataset where incomplete transcriptions are filtered out to avoid artificially high error rates that make the models worse. Although it is tempting with any low-resource language to

[5]More information on the content and accuracy of Standard Tibetan transcriptions was not available.

utilise as many transcribed utterances as possible, those with too much noise or interference are clearly creating more problems later on.

5 Conclusion

Our main goal was to present a first test of the most effective and efficient ASR pipeline to facilitate the documentation and preservation of endangered languages, which are often extremely low-resourced. For both Dzardzongke and Newar, model improvements are different for different masses of data, which helps to guide those who have to start transcriptions from scratch.

We tested different modification techniques to see which would be most effective for small-size datasets and carefully evaluated and discussed the results. Directions for future research include experiments with transfer learning for Newar and further modifications and corrections once word lists in standardised orthographies have been created.

Limitations

There are some limitations in the current datasets upon which the models were trained. First, they are still of limited size and the Newar set in particular is very heterogenous as it contains samples from four different varieties. The Dzardzongke dataset on the other hand is less robust since half of the data consists of recordings of narratives by one near-native speaker in a quiet, controlled environment. For both datasets, most speakers are old and there are very few women.

Additionally, the training took a large amount of processing time, and this might be prohibitive for many teams and communities. The models were trained using Nvidia Tesla K80 GPUs from Dartmouth's Research Computing, and training all the models took approximately 3972 hours of computing time. This was done in an HPC infrastructure, with 5$\sim$7 processes running in parallel. With this set up, the training took approximately one month. The inference per se does not consume so many resources, but a user would still need a GPU to actually get a transcription. While this can be done online with a number of free alternatives, the cost could be prohibitive for communities who wish to implement these transcription systems offline.

Ethics Statement

Ethics approval was obtained prior to data collection from the University of Cambridge.

Acknowledgements

We would like to thank Esukhia/Monlam AI for sharing their smaller Standard Tibetan dataset with us at an early stage allowing us to start training our transfer models. We also thank Charles Ramble, Nyima Drandul and Birat Raj Bajracharya for support with the Dzardzongke and Newar transcriptions. We also gratefully acknowledge funding for various parts of this project from the Endangered Language Documentation Programme (ELDP - G114548), the Cambridge Centre for Digital Humanities Incubator Grant 2023 and the Arts and Humanities Research Council (AHRC - AH/V011235/1). Finally, we want to thank Jianjun Hua, Elijah Gagne and the personnel at Dartmouth Research Computing for their assistance in setting up the experiments.

References

Timofey Arkhangelskiy. 2021. Low-resource ASR with an augmented language model. In *Proceedings of the Seventh International Workshop on Computational Linguistics of Uralic Languages*, pages 40–46, Syktyvkar, Russia (Online). Association for Computational Linguistics.

Alexei Baevski, Henry Zhou, Abdelrahman Mohamed, and Michael Auli. 2020. wav2vec 2.0: A framework for self-supervised learning of speech representations. *arXiv preprint arXiv:2006.11477*.

Sameer Bansal, Herman Kamper, Karen Livescu, Adam Lopez, and Sharon Goldwater. 2019. Pre-training on high-resource speech recognition improves low-resource speech-to-text translation. In *Proceedings of the 2019 Conference of the North American Chapter of the Association for Computational Linguistics: Human Language Technologies, Volume 1 (Long and Short Papers)*, pages 58–68, Minneapolis, Minnesota. Association for Computational Linguistics.

Martijn Bartelds, Nay San, Bradley McDonnell, Dan Jurafsky, and Martijn Wieling. 2023. Making More of Little Data: Improving Low-Resource Automatic Speech Recognition Using Data Augmentation. *arXiv preprint arXiv:2305.10951*.

Laurent Besacier, Etienne Barnard, Alexey Karpov, and Tanja Schultz. 2014. Automatic Speech Recognition for Under-Resourced Languages: A Survey. *Speech Commun.*, 56:85–100.

Sebastian Braun and Hannes Gamper. 2022. Effect of noise suppression losses on speech distortion and ASR performance. In *ICASSP 2022-2022 IEEE International Conference on Acoustics, Speech and Signal Processing (ICASSP)*, pages 996–1000. IEEE.

Central Bureau of Statistics (Nepal). 2012. *National Population and Housing Census 2011: National Report*. Central Bureau of Statistics, Kathmandu.

Ramon Corretge. 2012. Praat vocal toolkit. *Barcelona, Spain: Praat. Retrieved from http://praatvocaltoolkit.com.*

Rolando Coto-Solano. 2021. Explicit tone transcription improves ASR performance in extremely low-resource languages: A Case Study in Bribri. Proceedings of the First Workshop on Natural Language Processing for Indigenous Languages of the Americas (pp. 173–184). Association for Computational Linguistics.

Rolando Coto-Solano, Sally Akevai Nicholas, Samiha Datta, Victoria Quint, Piripi Wills, Emma Ngakuravaru Powell, and Isaac Feldman. 2022. Development of Automatic Speech Recognition for the Documentation of Cook Islands Māori. Proceedings of the Thirteenth Language Resources and Evaluation Conference (pp. 3872-3882). https://aclanthology.org/2022.lrec-1.412.

Raj Dabre, Tetsuji Nakagawa, and Hideto Kazawa. 2017. An empirical study of language relatedness for transfer learning in neural machine translation. In *Proceedings of the 31st Pacific Asia Conference on Language, Information and Computation*, pages 282–286. The National University (Phillippines).

G. Durantin, B. Foley, N. Evans, and J. Wiles. 2017. Transcription survey. *Paper presented at the Australian Linguistic Society Annual Conference.*

B. Foley, J. T. Arnold, R. Coto-Solano, G. Durantin, T. M. Ellison, D. van Esch, and J. Wiles. 2018. Building speech recognition systems for language documentation: The CoEDL endangered language pipeline and inference system (ELPIS). *SLTU*, pages 205–209.

Nils Hjortnaes, Timofey Arkhangelskiy, Niko Partanen, Michael Rießler, and Francis Tyers. 2020. Improving the language model for low-resource ASR with online text corpora. In *Proceedings of the 1st Joint Workshop on Spoken Language Technologies for Under-resourced languages (SLTU) and Collaboration and Computing for Under-Resourced Languages (CCURL)*, pages 336–341, Marseille, France. European Language Resources association.

Hugging Face. 2024. Transformer Documentation: XLSR-Wav2Vec2. `https://huggingface.co/docs/transformers/model_doc/xlsr_wav2vec2`.

Tej R. Kansakar. 1999. The Sociology of the Newar Language. *Newar Vijñāna*, 2:17–27. INBSS, Portland.

Tej R. Kansakar, Nirmal Man Tuladhar, Omkareshwor Shrestha, Shobha Kumari Mahato, Narayan Gautam, Sulochana Sapkota, and Kishore Rai. 2011. A Sociolinguistic Survey of Newar/Nepal Bhasa. A Report submitted to the Linguistic Survey of Nepal.

Tom Kocmi and Ondřej Bojar. 2018. Trivial transfer learning for low-resource neural machine translation. In *Proceedings of the Third Conference on Machine Translation: Research Papers*, pages 244–252, Brussels, Belgium. Association for Computational Linguistics.

Marieke Meelen and Charles Ramble. 2023. An Audio-Visual Archive of Dzardzongke (South Mustang Tibetan). Endangered Language Archive.

Boyd Michailovsky and Ramapati Raj Sharma. 1968. The Sahu Hari Das has many troubles. Audio recording, Pangloss: A CNRS Project.

Vikramjit Mitra, Horacio Franco, Martin Graciarena, and Arindam Mandal. 2012. Normalized amplitude modulation features for large vocabulary noise-robust speech recognition. In *2012 IEEE International Conference on Acoustics, Speech and Signal Processing (ICASSP)*, pages 4117–4120. IEEE.

Christopher Moseley, editor. 2010. *Atlas of the World's Languages in Danger*, 3rd edition. UNESCO Publishing, Paris.

Toan Q. Nguyen and David Chiang. 2017. Transfer learning across low-resource, related languages for neural machine translation. In *Proceedings of the Eighth International Joint Conference on Natural Language Processing (Volume 2: Short Papers)*, pages 296–301, Taipei, Taiwan. Asian Federation of Natural Language Processing.

Peter Norvig. 2021. How to Write a Spelling Corrector. `https://norvig.com/spell-correct.html`.

Emily Prud'hommeaux, Robbie Jimerson, Richard Hatcher, and Karin Michelson. 2021. Automatic Speech Recognition for Supporting Endangered Language Documentation. *Language Documentation & Conservation*, 15:491–513.

Syed Shahnawazuddin, KT Deepak, Gayadhar Pradhan, and Rohit Sinha. 2017. Enhancing noise and pitch robustness of children's ASR. In *2017 IEEE International Conference on Acoustics, Speech and Signal Processing (ICASSP)*, pages 5225–5229. IEEE.

Daya Ratna Shakya. 2019. Agreement vs Non-Agreement: Gradual Development of Inflectional Pattern, Assessment drawn from Ten Dialects of Nepal Bhasa. *Nevāḥ Prajñā*, 2(3):41–80.

J. Shi, J. D. Amith, R. Castillo García, E. G. Sierra, K. Duh, and S. Watanabe. 2021. Leveraging end-to-end ASR for endangered language documentation: An empirical study on Yolóxochitl Mixtec. *Proceedings of the 16th Conference of the European Chapter of the Association for Computational Linguistics*, page 1134–1145.

Ishwar Chandra Yadav and Gayadhar Pradhan. 2021. Pitch and noise normalized acoustic feature for children's ASR. *Digital Signal Processing*, 109:102922.

Barret Zoph, Deniz Yuret, Jonathan May, and Kevin Knight. 2016. Transfer learning for low-resource neural machine translation. In *Proceedings of the 2016 Conference on Empirical Methods in Natural Language Processing*, pages 1568–1575, Austin, Texas. Association for Computational Linguistics.

Akha, Dara-ang, Karen, Khamu, Mlabri and Urak Lawoi' language minorities' subjective perception of their languages and the outlook for development of digital tools

Joanna Dolińska
University of Warsaw
j.dolinska@al.uw.edu.pl

Shekhar Nayak
University of Groningen
s.nayak@rug.nl

Sumittra Suraratdecha
Mahidol University
sumittra.sur@mahidol.edu

Abstract

Multilingualism is deeply rooted in the sociopolitical history of Thailand. Some minority language communities entered the Thai territory a few decades ago, while the families of some other minority speakers have been living in Thailand since at least several generations. The authors of this article address the question how Akha, Dara-ang, Karen, Khamu, Mlabri and Urak Lawoi' language speakers perceive the current situation of their language and whether they see the need for the development of digital tools for documentation, revitalization and daily use of their languages. The objective is complemented by a discussion on the feasibility of development of such tools for some of the above-mentioned languages and the motivation of their speakers to participate in this process. Furthermore, this article highlights the challenges associated with developing digital tools for these low-resource languages and outlines the standards researchers must adhere to in conceptualizing the development of such tools, collecting data, and engaging with the language communities throughout the collaborative process.

1 Introduction

The region of Southeast Asia encompasses biologically and linguistically distinct countries. It is characterized by a high level of biodiversity (Tungittiplakorn and Dearden, 2002) and is renowned for its rich linguistic landscape (Enfield, 2021; Lee, 2019; Prasithrathsing, 1988).

However, biodiversity and multilingualism in this region are becoming endangered due to globalization, industrialization and intensive tourism. Available data suggest that the simultaneous disappearance of linguistic and biological diversity is correlated (Gorenflo et al., 2012). This article primarily focuses on six minority language communities in Thailand, located in the provinces of Chiang Mai, Chiang Rai, Nan and Krabi. It presents preliminary findings from interviews with representatives of the Akha, Dara-ang, Karen, Khamu, Mlabri and Urak Lawoi' communities, and discusses efforts to collect audio data for developing voice technology for some of these languages. The aim of this article is to explore concrete steps required to foster more effective collaboration between computer scientists, documentary linguists, and language communities in Thailand. It also proposes technologies for tasks in low-resource settings, particularly for the discussed endangered languages from four selected Thai provinces. Furthermore, it is hoped that the presented findings will initiate a discussion on how to approach the development of digital tools for endangered and low-resource languages.

Data collection has been conducted following the "data statements" practice developed by Bender and Friedman (Bender and Friedman, 2018). The aim of this practice is to create digital tools that avoid the risk of oversimplyfing the situation of any given speech communities and prevent their exclusion, underrepresentation and misrepresentation. The preliminary data presented here was collected in November and December 2023 across four provinces of Thailand: Chiang Mai, Chiang Rai, Nan and Krabi. This data includes approximately 18 hours of recordings and notes involving the participation of 16 adults (3 women and 13 men) aged between 30-94 years at the time of the recordings.

2 Data statements

Curator rationale: Interviews have been conducted with the representatives of language minorities in Thailand in order to learn about their subjective perception of the condition of their languages, to hear out their opinions concerning the needs of their communities and to inquire if these language communities would like to cooperate

Proceedings of the The Seventh Workshop on the Use of Computational Methods in the Study of Endangered Languages, pages 94–99
March 21-22, 2024 ©2024 Association for Computational Linguistics

Language	No. of persons	Province
Akha	2	Chiang Rai
Dara-ang	3	Chiang Mai
Karen	3	Chiang Mai
Khamu	1	Chiang Rai
Mlabri	2	Nan
Urak Lawoi'	5	Krabi

Table 1: Number of native speakers of each minority language that the authors interviewed in 4 different provinces[1] in November and December 2023.

with the interviewers on developing useful digital tools for their languages. **Language variety:** The represented speakers' variety includes everyday, contemporary, spoken language varieties of Akha, Dara-ang, Karen, Khamu, Mlabri and Urak Lawoi' from the Chiang Mai, Chiang Rai, Nan and Krabi provinces in Thailand. Interviews have been carried out with the support of three translators communicating with the interviewees in Northern, Southern and standard Thai. All interviewees are at least bilingual. Apart from their native languages, they speak Northern Thai in their everyday communication (9 persons), Southern Thai (5 persons) and standard Thai (14 persons). **Speaker demographic:** All 16 interviewed minority language speakers are adults aged between 30 and 94 years. There has been a noticeable tendency for men to be more willing to participate in the interviews than women, with 13 men and 3 women participating. This might result from the fact, that among the interviewed communities men tend to interact more with other social groups and villages. The speakers represent various professions: one community activist, one community activist/social entrepreneur, one healer, one farmer/pastor, five farmers, two farmers/hunter-gatherers, one fisherman/teacher, three fishermen, and one tourism sector employee. All interviewees with exception of one person have attended at least primary school and two conversation partners hold university degrees. Three interviewees migrated to Thailand several decades ago from Myanmar and Laos, while 13 have lived in their province, or a neighbouring province in one case, their entire lives. The interviewees represent diverse religious backgrounds: seven are Buddhist, four follow local beliefs, four are Christian and not known (1 person). Furthermore, all interviewees were asked the following two questions: **[1]** "How would you describe your identity? Are you *Akha /Dara-ang /Karen /Khamu /Mlabri /Urak Lawoi'* **and/or** Thai?" **[2]** "Alternatively, are you Thai and *Akha /Dara-ang /Karen /Khamu /Mlabri /Urak Lawoi'*?" Without exception, all interviewees answered that they feel first *Akha /Dara-ang /Karen /Khamu /Mlabri /Urak Lawoi'*, depending on their community of origin. Almost all interviewees have Thai citizenship, except for one person who has been actively applying for it for several years and continues to strive for full citizenship rights in Thailand. Three interviewees went through distressing refuge experiences in their early adolescence and adulthood periods. **Speech situation:** Twelve interviews took place in the village settings of the interviewees, two in a cafeteria, one at a school, and one in a church community area. The interviewees were informed about the interview topics beforehand and communicated with the interviewers in Northern Thai and standard Thai (10 persons), Southern Thai and standard Thai (4 persons) and English (two persons). The structured interview comprised four sections: general questions, questions about language use, question about the natural environment, and questions related to work and leisure domains. Almost all interviews lasted approximately one hour. All interviewees responded to questions concerning their subjective perception of the sociolinguistic situation within their respective communities. A preliminary set of audio-data has been collected for the Karen language, including a wide array of plant names, and for the Urak Lawoi' language, featuring names of celebrated Deities, basic vocabulary concerning time perception, human body parts, verbs for basic human activities, names of colours and natural phenomena, as well as terms related to fishery, as it is the most essential mode of subsistence for this community. Furthermore, it has been discovered that the Dara-ang community of Christian denomination in the Chiang Mai province has translated Bible into the Dara-ang language with the support

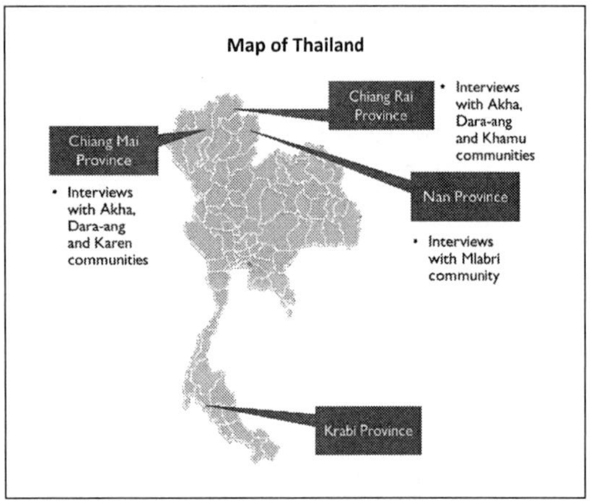

Figure 1: Interviews conducted with the representatives of language minorities in Thailand in November and December 2023.

of foreign religion activists and has supplemented parts of it with numerous audio-recordings which are available through electronic application.[2]

3 Data collection

3.1 Preliminary findings concerning independent efforts of the interviewed language communities to document and revitalize their languages

All interviewed representatives of language communities recognize the need to preserve their language for future generations. They acknowledged the primary role of **oral language** transmission within the family and among members of the same village. Furthermore, the Akha, Dara-ang, Karen and Urak Lawoi' communities each possess their own written standard, which has been developed by these communities with the support of researchers and/or missionaries. Notably, the Akha writing system encompasses Akha varieties spoken not only in Thailand, but also in neighbouring countries. The written forms of Dara-ang and Urak Lawoi' languages are based on the Thai script. However, it should be noted that the transmission of the **written standard** in these communities has not been consistent over the past decades, and not all community members can read it.

In fact, the aforementioned language communities primarily depend on oral transmission, which may also influence the potential development of **digital tools** for these languages in the future. Among the interviewed representatives of language minorities, the Akha group appears to have advanced its own language policy to the most successful stage, yet the motivation to preserve the language remains strong across all the encountered communities. Notably, the motivation to preserve the Dara-ang language among the Christian community in the Chiang Mai province seems to have been inspired by the desire to practice their religion in their first language.

When asked about any potential need for digital tools to preserve their community languages, interviewees from the Akha, Dara-ang, Karen, Mlabri and Urak Lawoi' communities expressed interest. Akha interviewees were primarily interested in developing digital tools for educational purposes, while the Karen speakers would like to use the digital tools to preserve the indigenous knowledge of the Karen community pertaining to the names and images of healing plants and their application. Mlabri and Urak Lawoi' interviewees both shared the views that it would be beneficial to use their native languages when using mobile phones and one of the Urak Lawoi' interviewees positively approached the idea of developing digital educational materials in Urak Lawoi' language.

3.2 Future plans for the development of voice technology

The interviewee from the Akha community has shown a considerable interest in creating a voice technology tool for the Akha language, especially in the speech-to-text tool. Given the existing abundance of the Akha language written materials for educational purposes, the authors of this article have drafted a plan with the Akha community representative to start Akha language recordings in 2024 in order to provide the data for the development of the audio tool. A positive outcome of this cooperation between sociolinguists, a computational linguist and language activist is to be expected, since it combines Akha community experience, professional academic knowledge and skills, as well as the self-driven motivation of the Akha community to create Akha language resources.

The second future opportunity to develop digital tools for one of the above languages is to create an offline and online educational brochure focused on the Karen language, especially on the plants with healing characteristics, which are applied in the

[2]The interviewers were advised by the Dara-ang community to ask the Christian Pastor about the need and feasibility of the development of digital tools, as he would have the knowledge about the authors rights of the translation and recording of the Bible.

traditional Karen medicine and constitute a component of the Karen indigenous knowledge. After consultations with the Karen healer, the authors of this article alongside with the Karen healer carried out video recordings of several dozen of plants, alongside their name in Northern Thai and Karen languages. These names have been recorded in the audio format as well. This initiative will be implemented at the beginning of the year 2024 with the active participation of the Karen community. Like in the case of the Akha community, the most important factor pointing towards the potentially positive outlook of this project is the strong engagement and motivation of the Karen healer to preserve the knowledge about healing plants and herbs that she inherited from her both grandfathers. Thirdly, the collected Urak Lawoi' data encompassing names of local Deities, basic vocabulary concerning time perception, human body parts and fishery, verbs for basic human activities, names of colours and natural phenomena could be the basis for the development of a basic audio dictionary for the Urak Lawoi' language in the future, if the Urak Lawoi' interviewees will be interested in a further cooperation.[3]

3.3 Outlook for multilingual ASR for these endangered languages

There have been recent efforts in the speech technology research towards developing tools which are not pre-dominantly text-driven to support many endangered languages which lack in textual resources (Ewan Dunbar and Dupoux, 2022). A range of strategies has been developed specifically for speech-to-text or automatic speech recognition (ASR) for low resource languages (Nayak and Kodukula, 2019). Multi-lingual and cross-lingual approaches (Schultz and Kirchhoff, 2006) have essentially led to effective use of limited resources of these languages for improved ASR performance. Specifically, the self-supervised learning based models such as wav2vec 2.0 which are pre-trained on large number of diverse languages make the development of speech-to-text simpler as the models aren't trained from scratch for such languages (Babu et al., 2021; Baevski et al., 2020). Also, the untranscribed audio data can be utilized for pre-training these models. Our future goal is to expand our database for these languages and build a common multilingual ASR model supporting these endangered languages utilizing self-supervised and transfer learning methodologies.

3.4 Challenges concerning the development of digital tools for the Akha, Dara-ang, Karen, Khamu, Mlabri and Urak Lawoi' languages

Having analyzed the interviews with the above-mentioned communities, the authors came to the following conclusions. First of all, asking the representatives of minority speech communities, if they would be interested in co-developing digital tools for their language needs to be preceded by a description of how their audio-data could be processed and what kind of benefit it would mean for the community.

A second question refers to the motivation to create such tools. Based on the interview results, it seems that the Akha community representative would like to promote and standardize the Akha language within the Akha community, whereas the Mlabri speakers offered to help acquire Mlabri language skills by the foreigners willing to learn it. Another challenge is the written standard of a given language. If a speech-to-text tool is developed, in which script does the text need to appear? Even if only one type of script has been consequently applied in the history of this language research, orthography variants can also induce complications while developing digital tools. Not only the motivation to develop particular tools is important, but also the target audience. An essential question to ask before developing digital tools for a given low-resource language concerns the data that it needs to encompass, whether they should be accompanied by pictures (if the tool is for children), whether it should include religious and worldview contents (but then which religion and which worldview, as the above-mentioned communities often follow various religions and beliefs within their groups).

Another question relates to the so called "heritage data" for a given language, which means data compiled by the community members themselves, researchers and missionaries in the past. The question which arises here is how to incorporate such data and how to understand the situation related to the authors rights in terms of these data (Blokland et al., 2019).

[3]Two Urak Lawoi' interviewees explicitly stated that they would like to have such tools for their native language in the future.

4 Ethical statement

The design of the project and its implementation follow the "The TRUST Code - A Global Code of Conduct for Equitable Research Partnerships" `https://www.globalcodeofconduct.org`. The participants of the research were both informed about the consent procedures and the goal of the research in Thai language (as all of them are fluent Thai speakers). Question concerning consents have been asked without recording. If the participants allowed the recording of the interview (which all of them did), they responded to the consent questions once again while being audio-recorded. After the interviews the participants received audio-recordings and photos from the meetings from the interviewers.

4.1 Limitations

Since the authors interviewed only 16 representatives of 6 various language minority groups in Thailand, the collected qualitative data understandably cannot be indicative of the whole speaker populations. Nevertheless, the presented results allow for determining the future direction of the research devoted to the self-perception of language minorities in Thailand. The qualitative research method in the form of a structured interview was perceived by the authors as the best choice for introductory field work research on the sociolinguistic status of minority languages in Thailand and the interest of their speakers in developing digital tools.

5 Acknowledgements

Joanna Dolińska would like to acknowledge the seminal role of the University of Warsaw New Ideas 3A Grant "Interdependence of multilingualism and biodiversity in the Chiang Mai and Satun provinces in Thailand" (2023-2024), as well as the Scholarship for Short-term Visiting Scholars at the Mahidol University for the conceptualization and implementation of this research project together with Sumittra Suraratdecha. Furthermore, Joanna Dolińska would like to acknowledge the importance of Short-Term Scientific Action (STSM) within the LITHME (Languange in the Machine-Human Area) COST Action at the Voice Technology Program, Campus Fryslân, University of Groningen, which inspired the cooperation with Shekhar Nayak on the development of voice technology tools for endangered languages, as well as the conceptualization of this article and future development of voice technologies for the described endangered languages.

References

Arun Babu, Changan Wang, Andros Tjandra, Kushal Lakhotia, Qiantong Xu, Namal Goyal, Kritika Singh, Patrick von Platen, Yatharth Saraf, Juan Pino, and Alexei Baevski. 2021. Xls-r: Self-supervised cross-lingual speech representation learning at scale. arxiv preprint.

Alexei Baevski, Henry Zhou, Abdelrahman Mohamed, and Michael Auli. 2020. wav2vec 2.0: A framework for self-supervised learning of speech representations. *Advances in neural information processing systems*, 33:12449–12460.

Emily M. Bender and Batya Friedman. 2018. Data statements for natural language processing: Toward mitigating system bias and enabling better science. *Transactions of the Association for Computational Linguistics*, 6:587–604.

Rogier Blokland, Nikko Partanen, Michael Rießler, and Joshua Wilbur. 2019. Using computational approaches to integrate endangered language legacy data into documentation corpora: Past experiences and challenges ahead. *Proceedings of the Workshop on Computational Methods for Endangered Languages*, 2(5).

Nick Enfield. 2021. *The Languages of Mainland Southeast Asia (Cambridge Language Surveys)*. Cambridge University Press, Cambridge.

Nicolas Hamilakis Ewan Dunbar and Emmanuel Dupoux. 2022. Self-supervised language learning from raw audio: Lessons from the zero resource speech challenge. *IEEE Journal of Selected Topics in Signal Processing*, 16(6):1211–1226.

Larry Gorenflo, Suzanne Romaine, Russel A. Mittermeier, and Kristen Walker-Painemilla. 2012. Co-occurrence of linguistic and biological diversity in biodiversity hotspots and high biodiversity wilderness areas. *Proc Natl Aca Sci U S A*, 22;109(21):8032–8037.

Hugo Yu-Hsiu Lee. 2019. Rethinking globalization, english and multilingualism in thailand: A report on a five-year ethnography. *3L – Language Linguistics Literature – The Southeast Asian Journal of English Language Studies*, 2(1):69–84.

Shekhar Nayak and Sri Rama Murty Kodukula. 2019. *Unsupervised speech Signal to Symbol Transformation for Zero Resource Speech Processing*. Doctoral dissertation, Indian Institute of Technology Hyderabad.

Amara Prasithrathsing. 1988. Sociolinguistic research on thailand languages. *Language Sciences*, 10(2):236–272.

Tanja Schultz and Katrin Kirchhoff. 2006. *Multilingual speech processing*. Elsevier, Amsterdam.

Waranoot Tungittiplakorn and Philip Dearden. 2002. Biodiversity conservation and cash crop development in northern thailand. *Pacific Linguistics*, (C-43):2007–2025.

Author Index

Association for Computational Linguistics
209 N. Eighth Street
Stroudsburg, Pennsylvania 18360

ISBN 978-1-7138-9452-0

CURRAN ASSOCIATES INC.
proceedings.com